T0271122

In a historically informed critique of the theory and practice of development assistance, Paul Kingston examines Britain's foreign aid programme in the Middle East in the 1940s and 1950s. After an initial assessment of the origins of what was dubbed the 'peasants, not pashas' policy – notably the link between development, sterling balances, and postwar imperial strategy – the author focuses on planning and policy debates in Iran, Iraq, and Jordan, between British development experts, their American rivals, and Middle Eastern technocrats. These debates, which centred on issues such as afforestation, irrigation, and rural credit, raise important questions about the nature and limits of the development process within the Middle East and the Third World more generally which the author explores in his analysis. These insights will be of interest to development practitioners and scholars in development studies, as well as to students of Middle East and imperial history.

Cambridge Middle East Studies

Britain and the politics of modernization in the Middle East, 1945–1958

Cambridge Middle East Studies 4

Editorial board
CHARLES TRIPP (General Editor)
SHAUL BAKHASH, MICHAEL C. HUDSON, DENIZ KANDIYOTI,
RASHID KHALIDI, NOAH LUCAS, BASIM MUSALLAM, ROGER
OWEN

Cambridge Middle East Studies has been established to publish books on the nineteenth- and twentieth-century Middle East and North Africa. The aim of the series is to provide new and original interpretations of aspects of Middle Eastern societies and their histories. To achieve disciplinary diversity, books will be solicited from authors writing in a wide range of fields including history, sociology, anthropology, political science and political economy. The emphasis will be on producing books offering an original approach along theoretical and empirical lines. The series is intended for students and academics, but the more accessible and wide-ranging studies will also appeal to the interested general reader.

1 Parvin Paidar, *Women and the political process in twentieth-century Iran*
2 Israel Gershoni and James P. Jankowski, *Redefining the Egyptian nation, 1930–1945*
3 Annelies Moors, *Women, property and Islam: Palestinian experiences, 1920–1990*

Britain and the politics of modernization in the Middle East, 1945–1958

Paul W. T. Kingston
University of Toronto

CAMBRIDGE
UNIVERSITY PRESS

PUBLISHED BY THE PRESS SYNDICATE OF THE UNIVERSITY OF CAMBRIDGE
The Pitt Building, Trumpington Street, Cambridge, United Kingdom

CAMBRIDGE UNIVERSITY PRESS
The Edinburgh Building, Cambridge CB2 2RU, UK
40 West 20th Street, New York NY 10011–4211, USA
477 Williamstown Road, Port Melbourne, VIC 3207, Australia
Ruiz de Alarcón 13, 28014 Madrid, Spain
Dock House, The Waterfront, Cape Town 8001, South Africa

http://www.cambridge.org

First published 1996
First paperback edition 2002

A catalogue record for this book is available from the British Library

Library of Congress Cataloguing in Publication data
Kingston, P. W. (Paul W.)
Debating development: Britain and the politics of modernization
in the Middle East, 1945–1958 / Paul W. T. Kingston
        p.   cm. – (Cambridge Middle East Studies: 4)
Includes bibliographical references (p.   ) and index.
ISBN 0 521 56346 1 (hc)
1. Economic assistance, British – Middle East.   2. Great Britain –
Foreign economic relations – Middle East.   3. Middle East – Foreign
economic relations – Great Britain.   4. Middle East – Economic
conditions – 1945–1979.   5. Rural development – Middle East
I. Title.   II. Series.
HC415.15.K558   1996
338.9′1′0956–DC   95-50934   CIP

ISBN 0 521 56346 1 hardback
ISBN 0 521 89439 5 paperback

To my family and especially to
my mother and dear, late father

Contents

Acknowledgements   *page* x

Introduction

1   Britain, peasants, and pashas: debating approaches to
    modernization in the postwar Middle East   10

2   Imperial dreams and delusions: the economics of promoting
    Middle East modernization   29

3   The British Middle East Office and the abandonment of
    imperial approaches to modernization   46

4   The British Middle East Office and the politics of
    modernization in Iran, 1945 to 1951   67

5   The British Middle East Office and the politics of
    modernization in Iraq, 1945 to 1958   94

6   The British Middle East Office and the politics of
    modernization in Jordan, 1951 to 1958   123

    Conclusion: 'hastening slowly'   154

    Notes   158
    Bibliography   184
    Index   189

Acknowledgements

The experience of researching and writing a book can often be a 'struggle'. Mine never was. This is in large part due to the support of the individuals I met along the way – financial, intellectual, moral, and otherwise. My first words of thanks go to my supervisor at St Antony's College, Oxford, Dr Roger Owen, who both suggested this topic to me in the first place and then patiently channelled my intellectual enthusiasm for it in appropriate directions. If this study is solidly grounded in a political economy framework, it is in large part due to Roger's influence.

I am also very grateful for the help of the Connaught Fund of the University of Toronto, the Social Science and Humanities Research Council of Canada, the Middle East Centre of St Antony's College, the Committee of Vice-Chancellors and Principals of the Universities of the United Kingdom, the Beit Fund, and the Alistair Buchan Fund. I would also like to thank the Social Science Division of Scarborough College and the Political Science Department of the University of Toronto for having the imagination to hire an historian and a Middle East scholar to teach in their development studies programme. I would also like to thank the always friendly and helpful staffs of the Middle East Centre at St Antony's College (especially Derek Hopwood, Dianne Ring, and Gillian Grant), the Public Records Office, and the Overseas Development Administration in London (especially Nigel Hoult, Alan Bonner, Anne Anker, Eve Henrick, Gloria Leveridge, and Caroline Phillips).

Special mention needs also to be made of several individuals, especially David, Lakshmi, Carol and Martha, Tareq and Jocelyn, the football team at St Antony's, and Paula and Rob who transformed the daily routine of travelling up and down the M 40 into a thoroughly enjoyable experience! I am also very grateful to Robert Satloff for sharing his discovery of the Green Papers with me and for his always informed comments on the Jordanian aspects of my thesis. For their warm hospitality and support while I conducted research in Jordan, I would like to thank the Tell family, particularly Moraiwid whose advice and reminiscences I found invaluable. I shall always have fond memories of my stay in Amman. I am

grateful for the assistance of former members of the Development
Division among them Paul Howell, Barry Hudson, and Donald
Davidson. Above all, however, I would like to thank Bob Porter who in
many ways made this study possible, having ensured the preservation of
the Development Division's papers after the evacuation of the British
Embassy from Beirut in 1975. From that first and memorable meeting at
his home in county Devon, his kind assistance and helpful words of advice
have always been most appreciated. Had he written a history of the
Development Division himself, I can only hope that what I have
produced here at least approaches the story he would like to tell.

My final words of thanks, however, must be reserved for my parents
whose ever-present support I will always appreciate and remember. As a
small token of my gratitude, I dedicate this book to them and, especially,
to my father who passed away before knowledge of its publication.

Introduction

In the last half of the twentieth century, the world community underwent a remarkable expansion. Sparked by the declining capacity of western powers to maintain the colonial project, the rise of colonial nationalist movements in Asia, the Middle East and Africa, and the more general changes in the structure and ideology of the international system epitomized by the creation of the United Nations in 1945, state after state on the periphery began to acquire its political independence. As this process of decolonization progressed, a new phase emerged grounded in the desire of these countries to back up their newly found political independence with economic viability. It is this – the development phase of the postwar world – which sets the scene for what follows.

Transforming these former satellites into modern states was a monumental task. Life for the majority of its people was insecure, 'nasty, brutish and short' with disease and starvation ever-present realities. In the West, it had taken a cumulative process over centuries to alleviate such conditions. With the onset of decolonization, however, which brought the plight of the non-western world to the doorsteps of the West, this past reliance on a 'natural' process of growth and development was no longer felt acceptable nor conducive in the long run to global stability. In its place, a more positivistic notion emerged that 'development' should be systematically pursued, induced and accelerated, a notion reinforced by the belief that 'modernity', soon to be represented in the Third World by planners, Third World technocrats, and foreign aid workers, now possessed the means to pull the 'undeveloped' world out of the depths of poverty. This book, a history of the Development Division of the British Middle East Office (BMEO)[1] between the years 1945 and 1958, is an evaluation of these ambitious and optimistic postwar attitudes towards the ability of any of these groups to accelerate the pace of economic development.

There were many factors which fuelled this postwar optimism. The West, eager to gain the political favour of the emerging nations of the world and thus prevent their drift towards communism, portrayed economic and technical assistance as being a crucial variable in the fight to alleviate poverty and disease. This was especially so after the 'loss' of China in 1949. They characterized the underdeveloped world as being a victim of a 'vicious circle of poverty' which, in the absence of external stimuli, would perpetuate indefinitely. Particularly strong emphasis in the early years was placed on the importance of technological transfer. This was embodied in the launching of two world-wide initiatives in the technical assistance field in the early postwar years: the Point Four programme of the United States in 1949 and the Expanded Technical Assistance Programme of the United Nations in 1950.

In the Third World, however, many doubted whether the mere transfer of resources from the rich states to the poor would be adequate in itself. Instead, it called for a concentration and a rational allocation of those resources and based this approach on the moral argument that the Third World could not afford the gradualness that typified change in the developed countries nor was such a strategy feasible. Economic development had to come quickly and, given the structural obstacles which existed both at the domestic and international level, such speed could only be achieved if one's strategy was based on a centralization of economic control. In other words, it was only the state which could provide the necessary impetus to break the 'vicious circle of poverty' which afflicted most of the Third World and this belief was backed up by the experience of *étatist* experiments in the USSR, the fascist states of Europe, and even in the Middle East where both Turkey and Iran dabbled with such policies during the interwar period. Moreover, while attractive enough in their own right, these ideas also captured the political imagination of Third World leaders who were eager to abandon old colonial models and adopt others more in keeping with a new spirit of nationalism which was emerging in the underdeveloped world, a political marriage which, as the pre-eminent Swedish economist, Gunnar Myrdal, stated, 'gave the idea of planning an emotional momentum that it never would have obtained merely as a rational conclusion from knowledge of the facts'.[2]

It was in the context of this emerging optimism about the prospects for accelerated growth in the 'undeveloped world' that Britain launched its development programme for the Middle East in 1945. In fact, Britain was the first country in the western world to do so. It was not a global initiative, being confined to the Middle East, nor should it be confused with policies of colonial development whose conditions and antecedents obviously go back much further. Nonetheless, it predated both Truman's Point Four initiative as well as those of the United Nations, including most of the specialized agencies. Its purpose was mainly political, aimed at and designed to win the support of political élites in the Middle East, particularly the younger more progressive ones who, given their increasingly radical, nationalistic, and anti-western tone after the Second World War, posed serious dangers to the old imperial order. As the Middle East was an area of extreme strategic importance to Britain, second only to the 'jewel in the crown' India, British policy makers were determined to preserve what goodwill towards them remained in the region – not considered negligible in the early postwar years – and thus maintain the region's stability and importance as a vital strategic component of its wider imperial system.[3] The postwar Labour Government in Britain and especially its Foreign Secretary, Ernest Bevin, was no different in that regard than the Conservative Governments which preceded it.[4] Moreover, the policy was based on the assumption of a positive relationship between economic development and political modernization; in other words, economic progress was expected to bring political stability. The agent of this development programme was to be the British Middle East Office.

The task and challenge of this work is to describe and evaluate the effectiveness of this pioneering British foray into bilateral development assistance. This will not be an easy nor conclusive task. Debates about the effectiveness of development assistance are both complex and notoriously politicized. Basic questions such as what is the real purpose of development, who are the most appropriate agents of development, and what is the best kind of development assistance remain unresolved and often endlessly debated in abstract, ideological terms separated from the real contexts in which they must be situated. This has clouded the even more complex task of trying to evaluate the often contradictory if not dialectical effects of development programmes. Often, there are real trade-offs to be made – between growth and equity, short-term impact versus long-term sustainability, central direction versus social participation. Rarely have the choices been easy and never has 'modernization' proven to be the kind of linear process predicted by the early optimistic development theorists.

Nevertheless, the evaluation of development assistance remains a necessary exercise and it is therefore important to establish some criteria which can guide our judgements. Three criteria stand out as being useful in providing at least a rudimentary framework for analysis: the political motivations behind the provision of development assistance, the economic model which guides development policy decisions, and the mechanisms used to deliver development assistance. It is generally accepted, for example, that the more strictly 'developmental' assistance is, the broader its socio-economic impact will be. This is particularly so with regard to 'tied aid' but it also applies to aid which comes as part of a geostrategic package, of particular relevance to this story set as it is during the early days of the Cold War. Geostrategic interests usually always place the need for political order above the desire for socio-economic development, leading to development programmes which tend to strengthen inequitable and élite-based structures of power. One of the most consistent and vocal critics of development assistance, Peter Bauer, has gone so far as to argue that development assistance is inherently political and, as a result, can rarely be effective as an agent of development.[5] This argument has proven useful to neo-liberals eager to attack and reduce entrenched aid budgets in the western world; it has proven less helpful to those who disagree with his blanket indictment of foreign assistance and are interested in improving its effectiveness. The real question,therefore, is one of minimizing the political factor in the formulation and implementation of aid programmes.

In this regard, Britain's programme of development assistance for the Middle East stands out as interesting. The programme was initially designed to fulfil some lofty imperial goals. But, Britain found itself unable to back it up with money, men, and materials. Moreover, subsequent events in Palestine in 1948 and the emergence of the Cold War altered the imperial equation in the Middle East, further reducing Britain's political capital in the region, and laid bare a more problematic relationship between development and politics. This political decline continued until it reached its symbolic nadir with the debacle over the Suez invasion in the fall of 1956. Left to pick up the pieces was the Development Division of the BMEO, no more than a handful of technical experts brought together in 1945 and based in Cairo. Originally designed to facilitate the infusions of large amounts of British technicians into the bureaucracies of the region, the BMEO soon found itself in the front lines of policy. It became Britain's main source of development assistance, an end result which must have confirmed the skepticism of Middle East states towards Britain's lofty declarations. However, the results were paradoxical, for the failure of London to back up the BMEO with technicians and finance in its formative years freed it from the political shackles which greater support from London would have entailed. Facilitated by its location within the region and by the presence of a small number of high quality experts on its roster, the BMEO came to acquire a reputation for impartial and quality advice. While this argument should not be taken too far – after all, its work remained confined to those states more closely allied with Britain in the postwar period, namely Iraq and Jordan, it did allow the BMEO to emerge as a distinct and more strictly 'developmental' arm of Britain's foreign policy arsenal in the Middle East.

What of the BMEO's approach? Here, the process of evaluation is a more complicated and contentious affair. The most dominant model in both the theory and practice of development has been that of modernization or, perhaps better termed, Westernization. In fact, this idea of replicating the experience of 'the West' in 'the East' is inherent in the whole notion of development and assumes the existence of progressive historical forces which operate on a global basis. The challenge becomes to duplicate the conditions which led to 'take-off' in the West. For the most part, this has encouraged the formulation of abstract and academic assumptions about the role of such factors as the state, technology, capital or the market which have often had little contextual meaning or relevance, especially for the poor. Peter Bauer, for example, was very critical of the statist approaches of the 1950s and 1960s with their emphasis on the importance of economic planning and state-led development, arguing that the state had never shown such attributes in the past. Instead, he advocated a limited and minimalist role for the state whose main purpose would be confined to creating a legal framework in which the 'determinants of development', namely local institutions and attitudes, could emerge and flourish. In Bauer's opinion, it had been the 'habitual neglect' of these determinants of development, in part due to an abstract and misguided faith in the state, which had left the Third World in worse shape than it might have been had there been no economic planning at all.[6] According to Bauer, Third World leaders have seemed 'anxious to plan' while being 'unable to govern'.[7]

Bauer, of course, takes his own critique of the role of the state in the development process too far by exhibiting an equally abstracted faith in the market mechanism.[8] Here lies the real problem. As John Toye concluded in his work *Dilemmas of Development*, '[o]versimplified "solutions", resting on little more than the political preconceptions of a distant ideologue, are incapable of resolving the real dilemmas of development satisfactorily'.[9] The challenge, therefore, becomes to move away as far as possible from abstract modelling of the development process which can lead to a very directive and 'top-down' approach and adopt a more responsive and open-ended approach based on the idea of learning about development based on the conditions and experience of local communities. In short, there must be a high degree of interaction between theory and practice, with the emphasis on the practice. How far development programmes move in this direction can have a direct bearing on their effectiveness.

The approach of the Development Division of the BMEO also is interesting in this regard for it was neither wholly statist nor dogmatically neoliberal. Certainly, the state features prominently in its own *ad hoc* analysis of the development process. This should not be surprising given Britain's experience as a colonial power in which the fostering of order was always a key priority. It was the lack of a public legal framework and the weakness of the state apparatus which was seen by most colonial officials as the most serious obstacle to economic progress.[10] On the surface, one could argue that these ideas are congruent with those of Peter Bauer but there are important and subtle differences, ones which become clear in the course of the text when the BMEO's approach is compared to the more society- and private sector-oriented one of the US Point Four programme. These subtle differences revolve around the question of how active a role the state should take in laying the groundwork for the effective functioning of markets. The BMEO advocated a more activist role for the state. In part, this was based on the orientalist-generated assumption of the day that Islam encouraged an 'excessive' sense of individualism; it was also strongly influenced, however, by actual conditions in the region, especially in rural areas where there were pervasive problems of land concentration, land fragmentation, inequitable divisions of scarce water resources, and restricted access to reasonable credit – all of which indicated that the public realm was weak. As a result, great importance was placed on state ownership of land and water resources, particularly with regard to new settlements brought about through irrigation.[11] One of the first tasks of the cooperative advisers was to convince the various governments of the region to not only adopt basic laws and frameworks for cooperative activity but also to play a catalytic role in their foundation. Some of the most effective if understated work of the BMEO was in the development of statistical services in the region which were of vital importance in subsequent state programmes of poverty alleviation and development, and great emphasis was placed on the creation of autonomous state structures which included central statistical offices, self-financing forestry departments, as well as development boards which became a major preoccupation throughout the 1940s and 1950s.

However, these 'statist' leanings of the BMEO should be distinguished from the development orthodoxy of the day. The latter called for 'big push' modernization strategies based on the dominant involvement of the state in programmes of infrastructural and industrial development (although pre-revolutionary Iraq's extensive programme of agricultural development which is highlighted later is an interesting exception to that rule). The BMEO's approach was more cautious and pragmatic. It criticized strategies of 'forced industrialization' and was more apt to target its development policies at the agricultural sector where the majority of the population of the region lived and worked.[12] It was not until the late 1950s that an industrial advisor appeared on the roster of the BMEO, this perhaps reflecting a calculation on its part that the region had progressed to the next 'stage of development'. Moreover, the BMEO looked upon large-scale projects, even in the agricultural sector, as unsustainable without first enhancing local administrative capacity. As a result, it tended to base its approach on small-scale pilot projects, appropriate technology, and the use of local rather than foreign resources. Thus, rather than assume the existence of a strong and effective state apparatus, something of which *étatist* planners and neo-liberals have both been guilty, the BMEO showed greater sensitivity to the institutional aspects of the development process, hitherto a neglected aspect of development planning.[13] This highlighting of the need to build up public institutions came as a direct result of the BMEO's more pragmatic and contextually informed approach.

A final factor influencing the effectiveness of development assistance revolves around the question of programme delivery. The premise here is that good approaches to development can be rendered ineffective by inappropriate administrative set-ups, a point which further reinforces the above assumption that the practical realm is more important than the theoretical. A recent evaluation of the effectiveness of USAID over the last forty years, for example, has made the interesting point that swings from 'liberal' to 'conservative' approaches to promoting development within the agency have had little effect on actual performance because both approaches were implemented for the most part using the same administrative mechanisms. The report goes on to suggest that the first priority for reform in the development business is 'to change the mode of delivery'.[14]

It is in this light that the approach of the BMEO comes out looking particularly distinctive. Most bilateral aid programmes to this day tend to send out large numbers of technicians, build up a large administrative apparatus, and use complicated procedures of project formulation, implementation, and evaluation. Rather than promote local capacity, however, these approaches often overwhelm it and create dependencies on foreign capital, experts, and technology. This is certainly the critique which is made in the following pages of the US Point Four programme in the Middle East. The BMEO, on the other hand, lacked the resources which characterized the US and UN aid programmes and was forced to adopt a *modus operandi* which placed great emphasis on the use of local financial and human resources. In other words, it had an in-built awareness of the importance of building up local administrative capacity and promoting sustainability. This was aided by its peripatetic style which meant that advisers were never in one country long enough to dominate any one project or programme, something which also had obvious political advantages given the BMEO's origins as an instrument of British imperial policy. Finally, the BMEO operated on an informal basis devoid of the need for agreements at every step of the way and, thus, it avoided the tendency to 'abstract, rationalize, standardize [and] control' which has become such a noted and self-defeating feature of the development industry as it now stands. Rather, it adopted a flexible and adaptive style of operating, sensitive to the weaknesses, limitations, and uncertainties of promoting development in Third World countries which is now recognized as being a prerequisite to development success.[15]

Thus, with regard to the above three criteria, the BMEO's report card comes out with high marks. It was able to acquire a significant degree of autonomy from the imperial imperatives coming out of London; it developed a strategy towards the promotion of development which seemed more influenced by experience and context than by doctrine and dogma; and it developed a *modus operandi* which seemed to maximize local participation in the development process. However, in making this favourable appraisal of the BMEO's approach, let there be no illusions about the extent of its economic impact. This was not very great, nor should this fact be surprising. Its resources were extremely limited, complaints about which the BMEO made repeatedly in cables and telegrams sent back to London. In addition, the resources that it did possess were spread over an expansive geographical mandate – the definition of its Middle East included such states as Ethiopia and Somalia. The BMEO also had to operate in an exceedingly inhospitable regional environment, particularly after the Suez invasion of 1956. This narrowed the opportunities for devising significant programmes of bilateral aid to those states firmly tied to Britain, namely Iraq and Jordan. Moreover, even if 'in theory' its approach might come out looking favourable, in reality the BMEO had little effect where it counted most: improved growth rates in the region and reduced rates of poverty (with the notable exception of Jordan).

Finally much of what this book seeks to examine and evaluate is of an intangible nature and is not subject to empirical verification. While based on extensive research, the conclusions presented here about the nature and effects of development assistance are at best anecdotal and, in large part, based on British sources. More material and research is needed, for example, before the effects and impact of the US Point Four programme in the Middle East can be properly evaluated; and there is an even more urgent need to uncover regional sources of material if we ever hope to come to a wider and more balanced appraisal of the effects of foreign development assistance on the economic and social development of the Middle East. What follows, therefore, is merely the opening chapter in that larger project.

The first part of the book will outline the difficult first years in the life of the Development Division of the BMEO. Chapter 1 examines the origin of the development initiative which goes back to the experience of the Middle East Supply Centre (MESC) during the Second World War before being revived by Bevin in the early postwar years. Chapter 2 looks at some of the innumerable financial difficulties faced by Bevin in trying to transform the development initiative into a viable tool of imperial policy. Subsequent chapters then turn to an examination of the Development Division of the BMEO itself. Chapter 3 looks in more detail at how its distinctive approach came to evolve and the remaining chapters provide case studies of its actual work within selected Middle East countries: Iran, Iraq, and Jordan. In the course of our analysis, it will soon become clear that while the BMEO's views towards development were not always the same nor unanimously held, those which eventually came to prevail, though perhaps forced upon it by a variety of political and economic circumstances, showed great sensitivity to the limitations as opposed to the opportunities of promoting development. With its emphasis on the personal rather than the political, on small rather than large technically perfect projects, and showing a keen awareness of the institutional constraints on the development process, the approach of the BMEO stood in contrast to and in fact cut across the grain of most development thinking of the time let alone past techniques of British imperial diplomacy. It is the existence of this counter-approach, born in the unique and highly charged circumstances of the postwar Middle East, which sets the BMEO apart and makes a study of its work in the 1940s and 1950s especially interesting.

1 Britain, peasants, and pashas: debating approaches to modernization in the postwar Middle East

The Second World War is seen as the decisive turning point in the 'decline, revival and fall' of the British Empire.[1] Nowhere was this more true than in the Middle East. With the crushing of revolt in Iraq, the making of cabinets in Egypt, the imposition of extensive economic control through the auspices of the Middle East Supply Centre, and the flooding of the region with British troops and personnel, British power in the Middle East had never been so visible nor so extensive and stood in stark contrast to the interwar period when the exertion of British power had been relatively indirect and restrained. This expansion of British influence intensified the already strong resentment in the region towards the British presence and gave impetus to a more radical strain of Arab nationalism whose footsoldiers were the lower and emerging middle classes most affected by the inflation and general economic dislocation of the war and postwar world. It was these – the economic sources of political discontent in the Middle East – which the British found particularly worrying and suggested to many the need for a new approach to the maintenance of British influence in the region. As Lord Altrincham, Britain's Minister of State in the Middle East during the latter part of the war, concluded: 'In the preoccupation of fighting for our life . . . we have allowed the contrast between wealth and poverty to reach a dangerous state . . . Another Arabi will arise if this long deterioration is not effectively reversed.'[2]

In order to find ways to counter these dangerous political trends, Bevin convened in London a conference of His Majesty's Representatives in the Middle East in September 1945. Its purpose was to survey the whole field of foreign policy in the Middle East in order to devise ways which would allow Britain to continue to assert predominant political influence in the area.[3] All aspects of British policy were discussed and, in every case, the conclusion was the same: Britain's involvement in the region was narrowly based, concerned for the most part with questions of oil and strategy with little attention being paid to questions of social and economic justice. With respect to Egypt, for example, Bevin was forced to admit that while 'we have added very great wealth to the country, it has never flowed down to the *fellahin*'.[4] This situation had been acceptable to imperial policy makers so long as their collaborators in the Middle East, a small governing class made up of old Ottoman notables, land owners, and bureaucrats often referred to as the 'old gang', could guarantee the relative security of British interests. The Second World War, however, broke the equilibrium of this arrangement and placed the 'old gang' increasingly on the defensive. If the security of British imperial interests was to continue, Britain would have to search for ways to broaden the base of its support. The conference decided one way to do this was to promote social and economic development in the Middle East; it was what Bevin called his 'peasants, not pashas' policy.

The strategy, of course, was not really one of transferring British loyalty to the peasants of the region. The interests at stake were too great to risk a complete reversal of imperial strategy. Nor can it be said that Bevin expected quick improvements in the standard of living of the peoples of the region. That could at best come in the long term after years of greater effort and more progressive reform. Bevin was after more immediate political results. He wanted the longstanding ties with Britain to be reappraised in a more favourable light, especially by the younger and more progressive politicians and technocrats. And, he needed to revitalize and, thus, relegitimate the existing systems of government in order to forestall the nascent revolutionary forces in the region. Moreover, he needed to accomplish these goals quickly, especially in light of the growing perception of a Soviet threat.

The focus on development seemed an ingenious way to do this. Certainly, early debates about development prospects in the underdeveloped world were characterized by a great deal of optimism. When created in 1950, for example, the US Point Four programme looked upon itself as playing an historic and selfless role in alleviating world poverty through the transfer abroad of American know-how and technology. Britain, however, found itself in a very different position than the United States. Its resources were limited, its economy was in decline, and its past record of imperialism laid bare any attempt to elevate British policy onto a higher moral plane. Thus, instead of embarking on a postwar Middle East policy buoyed by the limitless sense of possibilities, British policy-makers worked in an atmosphere coloured more by a sense of vulnerability and this would have interesting effects on how the 'peasants, not pashas' policy would come to evolve. Born out of the unique circumstances of a dying imperial power, what is interesting about Britain's Middle East development policy was its recognition and early appreciation of 'the limits to promoting growth' in the region. How this more cautious and skeptical approach to accelerating the pace of socio-economic development in the region emerged is the principle focus of this chapter.

Devising plans for postwar regional development

Britain's first experience in providing development assistance to the non-colonial world was in the Middle East during the Second World War. Largely due to controls imposed by the Middle East Supply Centre (MESC) on ingoing and outgoing shipping, the region became isolated from its overseas supply of foodstuffs, consumer, and industrial goods.[5] The result of this control had been a massive 4 million ton decrease in ingoing cargo by 1944.[6] To compensate for this loss, the MESC set up various divisions manned with a group of technical assistants whose primary concern was to help the governments of the region in increasing regional production. Their services were freely available and, as a result, they spent much of their time in the field on advisory missions. Upon assuming their duties, however, the first thing that struck them was the long-term nature of the development problems which faced the region. As Doreen Warriner, herself an employee of the MESC, stated: 'For the first time, the causes of poverty in the Middle East came under scrutiny [which] . . . threw into sharp relief the limiting factors in the way of any large immediate increases in production.'[7]

In keeping with the British colonial preoccupation with matters of administration and the state, the technical staff of the MESC saw the main barrier to economic development in the Middle East to be the inadequacy of technical and administrative expertise. The Middle East had always suffered from a lack of trained personnel and, in the case of areas under British influence, had been forced to rely for such knowledge 'on a small and decreasing band of contract Englishmen'.[8] Administrative weaknesses were diagnosed as even more glaring. Iraq, for example, did not have a Ministry of Agriculture at this time and only Egypt had any kind of statistical services.[9] Bureaucratic weaknesses were also revealed by the efforts of the various governments of the region to control inflation, the most serious possible consequence of wartime controls. Numerous methods of controlling inflation were available but 'most of these demanded a large and efficient civil service . . . [I]n the Middle East these prerequisites were lacking'.[10] In the territories under more direct British control, Egypt, Palestine, Sudan, and Cyprus, inflation was kept in check. However, in countries more reliant on their own administrations, Iraq, Iran, and the Levant states, control of inflation was less successful.[11] This lack of control meant that goods ostensibly imported for one purpose in order to get a MESC licence would often be used for other, more lucrative, purposes by racketeers. Hunter related the example of cork finding its way into high-priced ladies' shoes.[12] The lack of bureaucratic control also meant that price controls were easily evaded with badly patrolled borders proving easy prey for smugglers eager to take their goods from 'the Stygian regions of low prices to the Eldorados of inflation'.[13] With the breakdown of market forces during the war, governments of the region also had difficulty accumulating enough grain from the countryside to feed the region. In fact, the most severe grain crisis occurred in 1941 at the same time as Rommel's offensive in the Western Desert.

The MESC used its band of advisers in an attempt to compensate for these deficiencies in regional administration. Government-run grain collection schemes, for example, were initiated, the most well-known being the Offices des Cereales Panifiables (OCP) which was jointly run by the Free French and the British (as represented by the Spears Economic Mission) in Syria and Lebanon. Similar schemes were also set up in Egypt, Iraq, and Iran. As a result of these schemes, no severe shortage of food existed in the region during the wartime, with the exception of British Somaliland and the Hadhramaut which Wilmington described as 'exceptions to an overwhelmingly different trend'.[14] To ease inflationary pressures, gold sales were tried on a limited basis in the Levant states and Iraq. With regards to transportation, advisors assisted in regulating the use of tires, fuel and vehicles, implementing licensing programmes, and setting up Transport Advisory Boards.[15] To help develop the statistical services of the region, the MESC produced the monthly *Middle East Economic and Statistical Bulletin* in addition to sending advisors to Iraq, Syria, Lebanon, and Cyprus to assist in the establishment of statistical offices. To assist local doctors in their fight against disease, a 'Middle East Formulary' was distributed by the Medical Division of the MESC.[16] Coordinated regional action was also taken against the problem of locust plagues with the setting up of the Middle East Anti-Locust Unit.

Important though these contributions were, they were small in relation to the larger, more fundamental problems that remained. Wilmington's description of the MESC having 'nibbled here and there at the towering roadblocks to long-term progress in the Middle East' seems appropriate.[17] Realizing this, the staff of the MESC in the latter stages of the war turned their attention to the question of effecting lasting improvements in the economic conditions of the Middle East. There was concern to keep going the promotional work of the MESC 'lest the momentum of accelerated development which technical aid had infused into the social and economic structure of the Middle East become bogged down with the return to peacetime'.[18] In his closing address to the MESC conference on agricultural development, Robert Jackson, the Director-General of the MESC who later went on to become highly involved in the activities of the UN development system, spoke of turning 'swords into ploughshares'.

Several steps were taken subsequently by the MESC. First, a series of regional conferences were held on specific technical issues such as rationing (1943), statistics (1944), agriculture (1944), and locusts (1945). These conferences were designed to prod the governments of the region into a realization of the importance and usefulness of technical cooperation on a regional level. This purpose was clearly evidenced in remarks made by the Assistant Director of the Food Division, Dunstan Skillbeck, concerning the conference on agricultural development:

> To some it appeared that too many papers had been requested and that the agenda was too congested to be wholly satisfactory; that . . . was part of this conscious intention. It was intended to give the delegates a mild attack of intellectual indigestion and so convince them, in a kindly way, of the disease from which they were suffering. In other words, to show clearly that the subject was an enormous one, far too big to be tackled effectively by such a conference and fully warranting detailed and continuous study.[19]

To further encourage the governments of the region to take a more active interest in questions of economic and social development, the MESC also established a Scientific Advisory Mission whose purpose was to gain 'a comprehensive and objective appreciation' of some of the main scientific and technical problems facing the Middle East region as a whole. Four studies were commissioned of which three were published.[20] They have been described as one of the most lasting and fruitful legacies of the MESC.[21]

Finally, to cement these efforts, the MESC decided to try and institutionalize the various functional arrangements for regional cooperation. There was reason for caution here, however. As Skillbeck stated: 'Any attempt, however well meaning, to superimpose [upon the region] a new type of technical education system would be to court disaster unless the ground had been carefully prepared, suspicions allayed, and a fully cooperative spirit developed.'[22] This would not be an easy task. The MESC, for example, while it had been successful in fulfilling its wartime mandate, had not ingratiated itself with the governments of the region. Although it ostensibly worked on the basis of 'recommendation' only, the MESC was too often looked upon as 'dictating to' and 'deliberately infringing upon' the sovereignty of Middle East countries. In light of the wartime reimposition of imperial control in the region, seen most visibly in the crushing of the Rashid Ali revolt in Iraq in 1941 and the 'Palace Ultimatum' in

Egypt in 1942, this attitude towards an agency which had complete control over all supplies coming into the Middle East was not surprising. In Iraq, this resentment erupted when a Colonel Bayliss, a British officer hired in 1943 as Director-General of Supply in Iraq, tried to enforce a supply policy too comprehensively and quickly. While hired directly by the Iraqi Government, Bayliss was viewed as an 'economic dictator' who took his instructions from the MESC.[23] The conflict over Bayliss was subsequently defused after a visit by MESC officials to Iraq clarifying their role and by the eventual resignation of Bayliss himself. Nevertheless, the incident revealed the underlying resentment felt towards both the MESC and the reinvigorated British presence in the region. Thus, while the institutionalization of technical cooperation was desired, both because it could benefit the economic development of the region and because it would serve to enhance British influence albeit through more subtle, technical, and 'apolitical' means, it could not be seen to be imposed upon the region from the outside. It would have to be the result of indigenous initiative 'which would have infinitely better chances of survival in Middle East soil than a rather exotic plant imported, suspected and probably unsuited to local conditions'. Above all, Skillbeck emphasized the importance of resisting those who 'would rather have seen the British lion rise more immediately resplendent in bricks and mortar in the shape of a temple consecrated to the Goddess of Agricultural Research'.[24]

Initial events produced great optimism among the staff of the MESC as various proposals for the institutionalization of wartime regional cooperation emerged 'with complete spontaneity' from Middle East sources. There was talk of creating a regional statistical bureau and Lebanese interest in creating a regional capital market. The most concrete proposal, however, was that to create a Middle East Council of Agriculture (MECA), the result of a unanimous resolution passed at the MESC conference on agricultural development in February 1944.[25] A standing committee was set up consisting of three members of the MESC staff and a delegate each from Egypt and Iraq and, soon afterwards, a constitution was drafted creating an organization of an advisory nature. At all times during the process, the MESC tried to underplay its own role in the process and emphasize the initiative as entirely a 'technical' and Middle East one. Skillbeck wrote:

We deliberately followed a technique of building up the Standing Committee as an autonomous corporate body on the technical level. Contacts with Governments were normally conducted through their members on the Committee, and not through the conventional diplomatic channels. The influence of the MESC was kept in the background; for example, one of our first actions was to print special notepaper for the Committee's use. Our objective throughout was to place the initiative in the hands of the technical delegates themselves.[26]

Skillbeck was obviously pleased with the initial fast progress, expressing his delight at seeing the same sort of enthusiasm which had characterized the conference.[27]

In tandem with the regional technical councils, it was hoped that the MESC would continue to exist in an advisory capacity. This required a solution to the problem of Anglo-American cooperation. Britain preferred to keep its relationship with the regional institution that was to emerge, a purely bilateral one. However, it was realized both that the provision of capital for development work could not come solely from Britain and that an exclusive relationship with Britain might taint the whole venture as 'imperial'. It was, therefore, decided to seek the cooperation of the United States 'as a psychological counterweight'.[28] Initially, the Americans acquiesced to the idea of postwar involvement, in tandem with the British, on matters of economic development in the Middle East. James Landis, the Principal Representative of the American Economic Mission to the Middle East (AEMME), and Jackson made joint trips around the region as well as to Britain and the United States acquainting governments of the various proposals for postwar cooperation. Moreover, the United States Special Economic Mission to the Middle East, the Culbertson Mission, endorsed the idea of American postwar involvement in development activities in the Middle East, suggesting that some of the promotional services of the jointly run MESC be continued.[29] To diminish political suspicion towards the continued existence of the MESC, there was talk of handing the MESC over to the governments of the region with the provision that British and American advisors would remain as permanent members.[30]

However, none of Britain's wartime plans for the postwar institutionalization of technical cooperation in the Middle East materialized. The promotional activities of the MESC, for example, were not continued after the war. In fact, 'regional controls and coordinating arrangements were demobilized in the Middle East faster than almost anywhere else',[31] a demobilization brought about by the breakdown of Anglo-American economic cooperation. Landis, for example, felt that the MESC had worked to the disadvantage of American trading interests during the war. It had not gone unnoticed that as MESC controls tightened, the percentage of American exports to the region fell.[32] While necessary during wartime, Landis, looking into the future, was concerned that American acceptance of this situation would continue the past tendency of American policy in the Middle East to accept and 'underwrite' empires.[33] In the postwar world, Landis called for a reversal of traditional thinking on policy, for an end to the regional approach which worked on the assumption of empire in favour of a new American drive based on bilateralism: 'If Liberia and Bolivia can exist in their own right, so equally can Egypt, the Sudan and even Palestine.'[34] Needless to say, it was assumed that such an approach would bring home a more abundant commercial harvest. As these views were widely held in the United States, it was obvious that the MESC with its regional approach had little chance of surviving in the postwar world. Its fate was sealed with the resignation of Landis from the MESC, one which 'was a turning point in the evolution of the Centre and in many ways sealed its doom as a postwar project'.[35] The development arm of the MESC was the unfortunate though logical casualty of these emerging attitudes. Landis, Culbertson, and Hoskin, the postwar Economic Advisor on the Middle East for the State Department, did in fact make some efforts to revive American interest in the development aspect of the MESC's work by advocating the establishment of an exclusively American economic body there. This attempt, however, was blocked by the State Department both because it threatened the future operation and organization of the department and because, as one commentator stated, 'it obstructed the quest for the "Holy Grail" of free and private international trade'.[36]

At the same time that British plans for the continued existence of the MESC in peacetime were being thwarted, so too were its plans for the establishment of the MECA. Part of the blame lay with the British for this state of affairs who delayed their approval of the draft constitution of the MECA because of the initial exclusion by the Arab delegates of British mandates and colonies in the region as voting members, namely Cyprus and Palestine. By keeping the organization a 'technical' one, the British had hoped to minimize the significance of their inclusion. Led by the Egyptian delegates, however, the Arabs were suspicious of British 'technical' motives and demanded instead that the whole matter be raised to the 'dignity' of an international treaty. Skillbeck felt this was most unfortunate since what was meant to be a purely consultative and advisory technical body seemed destined to become a centre of political intrigue.[37] However, as Keith Murray, the Head of the Food Division of the MESC, stated, it was really Britain that had played the political card first.[38] In the meantime, the MECA proposal was superseded by a more comprehensive Arab initiative in regional coordination with the creation of the League of Arab States.[39] Some expressed hope that the League would take up the idea of promoting regional economic development. Indeed, Skillbeck remarked that 'for the League to do nothing would be virtually to convict itself of lack of interest in constructive action in the economic field'.[40] The League, in fact, did give voice to the idea of cooperation and coordination of policy between Arab states in economic and technical matters. Skillbeck attributed this to the work of the MECA Standing Committee, believing it had 'lit a candle which the Arab League could not afford to put out'.[41] Nevertheless, the failure of the MECA scheme itself was disappointing for the British. Any scheme of technical regional cooperation run by the Arab League would exclude the British territories in the Middle East and thus remove potential sources of British influence, particularly given the relatively wide development experience of Cyprus and Palestine. Moreover, there were strong doubts as to whether the League could follow through on its initial enthusiasm towards technical cooperation. As Skillbeck pessimistically predicted, 'having passed into the political field, the Council . . . is unlikely to be retrieved from it'.[42] Thus, by mid-1945, British hopes for the postwar institutionalization of the wartime system of technical cooperation with the states of the Middle East were still-born. If continuity with the work of the MESC was to be maintained, therefore, the British would have no choice but to build that British temple consecrated to the 'Goddess of Agricultural Research' which Skillbeck had so strongly warned against doing.

Reviving plans for postwar regional development

Bevin revived discussion of promoting development in the Middle East at the London conference of British representatives in the Middle East in September 1945. While finding its roots in the wartime work of the MESC, Bevin also hoped that the initiative would fit into his larger imperial design for the region, the goal of which was to transform the relationship between the Middle East and Britain into one of 'partnership' and 'equality'.[43] The main initiatives were to be taken in the strategic front through eventual offers of troop withdrawals and treaty renegotiation, all designed to reconcile imperial and nationalist interests. Ultimately, Bevin hoped to facilitate the creation of a regional defence system centred around the kind of joint defence board which had proved such an effective and cooperative arrangement in North America during the Second World War. The development policy was designed to enhance this initiative. In the long run, Bevin wanted to foster the creation of a parallel regional development system complete with a Middle East Development Board. It was a novel initiative, predating the formation of the Marshall Plan for Europe and one to which Bevin was firmly committed. For him, it represented a new departure in how Britain would conduct relations with the former colonial world. All in all, it seemed to fit nicely with

Bevin's wider regional schemes and meshed 'the siren calls of strategic imperative [with] a Labour version of the "white man's burden"'.[44]

However, the enthusiasm which surrounded the idea in theory waned when the practical problems of its implementation began to be considered by the conference. For example, in light of the MESC's failure to foster the creation of an indigenous system of technical cooperation into which foreign financial and technical assistance could fit, Britain was left to advance the idea itself which, as Skillbeck had warned, would prove very tricky indeed in the charged political atmosphere of the postwar Middle East, acutely sensitive to the interference of foreign powers. Lord Altrincham reiterated this point in a memo distributed to the conference, writing that 'there is a change of conditions under which our influence must be used in the Middle East. Nationalism will not abide the control which we exercised over the whole machinery of Government, nor will it any longer tolerate the open constraint of rulers and the arbitrary making and unmaking of Governments which we have thought desirable at some moments since Cromer's time.' If Britain was going to promote economic and social development in the Middle East let alone her more specific regional agenda, it was emphasized by Lord Altrincham that it would have to be done 'unobtrusively' and 'at request' with the accent at all times being on local initiative.[45]

It soon became clear that Britain's worsening financial position in the immediate postwar world also dictated the necessity of a cautious and quiet approach to economic development in the Middle East. Direct financial assistance for economic and social development in the Middle East was out of the question but there was some hope of using large sterling balances which the region had accumulated as a result of British wartime expenditure. Here, there seemed more than enough capital to finance large-scale development in the region for many years to come. Officials from the Treasury, however, warned the conference that too activist a stance could precipitafe an excessive and potentially disastrous demand for repayment beyond Britain's ability to supply either the goods or the foreign currency. If anything, therefore, this pointed to the need for limiting rather than hastening the pace of economic development in the postwar Middle East, something to which there are repeated references in the minutes of the conference. It also reinforced the point made earlier by Lord Altrincham that any British activity in this field would have to be based on local initiative. As William Iliff, who went on to become the roving regional Treasury representative stationed with the British Middle East Office in Cairo, explained: 'If we took the initiative in suggesting schemes to the local governments and were unable to meet their demands for imports, they could ask us for dollars with some justification. If, however, the initiative came from the governments themselves . . . our hands would be freed.'[46]

Where Bevin really hoped to make his mark on the economic and social development of the Middle East was through the provision of technical assistance. This was not a new policy for Britain in the Middle East but was part of a long tradition of providing advisers for many of the territorial bureaucracies of the region, notably Egypt and Iraq. In fact, the terms of the Anglo-Iraqi Treaty of 1930 actually guaranteed Britain a monopoly on all foreign advisers within the government administration. As has been shown, this tradition continued and was, in fact, intensified, as a result of the wartime work of the MESC. What Bevin, therefore, wanted was a more explicit British commitment to the revitalization of this tradition in the postwar world. Lord Altrincham even suggested the creation of an administrative service along the lines that existed for the Sudan and India.[47]

Here again, however, the conference moved with caution. Bailey, the former Deputy Director of the MESC, while pleased with the adoption of a more forward-looking development policy in the Middle East, warned of difficulties in finding an adequate number of qualified experts. Even the MESC with its wider wartime access to pools of experts had difficulties with recruitment.[48] In the postwar world, this situation was likely to worsen, something which Stonehewer Bird, the British Ambassador in Iraq, stated was already in evidence there.[49] The most economical solution seemed to be the creation of a small nucleus of regionally based experts who would operate much along the lines of those before them in the MESC. This idea had first been raised at an economic conference of British Middle East representatives held in Fayoum in April 1945 and was subsequently adopted by the conference in London. It was this regional pool which became the Development Division of the British Middle East Office. As a back-up to the BMEO in Cairo, the conference rejected Lord Altrincham's suggestion for the creation of a Middle East Service and established instead an administrative unit and a policy committee within the Foreign Office in London, called the Middle East Secretariat (MES) and the Middle East Official Committee (MEOC) respectively.

Even this fairly modest initiative, however, was fraught with political dangers. It was Bevin's intention, for example, that the BMEO would pursue his regional agenda which he considered such an important feature of his postwar strategy in the region. This meant continuing the compilation of regional economic information which would be incorporated into a region wide economic survey. It also meant continuing with the MESC's promotion of regional technical cooperation, convening technical conferences which ultimately would lead to the establishment of the Middle East Development Board. However, it was perfectly clear that in pursuing this agenda, the BMEO would have to be even more cautious than the MESC was before it. As was stressed repeatedly by Bailey, the success of this initiative would depend upon the degree to which the 'office' could maintain the kind of unobtrusive and disinterested approach which Lord Altrincham had spoken about. There could be no hidden agendas or undue pressure.[50] This warning was seconded by representatives from the British Embassy in Egypt where nationalist feeling was perhaps the strongest. In a post-conference note to the Foreign Office, they stressed that 'it is no good thrusting experts upon the Egyptian Government. The approach must be very cautious. Any suggestion that we want to run their country for them will make them turn elsewhere for assistance. The appropriate Egyptian Ministers etc. must be carefully worked on with the object of getting them to take the initiative in asking for British help.'[51]

The result of this cautious talk was a development policy dramatically reduced in scope. Certainly, the subject continued to be discussed in terms of grand possibilities. This was accompanied by vague promises to use sterling balances for capital development and the commitment to continue the provision of experts to the bureaucracies of the region. In concrete terms, however, the only provision of any novelty was the establishment of the BMEO with its Development Division, backed up by an administrative and policy support system in London and, even here, the initiative was described with a certain degree of circumspection. During a speech to the Anglo-Egyptian Chamber of Commerce on 1 November 1945, Bevin described the creation of the BMEO as an administrative exercise only, designed to improve upon an already existing system of British technical assistance. 'All I have tried to do', stated Bevin, 'is to introduce some organization behind the scenes in order to supply you with technical and scientific ability as you want it and as you ask for it . . . The benefit of the [BMEO's] experience may be available for any development schemes your Governments may have in mind.'[52] Above all, in keeping with the conference's cautious tone, Bevin countered those who looked upon the BMEO as a new forerunner of British imperialism by emphasizing the 'technical', 'apolitical' and non-interventionist nature of its work.[53] As he said in the House of Commons when first announcing its creation: 'I desire to make it quite clear that His Majesty's Government have no intention to interfere in the local politics of the different countries. Questions of government must be a matter for peoples in those territories. This is merely an attempt, as reconstruction and new production comes along, to do our best to assist our friends.'[54]

Revising plans for postwar regional development

The emerging skepticism surrounding the possibilities of effecting quick action on the development front seemed justified. In fact, two years after the inauguration of this policy, it seemed that little if anything had been accomplished. After the initial flurry of activity during which the BMEO was created, the American Embassy in London reported that further action had been 'spasmodic and piecemeal'.[55] For example, after an initial meeting in December of 1945, the MEOC, the policy arm of Bevin's development initiative, remained dormant and unused by the rest of the Foreign Office machinery.[56] This brought complaints from Sir Arnold Overton in Cairo, the first head of the BMEO, who was waiting for instructions from London[57] and a similar sense of dissatisfaction was expressed by Lord Altrincham.[58] Moreover, the administrative arm of this initiative, the MES, seemed to have been nothing more than a backwater in the Foreign Office and a small one at that. Complaints were heard very early on from those British officials interested in the initiative that its location in a 'far away part of the building' was making consultation and discussion about policy 'more difficult than it should be'.[59] An interview in late 1948 between Boardman of the American State Department and an administrative assistant in the MES, Miss Charlotte Waterlow, indicated that this state of neglect and bureaucratic isolation continued. This surprised the Americans who had gained the impression from Bevin's rhetoric that the MES was a major administrative arm of the Foreign Office. Indeed, the MES had started out with a strong head in Dennis Greenhill. Within two years, however, he was transferred to a diplomatic post in Sophia. A similar fate befell the MES one year later with the loss of Greenhill's replacement, Dundas who, in turn, was not replaced until the arrival of Trefor Evans in July of 1949. This left the MES without an administrative head for almost a full year. Moreover, the support staff was so minimal that with the out-transfer of an administrative assistant in 1948, Waterlow was forced to conclude to the American that, in fact, 'I am the Secretariat'.[60] This had an obvious effect on the dynamism of the MES. As Boardman concluded: 'The Secretariat is far less active than it was intended or than it was presently believed to be by many in the Department ... I do not in any way have a complete story, but I have a feeling that some in the Department believe that the Secretariat has far more grandiose and expensive ideas for the Middle East than it actually has. I do not think it is generally realized that the Secretariat is presently concentrating on personnel and not on various development projects.'[61]

Equally surprising to the Americans was the limited scope of activity in the field. While designed as the main instrument of Bevin's development initiative in the Middle East, the BMEO took longer to get its feet off the ground than was expected. Logistically, for example, while designed to carry on much of the roving technical assistance work of the MESC, it was forced in the postwar world to start from scratch. None of the technical staff associated with the MESC stayed on and it proved difficult to recruit a new team of experts. It was not until mid-1947 that the various positions for technical advisers – seven in all, were filled, almost two years after the original policy had been formulated.[62] Moreover, their progress was further delayed by the outbreak of a cholera epidemic in Egypt and the consequent ban on their foreign travel. Thus, when an American diplomat based in Cairo was asked about the work of the Development Division, he could do no better than describe its work in the Middle East as 'insignificant', adding that 'the agricultural expert was hard put to find anything to do for some time after his arrival'.[63]

These logistical problems were not helped by opposition within the British Government to the setting up of a regional economic representation of the Foreign Office in the Middle East. For example, one of the greatest institutional obstacles to the successful launching of the Development Division proved to be the ambivalence and, in some cases, outright jealousy of the various British embassies and legations in the Middle East towards its existence. This was a serious problem for an organization which, having lost the old personnel from the MESC, was only able to re-establish contact with the policy making élites of the various Middle East states through the liaisoning work of the embassies. Sir Miles Lampson, the British Ambassador in Egypt until mid-1946, while supportive of the idea in general, had warned of such opposition when the idea of maintaining a regional nucleus of technical assistants in the Middle East in the postwar world was first discussed with any seriousness. While a separate regional economic organization in the Middle East had seemed an 'awkward' but necessary expedient during the war, he looked upon its continuation in the postwar world as unwise. Not only was its political utility suspect but it was also administratively 'extravagant', complicated, and would create a two-tiered diplomatic structure.[64] As an alternative, he proposed the strengthening of local embassies and legations in such a way that technical advisers be made clearly subordinate and directly associated to them. If regional coordination of work had to be done, it should be left to London. What Lampson did not want to see was the creation of a system where British technical advisers worked directly with the local governments of the region. Writing to Eden, he stressed that 'I cannot but regard with considerable apprehension any British machinery for achieving this end which does not work under the direct cover of the local British diplomatic missions . . . I greatly hope that you will take the same view. This system of two Kings in Thule is not going to work at all satisfactorily.'[65]

However, with the establishment of the separately administered BMEO, Lampson's warnings were not heeded in London. The initial exclusion of the BMEO from involvement in 'political' matters and the accreditation of the BMEO's head as a member of each British mission in the region had in part been done in deference to his concern that its work not interfere with that of the diplomatic missions in the region. Advisers were meant to work in consultation with the appropriate local embassy. However, being given its own separate headquarters in the old buildings of the MESC in Cairo and its own lines of communication with London, the BMEO, in effect, became an autonomous instrument of the Foreign Office. Lampson's recommendations were even further trodden on with the decision to create a Political Division in early 1947.[66] The consequence of all this was an initial reluctance on the part of some British diplomatic representatives in the Middle East to openly cooperate with the BMEO, leaving Lampson's warnings as somewhat prophetic. The surprising degree to which this affected its work was revealed by Bill Crawford, the head of the BMEO's Development Division throughout the period of this study, who in retrospect reported:

Though it had the blessing and was indeed the child of the Secretary of State, it had more difficulties with our own diplomatic posts than with Arab Governments, suspicious as these were of this new brand of imperialism. There was a time at the start when the Embassy in Tehran was our only friend. Circumstances have altered but even now we are much at the whim of individual diplomatic representatives who may or may not believe in British technical assistance.[67]

The Treasury also proved a less than enthusiastic backer of the BMEO. It complained of the 'intangibility' of its work and refused to support it on anything more than on a year-by-year basis, creating a continual atmosphere of insecurity and dependence.[68] There were repeated difficulties over pay and allowances and continual resentment on the part of the advisers to the 'invidious distinction' made between them and the members of the regular foreign service. When this resulted in their being temporarily deprived of an increase in allowances given to all other British staff based in Cairo, many of the advisers considered quitting. As Crawford wrote: 'At this time . . . I had great difficulty in keeping the Division in being.'[69] There was also an on-going debate within Whitehall as to whether it would be better located in London. The result of this lukewarm commitment to the Development Division undoubtedly meant that Crawford and whoever happened to be the head of the BMEO at the time spent a good portion of their time justifying its activities in London rather than concentrating on the work at hand. The whole situation was infuriating to Crawford who in retrospect quipped that 'while we have had and still have our fervid supporters in parts of the Foreign Office, in other parts and, [in particular, in] the Treasury, [we have] only enemies'.[70]

Neither could the Foreign Office, in part due to Treasury opposition, devise a system or commit the resources needed to recruit experts to fill the bureaucracies of the region. In many ways, this went to the heart of the problem. The BMEO was created not so much to offer technical advice itself as to pave the way for the employment of a larger number of British technicians in the region and, in the early postwar years, there were encouraging signs of a significant demand. Iraq, for example, had established an Irrigation Development Commission and had made requests for over 100 technicians, a number which even the BMEO found staggering.[71] Bevin gave the scheme top priority and the MEOC declared it 'an opportunity which will not recur for consolidating our influence in the Middle East'.[72] However, Britain proved unable to attract 'upon demand' technicians of the highest calibre. The first progress report on the recommendations of the London conference, for example, reported that while Middle East Governments are prepared to accept British advice, no less than thirty-five requests covering a wide range of activities remain as yet unfulfilled.[73] Even the more concerted efforts to fulfil the Iraqi requests met with only moderate success with more than 40 per cent of the requests being left unfilled. These included some of the more important posts in agronomy as recommended by the agricultural advisor of the BMEO.[74] The situation was clearly a frustrating one. After reading a rather depressing report on the state of recruitment for the Iraqi Irrigation Development Commission, Bevin, for example, quipped 'Why is this?' and proceeded to demand swift and urgent action.[75] Throughout the late 1940s, however, things did not improve leaving the BMEO unable to fulfil the most significant part of its mandate. As Windett, the statistical advisor of the BMEO, stated in response to a request for estimates of need: 'As we have never had any to offer . . . we have never been able to test the real demand for them in M.E. countries, nor has it been politic to sound the market for them for fear of raising hopes of a supply from the UK which would either not be forthcoming at all or forthcoming too late . . . when the demand had been met from some other source.'[76]

However, it was the inhospitable political environment of the postwar Middle East which perhaps had the most important effect on the type of work undertaken by the BMEO and its pace. It soon proved pointless, for example, to pursue Bevin's regional agenda established at the conference,

Overton reporting very early on from Cairo that any hint of such a policy would be 'strongly resented' by the governments of the region.[77] Thus, shortly after the establishment of the BMEO, ideas to coordinate the use of scarce currency reserves in the region were dropped; so too were attempts to convene regional technical conferences; and, while there were some initial efforts to continue the collection of regional economic information in the form of the *Middle East Economic and Statistical Bulletin*, these too eventually fell by the wayside. By the middle of 1947, the MEOC formally recognized political reality by abandoning Bevin's policy of economic regionalism altogether.[78] Rather than operate on the basis of an agenda preconceived in London, the BMEO thereafter adapted its work to what seemed in demand from the Middle East itself.

These difficulties in pursuing Bevin's regional agenda are clearly seen when one examines the attempts by Waterston, the entomology adviser of the BMEO, to establish an International Desert Locust Security Service (IDLSS) in the early postwar years. During the war, the British had set up the Middle East Anti Locust Unit (MEALU) which had been remarkably successful in combating the effects of wartime locust plagues.[79] It was their hope that, with the end of the war, the Arabs would take over financial and administrative responsibility for the unit themselves, leaving the British to provide the technical support only. When no Arab initiative arose, however, London agreed reluctantly to continue financing the unit until 1948. In order to keep the idea of a regional organization alive, an entomology adviser was added to the roster of the BMEO.

By 1948, negotiations had recommenced on the terms of what became known as the Desert Locust Convention. As part of the agreement, the British wanted to establish a technical agency which would have full authority to inspect and destroy incipient locust swarms on a regional basis. By keeping the initiative a 'technical' one, they hoped to guarantee the possibility of quick executive action.[80] This emphasis on 'the technical' bore an uncanny resemblance to that tried earlier with the MECA. However, unfortunately for the British, an equally strong sense of *déja vu* was generated by the subsequent objections of the Arabs and, predictably, the Egyptians who, in a subsequent counter-proposal, recommended instead the creation of an advisory body which would leave actual work to the individual governments concerned. The Arabs did not believe British rhetoric about their 'technical' intentions and remained deeply suspicious of British motives, particularly when it came to locust control which would have allowed British technicians detailed access to Middle East territory. These suspicions were, if anything, intensified when Britain insisted on the representation of her mandates and colonies in any ensuing agency 'à la MECA'. A deadlock, therefore, developed which led to the abandonment of the desert locust convention and a return to more *ad hoc* methods of desert locust control. Most significantly for Britain, its demise also led to a reduction of British influence in this field in the Middle East. In late 1948, the main British technical team called the Desert Locust Survey was transferred to Nairobi and by 1952, the entomology adviser was dropped from the BMEO's roster altogether.[81]

These failed experiments with regional technical cooperation pursued both by Waterston and by the MESC before him had a great impact on the operational style which the BMEO quickly came to adopt in the postwar Middle East. During the war, the convening of technical conferences seemed an appropriate and 'non-political' way to promote technical cooperation. It soon became apparent, however, that in the postwar Middle East such formal ways of proceeding would no longer be effective and, in fact, would be resisted. As Overton reminded the Foreign Office, 'the end of our military occupation . . . has brought a situation where British assistance, to be effective, requires a new technique based on personal contacts which [are] being rapidly evolved'.[82]

It was this evolving emphasis on 'the personal' which is crucial to understanding how the BMEO operated. As experience with locust control showed, it would prove pointless trying to operate on the basis of worked out programmes and formal agreements; such would divert development from the practical to the political. A better approach seemed one based on personal contacts which could be activated by such informal means as a letter or a telephone call. It was this approach which the BMEO adopted and, thus, in the first few years of its life, much time was spent on building up an active clientele, especially among the technocrats and director-generals of the region.[83] This operational style was necessarily very time-consuming and, in some part, explains the BMEO's slow start. However, among those in its employ, it was the consensus that the political context of the postwar Middle East offered them few alternatives, much as Lord Altrincham had predicted. Overton made this point when he stressed in an early despatch to the Foreign Office that success in the field of technical assistance would not be achieved by 'spectacular methods' and 'ambitious schemes' but rather by 'unremitting, sympathetic and patient work from day to day and week to week'.[84] The point was emphasized further by Crawford who, in a retrospective defence of this philosophy, argued: 'There are two things I hold true of the Middle East: you can only get things done on a personal basis and the Almighty geared the development of the Middle East to a certain pace and not all the money and all the experts in the world can press it beyond that.'[85]

Thus, Bevin's 'peasants, not pashas' policy did not get off to the kind of spectacular beginnings which he might have liked. Resources in Britain in the postwar world were simply too limited, budgets too constrained. There was little direct finance available for overseas development schemes nor did the resources exist to set up an adequate system of recruiting experts for overseas postings. This had already led to a focus on local sources of capital and manpower to fill 'the poverty gap'. However, Britain also lacked the legitimacy to become actively involved in questions of internal economic policy, not surprising after almost a century of imperial manipulation and neglect. The nationalist impulse was strong and growing and would resist the imposition of this new kind of imperialism. This had proved equally the case during the early postwar period as it had during the Second World War. It is in this context of resistance and vulnerability that one begins to see the seeds of a new approach, more aware, and at times more sensitive to local conditions and realities, a sensitivity which bred a healthy skepticism about the ability of outside powers to accelerate the pace of socio-economic development in the region. Thus, while Bevin's greater vision would persist, a new vision, born out of a dying imperialism and cautious of the limitations of promoting socio-economic change, was beginning to take form.

2 Imperial dreams and delusions: the economics of promoting Middle East modernization

One of the most striking features of the postwar Middle East was the explosion of nationalist sentiment. Since the inauguration of the 'peasants, not pashas' policy and the establishment of the BMEO, the attitude of the Arab world toward Britain had deteriorated dramatically. Renegotiations with the Egyptians over the terms of the 1936 Anglo-Egyptian Treaty continued to flounder and this was joined by the Iraqi rejection of the Portsmouth Treaty in 1948 and the growth of nationalist pressure on the Shah in Iran to revise the terms of the concession of the Anglo-Iranian Oil Company (AIOC). Permeating all of these conflicts was the brewing storm in Palestine which erupted in 1948, severely weakening the existing political structures of the region and giving renewed life to the emerging nationalist opposition forces. When the development policy had been drafted in 1945, it was hoped that it would help to neutralize such political forces. It now seemed that economic and social development was dependent on the same factor which it was designed to promote. As John Troutbeck, Overton's successor as head of the BMEO, concluded upon completing his inaugural tour of the Middle East in late 1947: 'Quite apart from the obvious difficulties of world shortages, poor administration . . . corruption, indifference, etc., economic development is everywhere bedeviled by politics. It needs tranquility, but on the one side you have the Russian menace and on the other Palestine.'[1]

It was not that the political élites of the region were ignoring problems of socio-economic development. On the contrary, pressured by emerging nationalist forces, they embarked on a multitude of initiatives aimed at attacking deteriorating social and economic conditions in the region. Iran made the furthest advances by formulating and passing a Seven Year Plan in early 1949 to be implemented by the newly created Plan Organization. Similar plans for economic development were being completed in Iraq, most notably the report of the Irrigation Development Commission with approval in principle also being given to the creation of a development board. Even Egypt seemed to be making some progress in this direction by setting up a Higher Economic Council for combating 'poverty, ignorance and disease' and passing a modest Five Year Plan.[2] Bevin found all of this activity encouraging and looked upon these 'boards and blueprints' as having laid the foundations for success in the next stage of policy implementation.

However, all of this planning and 'development-mindedness' in the region was having little payoff for Britain. Bevin's policy demanded that Britain play a leading role in the promotion of development in the region. For this, it would need to provide manpower, machines, and capital if it was going to have any effect in convincing the emerging more radical and progressive social groups in the region of the benefits of maintaining ties with Britain and the West. Capital was felt to be especially important because it would facilitate the completion of large impact projects from which would radiate a whole series of backward and forward economic linkages. In the Middle East, many of these so-called impact projects revolved around the development of irrigation facilities in such areas as the Tigris and Euphrates rivers, the Khuzistan region of Iran, the Nile valley, and the Jordan River basin. Bevin showed a constant interest in promoting British involvement in these large development projects and, indeed, British firms such as Sir Alexander Gibb and Partners and Balfour Beatty and Company became quite active in the Middle East, especially with regard to the construction of dams and irrigation facilities in Iraq.

However, there is a difference between parasitically reaping the fruits of someone else's development programme and actively promoting and facilitating local enterprise and initiative. Britain was never able to do the latter and certainly not on a regional basis. In fact, for the most part, Britain was seen to be blocking rather than promoting progress: it had abandoned Palestine and the Arabs to their Zionist fate in 1947; it continued to dominate the region through the control of key military installations; and despite musings about the promotion of reform, it continued its underlying support for 'pashas rather than peasants', thus thwarting if not repressing more broadly based and progressive alternatives. In short, promoting the long-term development of the Middle East seemed to be in direct conflict with Britain's more immediate need of protecting the status quo. In true patrimonial logic, only one factor might have allowed this contradiction to persist: the provision of large amounts of capital, much along the lines of the large US aid programmes to several Middle East states in the 1980s and 1990s. Bevin recognized this important link and tried repeatedly to secure greater amounts of capital from the Treasury for Middle East development schemes. Apart from the aberration of Suez, it was one of the last gasps of British imperialism in the region. Much to the disappointment of

Bevin, it was also one which proved well beyond the means of Britain's fading imperial power. This will become readily apparent through an examination of British policy towards sterling balances, the World Bank, and proposals for the creation of an Arab Development Bank in the early 1950s.

British debt, sterling balances, and Middle East development

The first postwar Middle East conference had expressed caution about pledging British finance for Middle East economic development. It was hoped that local sources of capital would suffice and, for this, they pointed to the existence of large sterling balances which various states in the region had accumulated during the war. However, for sterling balances to be a valid form of development capital in the Middle East, an assumption which had been accepted by the conference, Britain had to be able to honour her debts either in the form of capital goods or foreign exchange. In the immediate postwar world, both proved beyond Britain's financial capabilities, in part, removing the assumptions upon which Britain's concentration on technical assistance had been based.

Originally, for example, the conference had predicted that sterling balances would provide 'golden opportunities' for British exporters in the Middle East.[3] However, the transition to a peacetime economy proved harder than expected. Britain had enough trouble supplying her domestic needs for capital goods, let alone her export markets. If exports were to be considered, they had to go to markets which surrendered hard currency (i.e. dollars) in exchange. With its large supply of sterling, the Middle East was not considered by the Treasury and the Board of Trade to be one of those high priority export markets. Hence, the existence of sterling balances, in fact, proved to be a liability and not an advantage to any dramatic 'take-offs' in capital works development in the Middle East. Until British domestic production increased, sterling balances dictated that, in most cases, the Middle East would in fact be denied capital goods needed for development.

Attempts were made by the Foreign Office to raise the priority of the Middle Eastern market by highlighting it as a potential source of foodstuffs. There was a general shortage of food in the early postwar period, particularly in the Commonwealth which was accentuating its worldwide shortage of dollars. By presenting the Middle East as a food supplier and, thus, a dollar saver, the Foreign Office hoped to enhance its attractiveness in the eyes of the Treasury and the Board of Trade. The Treasury were initially interested in the idea, Rowe-Dutton very conditionally suggesting that '*if* we had the money to spare and *if* we could make releases from their sterling balances, I should be very tempted to give pretty high priority to the Iraqi irrigation scheme in the hopes of securing a real increase in cereal production in Iraq'.[4] Before any conclusions could be reached, however, a full investigation would have to be made to determine how long it would take to get results, how much internal and external finance would be needed, and how much equipment would be needed from the United Kingdom. Bevin correspondingly ordered a wide economic survey of the region, a responsibility taken up by the Ministry of Food with help from the advisers of the BMEO. Overton also hoped that a Food Mission would be sent to the Middle East along the lines of the expert committee which had already visited East Africa.

Initially, there were high hopes. The MEOC threw around the idea of Iraq being a granary for the whole of the Middle East and potential was also seen for the Jezira in Syria, the Blue Nile Province of the Sudan and the north of Iran.[5] The results of the initial surveys, however, proved disappointing, a Ministry of Food report concluding that any short-term prospects for an increase in food production were remote.[6] Sir Herbert Stewart, the Agricultural Adviser of the Development Division, reached similar conclusions after having examined the potential for the production of linseed, cotton, rapes, and groundnuts in Iraq.[7]

Apart from problems with the general practicality of the proposal, there were some who felt it conflicted with the original purpose of Bevin's policy. Believing that the primary objective was to raise the region's standard of living, one Foreign Office official concluded that a move to promote the export of food might well have the reverse effect of what was intended by reducing the level of local consumption.[8] Crawford was in complete agreement, writing that 'the policy of promoting the Middle East as a source of food supply seems to me to be getting very far away from the original policy . . . to give all possible help to raise the standard of living in the Middle East'.[9] Though more out of disappointment over the lack of potential for quick large-scale increases in the production of foodstuffs than out of any concern for the well-being of the Middle East, London in the end abandoned this policy initiative. The result was that the Middle East remained, for the most part, a low priority region when it came to the release of sterling balances.

The ability of Britain to guarantee the convertibility of sterling balances and, thus, allow its Middle East creditors access to dollars was even more problematic. An impossibility immediately after the war, doubts remained as to its feasibility even with the signing of the Anglo-American loan agreement which called for full convertibility in July 1947. Eager to prevent a flood of sterling onto the market, Britain embarked on a series of negotiations with members of the sterling area to determine the degree to which sterling balances would remain blocked. London even hoped that some might agree to write off a portion of the debt altogether. As Judd Polk, the American Treasury Representative in the Middle East at that time, remarked: 'the more extreme British optimists saw a good part of the leaning tower of sterling balances . . . being cut off in a sportsman-like recognition of the excessive burden borne by the British for all associated countries during the war'.[10]

The course of these pre-convertibility negotiations in the Middle East offer a clear indication of the conflict which existed in the logic of Britain's attempt to promote economic development in the Middle East and her need to protect her domestic economic situation. As that policy unfolded, it became increasingly clear that London's approach was anything but 'development' minded: Syria was denied entry into the sterling area; Egypt, unhappy with the terms of London's offer, decided to leave the sterling area altogether; and releases were only given to Iran with great reluctance as a result of the importance of that country with respect to oil. However, perhaps the most telling negotiations took place in Iraq, a country which, as a result of the recent formation of the Iraqi Irrigation Development Commission, was being touted by Bevin as the 'most promising' development prospect in the Middle East.

The negotiations were undertaken by a Treasury mission headed by Sir W. Eady.[11] It opened the negotiations by offering the Iraqis a L 15 million release in convertible sterling over a five-year period on the condition that Iraq scale down their size. It estimated that with 'careful management' of imports and the maintenance of appropriate price levels at which the products of Iraq could be sold on the world market, current account needs could be met by domestic revenue leaving sterling balances for expenditure on capital development whose demands would not be so immediate.[12] However, the Iraqis questioned Britain's right to limit releases and refused to consider the possibility of scaling down sterling balances arguing that British assumptions about Iraq's fiscal capabilities were mistaken. For example, the likelihood of a balanced budget was slim in a country where floods and harvest failures were commonplace. In addition, with consumer imports already below the pre-1939 level, it was pointed out that British negotiators were, in effect, calling for the imposition of severe austerity in Iraq.[13] As an alternative, therefore, the Iraqis accepted the British offer of L 15 million for capital development but requested a further release of L 17.5 million in order to meet minimum consumption needs. As justification for what turned out to be a request for half of Iraq's sterling balances, the Iraqi delegation reminded London that:

Iraq has now experienced five years of continuing economic crisis. Agricultural workers and labourers in Iraq at the best of times were only barely above subsistence level. The cost of living had risen from 100 in 1939 to over 600 in 1945 and was now 550. All classes of employees, including Government employees, were underpaid in relation to the rise in the cost of living . . . [This] could only fall if sufficient imports of consumer goods were received which could absorb purchasing power.[14]

The British refused to budge from their offer of L 15 million leaving the Iraqis little choice but to accept what was, in effect, a unilateral rescheduling of debt. Some have described the agreement as generous in relation to similar ones in the 'dependent' sterling area[15] and, in theory, the British granted Iraq's request for L 15 million for capital development. However, it was recognized that without additional releases for current consumption, this attempt at 'targeting' sterling balances for development was pure semantics. Having spoken repeatedly of the 'extremity and impressiveness' of Iraq's poverty, the Iraqis, therefore, left the negotiations deeply concerned about their effect on the political state of the country. 'There was comparative stability in Iraq, based only on the hope of improvement, and if we were not to be allowed means for repairs, renewals and reconstruction, that hope would be replaced by despair. It was for this that [we] wanted the sterling balances.'[16]

The convertibility crisis in July, 1947, which resulted in a dramatic drain in foreign exchange reserves, forced Britain to renege on even these relatively restrictive agreements. In the return to the bargaining table, discussion no longer centred on the question of development but concentrated instead on maintaining adequate levels of consumption, a far cry from the original pledge made by Bevin that sterling balances would be used as investment capital in the Middle East.[17] What is even more indicative of this decline in policy expectations was the fact that sterling balances were not even adequate to cover shortfalls in current expenditure. In 1948, for example, Iraq was rocked by a severe financial crisis. Repeated requests were made by the Iraqis for more generous releases of convertible sterling, all of which London refused, recommending instead the hiring of a 'high-level' foreign financial advisor to solve what the British diagnosed to be mainly problems of internal revenue collection.[18] Coming in the wake of the Portsmouth Treaty fiasco, however, this negative response was not appreciated by the Iraqis. As Mack, the British Ambassador in Baghdad, reported: 'There is a growing bitterness against us . . . There is danger of a strong growth of feeling that while we are out to exploit Iraq materially and strategically, we are not prepared to do more than to make vague promises to help in economic development.'[19]

In 1949, a similar financial crisis threatened to grind to a halt many important government services. In the Department of Agriculture, for example, there was a proposed 30 per cent cut in the budget prompting Baghdad to remark that if these cuts go through, 'it will be a severe setback to development plans in Iraq'.[20] With the Government being unable to pay the British construction engineering firm of Balfour Beatty and Co. who were working on the Habbaniyah Storage Basin, a stoppage in work was threatened with the resultant dismissal of 700 workers.[21] The crisis had even resulted in the discharge of four engineers from the Iraqi Irrigation Development Commission and there was talk of closing it down entirely.[22] Finally, the government began to consider the sale of state lands, despite the importance which the advisers of the BMEO placed on state ownership of land.[23] In the case of Iraq, therefore, it was obvious that the restrictions on sterling were conflicting with Bevin's policy of promoting social and economic development in the Middle East. London, of course, continued to emphasize that the problem was mainly one of policy within Iraq. While this was to some extent justified, it should not obscure the fact that Baghdad was being denied capital which was rightfully hers and which could have helped to compensate for the crisis.

If sterling balances were not freely available in the immediate postwar period and if Britain's industrial capacity was far from being able to supply the Middle East with capital goods needed for development, why make the link between sterling and development in the Middle East in the first place, particularly if these constraints were recognized when the original policy was formulated? It was obvious, for example, that the British had no intention of promptly releasing vast sums of sterling amassed during the war in the Middle East for development. The policy had always been one of conservation.[24] Nevertheless, since no one expected development to take off quickly in the region, there seemed no danger from a financial point of view and every advantage from the political to make the link. The unforeseen element in these calculations was the extent and depth of the postwar financial crisis which exposed the contradictions in policy for all to see.

As during the days of the MESC, there was a lingering hope that the Americans might somehow agree to underwrite British economic policy in the region and thus compensate for British financial weakness. These were encouraged by reports from the British embassy in Washington in early 1946 of a growing American interest in the region, both as a strategic buffer against the emerging Soviet threat and as an area with great potential for trade and development.[25] This spawned initial interest in the Foreign Office in holding formal Anglo-American discussions on the subject though little came of it at this time due to sober second thoughts about the political and commercial implications of cooperating with the more well-endowed Americans.[26] However, a more serious approach was made one year later which resulted in a series of informal meetings between the two parties in Washington in the fall of 1947. These were conducted by Greenhill who was himself deeply frustrated by the Treasury's inability to support Bevin's Middle East economic policy. Believing that the limits of that policy had been reached with the creation of the MES and the BMEO, he suggested in private in the run-up to the discussions that only the Americans could provide the kind of practical help which the Middle East needed.[27] The talks themselves, however, resulted in nothing more than a non-committal exchange of ideas; no schedule or agenda for future discussions was laid down.[28] The British continued to 'weigh carefully' the extent to which cooperation with the United States was desired and the Americans were more apt to go it alone anyway. In fact, the Americans were doubtful of their own ability to finance capital development in the Middle East. In an implicit criticism at what the British were doing, they rejected the idea of drawing up a 'balance sheet' on Middle East development on the grounds that 'it does not seem appropriate to draw up one side of the balance sheet when we have nothing to offer on the other'.[29]

Britain, capital assistance, and Middle East development

By the spring of 1949, Bevin's 'peasants, not pashas' policy lay in tatters. Articles in *The Economist* called it 'bankrupt' and, in the wake of the Palestine fiasco, even Troutbeck was describing it as a 'vain hope' in the absence of more profound political solutions.[30] Bevin, however, refused to abandon his vision. At a reconvened conference of British Middle East representatives in London in July 1949, he spoke with some urgency about the need for a more energetic approach to the promotion of socio-economic development in the region, particularly now that the 'boards' and 'blueprints' had been put in place. Using a tentative proposal prepared by Crawford, Bevin called for the formulation of a 'great and imaginative' development plan covering the area from Pakistan to Turkey along the lines being formulated for South Asia – the 'Bevin Plan' as it was called in the Middle East.[31]

The big question mark was finance and, although there was some loosening of the Treasury's purse-strings, no dramatic policy shifts occurred. The conference did give their official sanction to an 'Interim Report' which had been produced by Crawford before the conference but it was really nothing more than an *ad hoc* list of projects with no time frames nor any commitments to provide finance.[32] When another of the oft-repeated appeals to the Treasury was made for greater finance, all that resulted was an agreement in principle to grant development loans to the governments of the region although this was supplemented by a commitment to grant 1.25 million pounds to the newly created United Nations Relief and Works Administration (UNRWA).[33] Thus, with the exception of UNRWA, the agreement 'in principle' did not represent an actual commitment of financial aid. The Treasury continued to bank on the misguided assumptions that most of the finance for the projects listed in the 'Bevin Plan' would not be needed until at least the mid-1950s and that internal sources of revenue, including sterling balances, would be able to make up the bulk of that which was needed.[34] When actual loans were still felt essential, they would at best be given on an *ad hoc* basis and be made dependent both on the economic and financial capacity of the British economy at that particular time and on commitments elsewhere, particularly in the Colonies.[35] What this implied, in effect, was that British financial assistance towards economic and social development in the Middle East could at best be looked at as a way of 'priming the pump'.[36]

This was a very weak policy foundation for Bevin's new initiative which meant that his reinvigorated vision for promoting socio-economic development in the region remained without any real substance. Numerous case studies reveal the emptiness of his rhetoric. Syria, for example, a state at the heart of the new regional refugee problem whose instability fuelled the political volatility of the Middle East, was an obvious target for development aid.[37] Along with Jordan, it had been defined as a 'capital-poor' country whose development Bevin wanted to make a priority. The Foreign Office repeatedly stressed the importance of assisting Syrian plans for economic development, Furlonge at one point arguing that 'even if there were no refugees, Syria's problem of underdevelopment, which is to a large extent responsible for its political instability, would have to be tackled and in view of our responsibilities, it is in our interest to see that it is tackled quickly'.[38] Whether Syria would have accepted British financial assistance is extremely problematic given its extreme suspicion of outside interference in its internal affairs. There had been a tentative offer of assistance to the more accommodating Zaim government in late 1949 but that offer was small and fell through with his overthrow later in that same year.[39] No further offer by the British was ever made to the Syrian Government. Lacking both a strong economic rationale and the security of British ties, the Treasury were unable to bend their rules and accept the political logic of providing it with development assistance, even despite appeals from the Foreign Office that the economic development of Syria was of utmost political importance, second only to Iran.[40] The effect of these refusals on Bevin's wider Middle East economic policy was clear to Evans, the administrative head of the MES, who concluded:

It would appear that the Treasury are not prepared to give aid *in extremis* and that they are not prepared to anticipate events and thereby avoid for ourselves trouble and possibly far greater financial commitments later on. This does not augur well for the attempt which we are making to secure general approval for United Kingdom assistance for economic development to the Middle East countries as a whole.[41]

Not only was Bevin's Middle East economic policy never used to forge new bilateral relationships in the region, it also proved inadequate as a mechanism to protect relationships already established, notably with Iran, a country of tremendous strategic importance to Britain. After a breakdown in negotiations between the Iranian Government and the Anglo-Iranian Oil Company (AIOC) over the issue of royalty payments, one which threatened to bring to a grinding halt the nascent Seven Year Plan, the Iranians requested temporary assistance to fill in the gap. If ever there was a case for 'priming the pump' in the postwar Middle East, this was it. Although momentarily immobilized for political reasons, the country had plenty of untapped local finance, an advanced programme of economic development in which three advisers from the Development Division of the BMEO had been closely involved, and with the appointment of the new Prime Minister, Ali Razmara, Iran had the type of strong man which many believed was needed in order to push through a development programme in the politically unstable Middle East. Strong appeals were, therefore, made by the Foreign Office to the Treasury for development assistance with Shepherd, the British Ambassador in Tehran, going so far as to predict a 'turning point in Persian history' if no assistance from either the AIOC or the British Government was forthcoming.[42] While this view probably overestimated the significance of financial aid in the face of strong nationalist sentiment in Iran, it nonetheless corresponded to the political logic of Bevin's Middle East development policy. As was the case with Syria, however, that logic was never tested. Delayed by bureaucratic infighting within Whitehall, the efforts to grant a loan to Iran which Bevin personally spearheaded were eventually overtaken by events on the ground, namely the assassination of Razmara in March 1951 and his replacement by a nationalist government under Mossadeq who shortly thereafter nationalized the AIOC. This brought Britain's involvement in the activities of the Plan Organization of Iran abruptly and effectively to an end. While Britain was able to resume her assistance to Iran in the late 1950s, the Development Division which had played such an important role in the first Seven Year Plan was never able to regain its foothold there.

Initially, a similar attitude was also taken towards Jordan, a state whose subsistence economy was on the verge of collapse in 1949 due to the influx of almost 500,000 refugees. Among the hardest hit were the *fellahin* of Arab Palestine, the economic refugees, whose predicament was described as 'desperate' with 'many slowly starving to death'.[43] If any country was to be a test case, if only a minimalist one, it would be Jordan which had become by default Britain's staunchest ally in the region and the home of Abdullah, 'Mr. Bevin's Little King'.[44] What awoke London to the need for financial aid was the dramatic reduction in Jordan's sterling balances in 1949. Eager to avoid the need to directly subsidize the Jordanian economy, London sought to slow the drain by tightening up financial control. This resulted in the appointment of a British exchange control expert to the Jordanian Government and the establishment of a Currency Board in London to regulate the pace of sterling releases, all designed to place the blame for the situation on Jordanian 'profligacy'.[45] However, British officials in the field, namely Kirkbride, the British Ambassador in Amman, felt this approach was intolerable. Profligate or not, the Jordanian Government was confronted with real problems which were directly related to the influx of 'unproductive hoards' of refugees whose needs were being inadequately looked after by all concerned.[46] What Jordan needed was immediate assistance and, in the end, Kirkbride's insistence paid off. In late 1949, London agreed to a more flexible policy on sterling balance releases and, most significantly, offered Jordan a development loan of one million pounds, an offer which was to mark the beginning of the rather extensive involvement of Britain, and in particular the Development Division of the BMEO, in the economic development of Jordan.

Iraq also experienced a tentative loosening of the Treasury's purse-strings. With sponsorship from the Export Credit Guarantee Department, Iraq was allowed to raise 3 million pounds on the London capital markets[47] and this was followed by an agreement one year later to release $5.6 million from the sterling area's pool of dollars to the Iraqi Government to help finance the building an oil refinery at Kirkuk. However, while this decision was the first example of sterling balances being used for a capital development project in the region six years after the policy was first formulated, there was little in the way of political reward for Britain given that the arrangements with Iraq were conducted in secrecy and received little or no publicity in the rest of the region.[48] Finance was given only reluctantly and, in the case of Iraq, reflected in large part her increased bargaining position within the sterling area.

The key issue here, however, does not concern the size of assistance so much as its destination. While Bevin had initiated a development policy to broaden the basis of British influence on a regional basis, that goal was not achieved by confining contributions to the two states, Iraq and

Jordan, which were already well established, if declining, centres of British influence. If anything, it had the exact opposite psychological effect of hardening cynicism in the Arab world towards British policy, a problem which would continue to affect British aid policy in the region in the 1960s.[49] Therefore, what was originally designed as a forward-looking and interest-creating policy proved in the long run unable to break out of the narrow confines of traditional British diplomacy in the region and create the kind of political goodwill on a regional basis, the attainment of which had been such an integral component of British strategic thinking of the time. Blocked by the Treasury's continued intransigence and more significantly, by Britain's financial problems, Bevin's policy was never allowed to get past the starting blocks.

Britain, the World Bank, and Middle East development

The Foreign Office hoped that the IBRD would be able to compensate for their limited ability to provide direct financial assistance to the Middle East. From the beginning of the IBRD's interest in the region, there had been a great deal of consultation and overlap between it and those British officials associated with Britain's development initiative in the region. Illiff, the former Treasury representative in the Middle East, became head of the Loans Department for the IBRD in 1948, later becoming a Vice-President in 1952. Development Division advisers often accompanied IBRD country missions in the region.[50] When visiting the Middle East individually, IBRD officials regularly visited officials of the Development Division, Crawford commenting that 'it is interesting that these IB people make straight for us'.[51] A particular point of attraction was their library, one of best collections of material relating to the economic development of the region that existed at that time.[52] This was all in addition to the constant communication between London and the headquarters of the IBRD in Washington.

Following up on a conference resolution to stimulate greater IBRD interest in the Middle East, the Foreign Office sent Wright to Washington in November to meet with officials from the Bank. Using the 'Interim Report' as the basis of discussion, Wright received assurances of the IBRD's general interest in the Middle East. Rowe-Dutton of the Treasury followed up on these meetings in a return visit to Washington in early 1950. However, the tangible results of this lobbying proved in the long run disappointing as the speed and extent of IBRD assistance was limited. The IBRD did make its first loan to a Middle East country in 1950, a $12.8 million loan to Iraq to finance the foreign exchange needs of the Wadi Tharther project. However, with the exceptions of Turkey and

Ethiopia, this remained the only Middle East loan from the IBRD until 1957 when several were made to the Plan Organization in Iran, including the first programme loan to a developing country.

Part of the problem stemmed from stringent financial conditions laid down by Britain who restricted the use of her 18 per cent prescription to the Bank and refused to allow the Bank to raise sterling on the London money markets. This resulted in London's refusal to allow the IBRD to even consider a loan to capital poor Jordan.[53] A greater problem, however, was IBRD 'conditionality' which proved too strict for most developing countries. Crawford himself wrote that 'to get a loan from the IB was just as difficult as it would be for an impecunious subaltern to get an overdraft from his bank'.[54] Because the IBRD was a commercial institution dependent for its funds on the New York money markets, it could take limited risks. Governments would have to prove their ability to provide the internal financing; projects would have to pass the test of eventual self-sufficiency. Unless governments changed their policies to meet these conditions, no loan would be forthcoming. In other words, the IBRD made reform a prerequisite for development. These conditions obviously proved financially difficult for many countries in the region to meet. Even oil-rich Iran was refused an IBRD loan in 1950.[55] Eventually, complaints from the less-developed countries about this restrictiveness led to a campaign in the 1950s for the creation of a more concessionary development fund.[56]

Attempts were also made by the British to liberalize the IBRD's terms. In a meeting between IBRD officials and the BMEO in Cairo in April 1949, for example, Crawford warned them against setting 'too high a standard' and suggested that, in some cases, finance should precede reform.[57] Troutbeck echoed Crawford's remarks, adding that the potential future of oil revenues should dramatically reduce the risk of such a lending policy, at least with regards to Iraq and Iran.[58] Realizing that in their present financial state, Syria and Jordan would never warrant an IBRD loan, Troutbeck also tried to alter IBRD policy as regards the Levant states proposing a bargain of 'money for settlement' based upon political rather than financial considerations.[59] Finally, to improve the Bank's image in the region, the BMEO continually emphasized the importance of setting up a regional office as a sign of a more positive approach: 'No one can do business in the Middle East unless he has a permanent representative here.'[60] Crawford also hoped that this step might serve the additional purpose of persuading the IBRD to be more flexible.[61]

The IBRD followed up on this latter suggestion and set up a regional office in Beirut in October 1953. However, the remainder of the suggestions were rejected outright. Projects had to be bankable and 'bankability' depended on the ability of the government to raise enough local capital. It was the general consensus of the IBRD that local private enterprise could and had to do much more in the region. The IBRD likewise rejected Troutbeck's desire for their direct involvement in resettlement schemes; their contribution could at best be 'later on' and 'incidental'.[62] The IBRD, therefore, maintained their cautious approach to lending in the Middle East during this time period and did not compensate for the straitened conditions of the British economy.

Early proposals for an Arab Development Bank

In the early 1950s, heated controversy arose over the possibility of using Kuwait's ever-increasing oil revenues to finance social and economic development in the Middle East. Hitherto on the periphery of British imperial concerns, Kuwait's importance skyrocketed with the conclusion of a 50–50 profit-sharing agreement between it and its foreign oil companies in late 1951. Given Kuwait's limited potential for development, there emerged the inevitable suggestions that revenue surpluses should be recycled to finance development in the region as a whole. An early report by a British Treasury representative in the Middle East had floated the idea of setting up a Middle East Development Corporation with guidance from the IBRD in order to recycle oil revenues to the 'have-not' states of the region.[63] Later, spearheaded by the new revolutionary government in Cairo, the Arab League would call for the creation of an Arab Development Bank, a call motivated as much by the desire to confront British imperialism in the Persian Gulf as it was to promote regional economic development.

Well before the challenge posed by the Arab League, Britain recognized the potential political and financial danger which surplus oil revenues in Kuwait presented. Prompted by early reports from the likes of Sir Rupert Hay, the Political Resident in the Persian Gulf, who had described the situation as frightening,[64] the Foreign Office decided to send Sir Roger Makins on a tour of the Gulf region in February, 1952 to devise ways to contain any potential dangers.[65] His conclusions reveal much about the degree to which British interest in promoting economic development in the Middle East continued to be plagued by the weakness of the sterling area well into the 1950s.

Reminiscent of Britain's initial response to Jordan's financial crisis in the late 1940s, Makins' first recommendation was to 'stiffen' the Kuwaiti administration by instituting a strong system of budgetary and financial control through the creation of a development board and, if necessary, to

be maintained by British political interference. While advocating a quick-
ened pace of economic and social development in Kuwait itself, the main
and explicit purpose behind Makins' recommendations was to minimize
current expenditure and, thus, maximize surplus revenue. With what
remained, Makins recommended that it be 'frozen' or 'sterilized' in the
London capital market, a recommendation which would lead later to the
creation of the Kuwait Investment Office.

Makins' report was favourably received within both the Foreign Office
and the Treasury. A tighter administration would help to contain the
potential local destabilizing effects of increased revenue; it would prevent
a 'frittering away' of resources as had happened in Saudi Arabia; and,
most importantly, it would help to minimize any uncontrollable drains
from the sterling area's dollar pool.[66] It also had the added political
benefit of isolating Kuwait from involvement in wider Arab affairs.[67]

But, was this such a benefit? Some within the Foreign Office thought
not and warned that this degree of British interference might well precip-
itate a political backlash among emerging Kuwaiti nationalists.[68] 'Can we
assume', cautioned one official 'that Kuwait will tamely follow our advice
on how to deal with her sterling surplus when that advice is patently
designed to freeze her money in some way which will not put too great a
strain on the sterling bloc or on UK resources?'[69] Of greater potential
danger was the extension of that conflict to the regional level which would
have placed London's policy in direct confrontation with the Arab world
who were beginning 'to cast their greedy eyes on the wealth of their
nouveau riche brethren'.[70] Black, the President of the IBRD warned, for
example, that 'if that money [is kept] in London, there'll be a yap from the
Middle East – sure as shootin'.[71] This concern became a reality with the
decision of the Economic Committee of the Arab League in May 1953, to
set up an Arab Development Bank (ADB) with the intention that its
capital would come from Kuwait's surplus oil revenues. Murray, Deputy
Head of the Development Division, wrote to London asking for a clarification of policy. There was obvious opposition to the idea of an ADB
operated by the overly political Arab League but what about 'development' in general: 'Do we intend to freeze these monies and thereby create
a new sterling balance problem?'[72]

Since the answer to Murray's question was probably 'yes', the Foreign
Office was not interested in a public clarification of policy. To duck the
issue and avoid a confrontation with Kuwaiti or Arab nationalists, the
British emphasized that the newly formed Investment Board was a
Kuwaiti institution but, as Troutbeck reported from Baghdad, attempts
to justify British policy along those lines 'merely draws a skeptical smile',
particularly in light of the fact that Kuwaiti nationals were not actually

represented on the Board.[73] Similar attempts to justify British policy by investing limited amounts of Kuwaiti revenue in the development of the Trucial States likewise carried little weight.[74] In the end, nothing came of the Arab League proposal to form an ADB, in effect, letting Britain off the hook and leaving her free to continue the *de facto* policy of freezing the Kuwaiti oil revenue in the London money markets. Later efforts to 'discourage' loans to Iraq and Syria bear this out.[75] It was very clear, therefore, that instead of being used for economic development in the Middle East, Kuwaiti oil revenues were to be used to protect Britain's international financial position. This gives us perhaps the clearest example of the gap which existed between the rhetorical support for economic development in the Middle East and the actual pursuit of more parochial economic interests.

This lack of financial assistance left a fundamental pillar of Britain's development policy unfulfilled. As so often happened, those responsible for British policy in the field felt the contradictions most acutely. The third head of the BMEO, Sir Thomas Rapp, complained, for example, that South-East Asia under the Colombo Plan had received a much better deal than had the Middle East, a fact confirmed by a subsequent Foreign Office study.[76] During a conference of the Development Division at the end of 1950 which was called in response to the emergence of much larger and more well-endowed technical assistance programmes into the region, Rapp predicted that the very survival of the Development Division would depend, first and foremost, on Britain's ability to provide development capital.[77] Without it, advice from them, or from any technical assistance agency for that matter, was of little positive value. Crawford himself echoed this feeling in reflecting that 'there must be a comic side to the Middle East . . . for they now are being hotly wooed by at least four suitors . . . and the cry goes up on all sides "You want the best experts, we have them!". Yet . . . without . . . the capital sums which are necessary for pilot and larger projects . . . Technical Aid has as little meaning as the training of a crew for a boat race which will never take place.[78]

   This lack of western financial assistance did not mean that economic development in the Middle East stagnated. Syria, for example, a state which did not receive any western aid to speak of during this time period, had perhaps the highest growth rate of any state in the region.[79] What it did affect, however, was the role that the West and for our purposes, Britain, played in that process. London had never realistically come to grips with its general policy of supporting economic development in the Middle East and the contradictions which existed between rhetoric and reality. Bevin, in a burst of wishful and well-intentioned feeling, might have desired British policy to contribute to large-scale development projects in the Middle East. Without the finance to back that policy up, however, such 'big push' tactics were simply inappropriate and politically counterproductive. Why British policy makers continued in their grand illusions despite repeated refusals from the Treasury to grant capital when and where it was needed is hard to know. It certainly helped lend an air of unreality and inconsistency to the debates which surrounded the issue of economic development in the Middle East. As Troutbeck observed from his post in Cairo, it gave the impression that Britain was 'trying to ride two horses at the same time which were galloping in opposite directions'.[80]

What is interesting at this stage is that British development policy in the Middle East took a new turn and, in a sense, gained an air of reality. With London unable to back up its ambitious policy, the initiative was quietly taken over by the Development Division which remained to work in the region, whether London was providing it with capital or not. Gradually, one saw a switch from London's emphasis on large-scale projects to the emerging emphasis of the Development Division on small-scale pilot projects and direct technical assistance, neither of which needed large amounts of capital. Indeed, much of this work had already come to fruition. From a political point of view, this switch symbolized the failure of Britain's development initiative in the Middle East. From the point of view of effective development, it was a new and definitely more realistic beginning and it is to this, based upon the local initiatives of the Development Division of the BMEO rather than on the more grandiose political initiatives of London that we now turn.

3   The British Middle East Office and the abandonment of imperial approaches to modernization

The problems associated with Bevin's imperial-driven 'peasants, not pashas' strategy were numerous, if not overwhelming. Without finance, without the experts, and without the goodwill and receptivity on the part of Middle East governments, Bevin's dreams of promoting a more socially just relationship between Britain and the region lay shattered. Imperial dreams may have died hard as we have seen, but it was inevitable that they would do so given the dynamics of the postwar world. Yet the small, seemingly insignificant core of Bevin's policy, the Development Division of the BMEO, remained in place – beleaguered, underfunded, undermanned, yet still in place. Indeed, if its regional reputation among certain British and Middle East officials by the end of the 1950s is anything to go by, it seemed that, in its own small way, the BMEO flourished. This success was recognized when Britain chose the example of the regionally located development division as the administrative model on which to base its global development programme inaugurated with the establishment of the Department of Technical Cooperation in 1961.

To understand why the seemingly insignificant BMEO retained such relative importance, one needs to change the parameters upon which one judges a development programme. If measured exclusively by inputs and outputs, by increases in GNP and the standard of living in the Middle East, the BMEO was of marginal significance although it did have some unqualified success stories, most notably in Jordan. If reappraised on its ability to generate local initiative and development, necessarily more gradual and incremental, then the work of the BMEO comes out looking more interesting. Most development programmes began their operations with a preconceived strategy, independent resources, rigid procedures of implementation, all backed up by the power to enforce them. The BMEO had none of these attributes. In fact, when it became clear that no development capital of any significance would be forthcoming, the BMEO was virtually abandoned by London. As a result, it was able to devise flexible strategies and procedures more in tune with local conditions and capacities. This did not emerge immediately but rather gradually in response to the many challenges which it faced, both material and political. Through an examination of some of these challenges faced by the BMEO in the postwar Middle East, it is hoped to come to a fuller understanding of just how this more 'adaptive' approach to development came to the fore.

Adjustment and survival in the formative years

The formative years of the BMEO were ones of adjustment and survival. We have already seen its difficulties in getting started and in establishing contact with the British embassies and local governments of the region. For the most part, its activity remained confined to the Levant states of Lebanon, Syria and Iraq with the one notable exception of Iran where their presence was described by Troutbeck as 'our greatest assets'.[1] Owing to the intensity of political resentment towards Britain and to the greater sophistication of the Egyptian bureaucracy, the BMEO never did get a foothold in Egypt. This was certainly not helped by the fact that the BMEO was housed in the old wartime headquarters of the MESC on Shari'a Toulambat. Moreover, it had a difficult time in breaking into some of the fields in which it was supposed to specialize. We have seen the problems in the field of entomology. The health adviser had the unenviable task of trying to promote British technical expertise in a field where Britain's position was either declining, such as in Egypt, or where more entrenched European interests already existed, such as in Syria or Iran.[2] And, while the agricultural adviser wrote some useful surveys on the state of agricultural development in the region, these on the whole were all too general to warrant specific action. As we shall examine later, its most active fields were forestry, statistics, and rural credit and cooperative development.

Nevertheless, meagre as this foothold was in the region, the position of the BMEO became even more tenuous with the emergence of competitors in the technical assistance field. The Food and Agricultural Organization (FAO) of the United Nations represented the first competitor. At their conference in Geneva in August 1947, a decision was taken to set up a regional office, much along the lines of the MECA which the British had tried to establish near the end of the Second World War. The proposal, in fact, came from Lloyd, who was formally an employee of the MESC.[3] It was also strongly supported by the Iraqis and the Egyptians whose national Mahmud Tawfiq Hafnawy was to become the FAO's Middle East regional representative. This was a genuine threat to the existence of the BMEO for it was felt that Middle East governments might prefer FAO advice for both political and financial reasons. There was widespread belief, for example, that association with the FAO might facilitate a loan from the IBRD. There was also concern that the Egyptians might use their dominant position in the regional office to politicize the technical assistance field.[4] 'We must be ready', wrote one Foreign Office official 'to avoid a situation in which Middle Eastern countries . . . could attempt to play off FAO and BMEO against each other.'[5] Of even greater concern to the BMEO was the emergence of some ambivalent attitudes within London. The Cabinet Steering Committee on International Organizations had already suggested the eventual merger of the Development Division with the various functional agencies of the United Nations[6] and this was not welcomed unsympathetically by many in the Foreign Office. Even Dundas, the administrative head of the MES, intimated that experts might be more effectively placed with either the regional embassies or in London.[7] When the FAO finally established its team in August 1947, and in Cairo, the BMEO's own back yard so to speak, the Foreign Office went so far as to garner opinions from the regional embassies as to what they felt the future of the BMEO should be.

Crawford responded by immediately trying to defend his team of experts in Cairo. He doubted whether the FAO could produce experts 'better or as good as his own' and surmised that the 'FAO, like so many other UNO bodies, may sooner or later have to draw in its horns for financial reasons and become not much more that a data-collecting agency'.[8] He felt it would be much better to talk of coordination and cooperation rather than amalgamation and dissolution since the Development Division was already established and had accumulated much practical information on the Middle East which FAO technicians would otherwise be without. This might even result in advisers from the BMEO working alongside Egyptian FAO technicians which could prove of tremendous importance symbolically.[9] Moreover, the nascent talk of amalgamation seemed to ignore the political justifications for the existence of a development division. As Crawford stated, the whole issue 'raises a point which has been worrying me for some time. BMEO was set up on the practical side to do much that FAO also sets out to do . . . On the other hand, [it] was set up to maintain British prestige and influence in the Middle East. If we allow ourselves to be ultimately swamped by FAO, the latter aim is lost.'[10]

Luckily, and perhaps surprisingly, for Crawford and the BMEO team, several of the regional embassies came to its defense. Troutbeck, the newly appointed head of the BMEO, wrote to Bevin vigorously defending the *status quo* and his views were also strongly endorsed by British representatives in the field. In Beirut, Houstoun-Boswall paid a warm tribute to the Development Division describing it as a valuable political and developmental asset.[11] Similar support was received from Tehran which stressed the importance of keeping the Development Division regionally based.[12] Perhaps the strongest endorsement came from Baghdad which wrote that 'any change which would reduce the intimacy of contact with Iraq is ... to be avoided at all costs ... [T]he loss of "atmosphere" which a transfer ... would entail ... would almost certainly be fatal to its usefulness.'[13] Above all, Mack, the British ambassador in Baghdad, wrote that its existence should not be open to question: 'Its experts are by this time well known ... to senior civil servants, to politicians and in some cases to the Regent himself. Their visits are welcomed and their advice listened to with respect and it is no exaggeration to say that our hopes of the economic and social development of this country would be seriously diminished if for any reason their services ceased to be available.'[14] This overwhelming on-the-spot support for the Development Division seemed to disarm for the time being those in London who were more skeptical of its value.

However, just as one review ended, the emergence of a new competitor in the technical assistance field led to the start of a new one. This time, the threat came from the work of private American consulting firms. The United States had always preferred the private sector approach to economic development and had, in part, rejected participation in a jointly run MESC at the end of the Second World War for that very reason. In fact, Landis, one of the principal architects of the demise of the MESC started his own private consulting firm called the Middle East Company designed to provide technical assistance to Middle East governments interested in expanding their economic horizons.[15] Before long, his was joined by others, notably Overseas Consultants Incorporated (OCI), a conglomerate of engineering firms represented by the enigmatic Max Thornburg, an oil magnate who had himself been involved in advising the Turkish Government on its plans for economic development.[16] Having first been involved in the initial stages of reconstruction in Japan, OCI subsequently turned their attentions to the Middle East and, in particular, Iran where a grandiose plan of national economic development was being formulated.

What activated British fears was the initial success of the OCI's approach – more comprehensive, team-oriented and openly commercial – which threatened to reduce the BMEO's influence in the field of technical assistance in the Middle East dramatically. This challenge materialized in Iran in 1948 when OCI were awarded the contract as official consultants for the Plan Organization. Having previously done much preparatory work for the newly drafted Seven Year Plan, the Development Division was now forced to scramble to maintain its influence. Two advisers did manage to secure high level appointments but

Stewart, the agricultural adviser, was excluded in favour of experts from OCI. With Thornburg openly beginning to consider the expansion of OCI's operations to the rest of the Middle East, the Development Division felt the situation serious enough to inform Bevin:

Our aim is to promote economic development in the Middle East so as to raise the standard of living of the common man. It is highly desirable that the Americans should be committed in the area on the same lines; at the same time, in view of our great interests there, I assume that it is our policy to keep abreast of them. The point which I wish to make is this – that if Overseas Consultants or similar groups are to be used . . . as the hands of the State Department in the economic development in the Middle East, we shall no doubt wish to employ parallel – or joint organization for our share in the execution of such development. The future structure of the Dev.Div. may well have to be reconsidered in this connection.[17]

This letter reopened the debate surrounding the usefulness of the BMEO, only months after a past review had been completed. This time, however, the emphasis was on how to strengthen its presence in the region. Some advocated closer ties between it and British industry which would improve the ability of the latter to compete on a commercial basis with the likes of OCI.[18] Others suggested setting up a British counterpart to OCI parallel to the BMEO to be headed by Sir Alexander Gibb and Partners, already active in the region.[19] What the BMEO most wanted, however, was an expansion of their already existing operations. At a meeting at their Cairo headquarters in April 1949 it was generally concluded that their greatest need was for more advisers in the agricultural sector to allow them to better compete with OCI's five-man team with special mention being made of the need for a water engineering expert. Some advisers also argued that the Development Division should work more as a team.[20]

In the end, the BMEO's requests for more advisers was put on hold until the more wide-scale review of Middle East economic policy which Bevin had ordered in early 1949 was completed. As for the idea of a British equivalent to OCI, this was ultimately rejected in large part because the interest on the part of private British firms was simply not there. However, there were also interesting political objections to this idea from some British representatives in the field. From Iraq, Trevelyan argued that an OCI-type organization would give the impression that Iraqi policy on the economic development of the country was being decided by western technicians. Stressing the importance of maintaining an Iraqi policy framework, Trevelyan argued that the quiet and inconspicuous manner in which the BMEO operated was really much more appropriate for the Iraqi context.[21]

Suggestions of a more team-oriented approach for the BMEO probably fell by the wayside for similar reasons. Crawford for one was very wary of too institutionalized an approach to technical assistance in the region. He tended to give his advisers complete liberty in working out their schedules and priorities. This, no doubt, was somewhat imposed upon Crawford by the nature of the team which was assembled in Cairo. All very distinguished in their own right – a bunch of prima donnas as one former adviser commented, they would not have taken kindly to a central-ization of control and a limitation of their independence.[22] Therefore, for both professional and practical reasons, it was felt better to keep the oper-ations of the BMEO both loosely knit and largely uncoordinated. The emphasis on team-work along with more elaborate suggestions of an OCI set up were, therefore, for the time being abandoned. Despite the initial threat posed by OCI, no changes were, in fact, made in the late 1940s to its basic structure.

Times changed for the BMEO in the 1950s. Having been a trail-blazer in the technical assistance field in the late 1940s, it now saw its relative place in the Middle East completely overrun by the emergence of larger and more lucratively endowed organisations. The IBRD began to com-pensate for its strict conditionality in the 1950s by sending out technical teams to undertake country-wide economic surveys. One had already been to Iraq and additional ones were being seriously considered for Ethiopia and Syria. The United Nations had also established its own Middle East Economic Survey Mission to examine the possibilities of resettling Palestinian refugees. Their report, published in December 1949, recommended the establishment of a United Nations Relief and Works Agency (UNRWA) whose task in part was to implement some so-called pilot (but in fact very large) projects most of which revolved around irrigation development on the Litani River Basin in Lebanon, the Ghab Depression in Syria and the Wadi Qilt and Wadi Zerqa Basins in Jordan. This was paralleled by a United Nation's global initiative with the launch-ing of the Expanded Programme of Technical Assistance (EPTA) in June 1950.[23] The most significant initiative, however, came from the Americans who, in response to Truman's pledge to fight communism through the promotion of a better world-wide standard of living – the 'fourth point' in his inaugural address of January 1949, established the Technical Cooperation Administration (TCA), an international technical assistance agency, commonly referred to in the region as *al-nuqt al-rab'ia* (Point Four).

In the post-Palestine Middle East, these initiatives provided a few kernels of hope in an otherwise desperate situation, hope bolstered by the apparent receptivity of the Arab states to these new initiatives. Iraq seemed poised to accept an IBRD loan and had agreed to set up a development board on which would sit foreign representatives; Syria seemed well disposed to western offers of assistance; and even the Wafdist Government in Egypt had expressed interest in using technical advisers from the West.[24] However, the BMEO did not share in the tentative sense of optimism and predicted the marginalization of its relatively meagre operation at the hands of these more lucratively endowed ones. Threlkeld, an animal husbandry adviser with the BMEO, complained, for example, of the lack of essentials needed to face the forthcoming work in the Middle East. While the BMEO's role of advising and stimulating local governments into working along new lines was a good one, it was one which automatically opened up avenues that demanded more experts and capital investment, neither of which the BMEO was in a position to provide. The Americans, on the other hand, seemed to have drawn up a programme which could offer all these things: preliminary advice, technicians to implement it, and money to pay for it. While he 'held no brief for the American technique' as such, Threlkeld admired the American clarity of purpose and determination which stood out in stark contrast to, what he termed, the muddled and unrealistic British thinking on the subject.[25] When it became known that Point Four would have an initial budget for the Middle East of $5 million, Threlkeld remarked: 'It would appear to me that, within a comparatively short period, the Americans will enter the M.E. sphere in earnest and British interests, due to the smallness of our "Point Four" staff . . . will be completely side-stepped and left the pickings from the rich man's table.'[26]

The crisis for the BMEO was real. In order to come to grips with their now more vulnerable position, the BMEO held a series of 'in-house' conferences at its headquarters in Cairo at the end of 1950 and 1951. A number of issues were discussed including the need for finance and a larger number of experts, and the importance of trying to coordinate the increased activity in the technical assistance field. However, most felt that the viability of the BMEO's position ultimately depended upon London's ability to improve the system of technical recruiting. 'The crux of the whole position', wrote Crawford, 'is our ability to get the bodies.'[27] In 1950, it was estimated that Britain had close to 350 technicians working in the region, the majority based in Egypt and Iraq.[28] While this was not an unsubstantial number, it was not an accurate reflection of Britain's position in this field. Most of these advisers were under private contract with Middle East governments themselves, making their categorization as a British contribution somewhat tenuous. Attempts by officials to officially associate these advisers with the Development Division had been previously rejected to avoid accusations from the 'xenophobic press'.[29] The Americans, in contrast, were talking of sending out hundreds of advisers directly employed by Point Four in addition to those under the EPTA of the United Nations. What most worried the British, however, was their inability to maintain their relative position. Many requests for experts were going unfulfilled and in Iraq, there had been no new appointments for over a year.[30] With the United States about to sign Point Four agreements with many states in the region complete with their offer of free experts, equipment, and money, it was clear to the BMEO that unless Britain was ready to compete with the Americans on the same terms, there was a clear danger that their own work in the region would prove redundant. Therefore, they stressed in a pre-conference despatch to London that 'if we are to keep our influence alive in the Middle East and incidently fulfil our boast we have so often made that, though we can in our straitened circumstances give little material assistance, we can supply technical and expert assistance, something must be done and done quickly before the US have it all their own way'.[31]

In 1949, some attempts had been made to improve on the very *ad hoc* system by transferring responsibility for it from the MES to a committee in the Ministry of Labour. This, however, proved no more efficient with more than half of the requested posts being left unfilled more than one year later. Between June 1949 and March 1950, the unit made one appointment and, by the beginning of 1951, only twenty-one of forty-five posts had been filled.[32] An alternative suggestion of Crawford's was to push for the creation of a permanent floating staff of experts in the Middle East which would prevent continual reference to the Treasury and allow the BMEO to react to demands for British advice with a great deal more confidence.[33] Chapman suggested that this was particularly suited for forestry given that advisers were already stationed with the colonial government in Cyprus.[34] In the long term, both saw these pools being amalgamated into the overarching Overseas Technical Service which was being strongly recommended by Sir John Sargent of the British Council following the Colombo Conference in 1950.[35]

The Treasury, however, was unwilling to agree to any of these steps. The existing *ad hoc* manner of recruitment, for example, allowed it to maintain maximum control over allocations towards technical assistance. While it did agree to subsidize certain politically important positions in the Middle East with the hope of attracting high-level British experts[36] and acquiesced in the formation of a more elaborate body for recruitment in the Ministry of Labour in July 1951 – a development which Waterlow described as 'the one door that has so far begun to open on the possibility of getting really rapid action taken to improve the situation',[37] it continued to reject the idea of an Overseas Technical Service along with the

more modest proposal from the BMEO for the creation of supernumer-
ary posts in the Middle East.[38]

It is here where the lack of resources may, in fact, have proved an advantage when it came to promoting development though it certainly was not
readily apparent at the time. In order to compensate for the lack of British
technicians, the BMEO increasingly began to stress the importance of
making greater use of local personnel. This contributed to the development of a local administrative and technical expertise while at the same
time had the additional advantage of fitting in nicely with the political
importance of maintaining the appearance of a local initiative. However,
here again, resources were needed to facilitate local training, especially in
the fields of forestry, statistics, and cooperatives where, as we shall see, the
BMEO was launching regional training schemes. Crawford made a
repeated point of requesting more finance for local training. However,
while London did agree to help finance the regional training centres and
later sent out the Mowatt-Jones mission to investigate the state of technical education in the region, more comprehensive support for local training in the Middle East did not materialize until the creation of the
Department of Technical Cooperation in 1961.

Another issue which began to receive an increasing amount of attention
was that of coordination. In fact, some saw coordination as saving the
BMEO by locking it into a regional coordinating mechanism. Originally,
some in London and in Cairo had pushed the idea of a joint development
division with the Americans, much along the lines of the MESC. The idea
was discussed several times but was not formally considered by the
Americans until a conference of US Ambassadors in the Middle East
held in Istanbul in December 1949.[39] At that point, however, it was not
received very enthusiastically. The Americans were not impressed with
Britain's past record in this field, an attitude no doubt reinforced by the
disastrous Groundnuts Scheme in East Africa, and its approach to economic development was seen as too conservative and 'stick-in-the-
mudish'.[40] Their view of the Development Division was especially dim,
its mode of operation felt too passive to have an effect on the 'lethargic'
governments of the region.[41] Crawford, in fact, reported that Clapp, head
of the Middle East Economic Survey Mission, who had requested the
secondment of some of the Development Division's advisers, was the
only one at the conference to speak up on its behalf.[42] There was also
concern lest it appear as though the Middle East was once again being
carved up into spheres of interest. As a result, British efforts to revive
close Anglo-American cooperation in matters of technical assistance in
the Middle East were not surprisingly rejected by the Istanbul conference, a rejection which effectively put to rest those lingering ideas of

recreating the MESC. In line with the American insistence on directing its programmes from Washington as was the case with Latin America, some tried to keep the idea of Anglo-American cooperation alive by suggesting the parallel transfer of the Development Division back to London. This too, however, was ultimately rejected as being too remote and impractical from an operational point of view.

Another idea being bandied about the Middle East at this time was the use of UNRWA as a kind of regional supercoordinator. To discuss the proposal, two meetings of those involved in the Middle East technical assistance game were held at Alexandria on June 29 and August 3 1951. The Development Division were not enamoured by the idea of a supercoordinator and, in fact, missed the first meeting in Alexandria. It smacked of over-institutionalization which they felt would only serve to arouse the antagonism of Middle East officials to the whole business. As was clear from their own experience, it would be better to keep any future arrangement informal. 'Much of the success of the efforts of the Development Division', wrote Rapp, 'has been due to the informality of its approach and its deliberate avoidance of the limelight. I consider that local coordination will also get off to a better start if it too is allowed to develop informally and unobtrusively.'[43] As it happened, the meetings were not very productive. Apart from a general exchange of information, no arrangement for coordinating technical assistance efforts in the region were made. To start with, there were too many logistical problems in bringing about greater cooperation: the absence of standardized contracts for experts, the difference in administrative approach, and the variation in constitutional powers held by the regional offices of the various organizations.[44] Moreover, the agencies themselves were not willing to tolerate interference in their day-to-day operations nor would governments of the region welcome any restrictions on their freedom of choice, particularly if that interference came from UNRWA. Thus, the Alexandria meetings disbanded without result. While the UN eventually became involved in coordination at the country level by setting up local Technical Assistance Boards to act as clearing houses, the onus for organizing the activities of foreign experts continued to remain with the local governments themselves.

As was to be expected, coordination was thus achieved on a more informal basis. The Development Division had already been highly involved with the IBRD in the Middle East and, as we have seen, had also participated in the MEESM. The continuation of this approach was encouraged not only as a way of fulfilling the Foreign Office's desire of holding 'a watching brief' on the activities of the other agencies but also to provide an opportunity to extend its own activities by transforming those agencies into unknowing agents of its own approach.[45] Cheesman, the cooperative adviser, spoke of his use of FAO experts in Syria to follow up on preliminary work already done by him and he later pursued the same strategy in Iraq. In line with the political concern with the issue of Palestinian refugees, there was also talk of gaining a foothold within UNRWA. Finally, in order to facilitate this new emphasis on networking, a decision was made to transfer the Development Division's operations to Beirut in 1952, a city fast growing into a regional centre for most western organizations with interest in the Middle East.[46]

In light of the absence of any policy of coordination and given the inability of London to devise a more effective system of recruitment, the BMEO was left to determine how best to proceed on its own. Threlkeld felt that the BMEO should adopt a more intensive approach to technical assistance if it was going to be able to compete at all. He argued for a greater emphasis on the execution of projects, the adoption of a more team-oriented approach, perhaps more specialization in one country, more meetings among experts at their headquarters in Cairo, as well as greater contact with the Heads of Mission in particular countries.[47] On the present footing, he complained that experts worked in 'watertight compartments', frequently on aspects of work which was not sufficiently related to a main policy goal.[48] Chapman, on the other hand, did not see any great need to alter the strategy of the BMEO, particularly along the lines advocated by Threlkeld. He felt that the BMEO had an important role to play so long as it continued its emphasis on prodding, stimulating, and liaising with local governments. A forestry adviser, he argued, should not indulge in long stays in any one country but should try 'to keep the activities of local forest services directed towards important and primary needs. He should pass on development news from one country to another, trying to stimulate a healthy rivalry in development, and he should try to arrange the exchange of visits of forest officers and local meetings for the exchange of ideas.'[49]

The decisive intervention at this stage was that of Crawford. He argued that Chapman's emphasis on liaison work and short-term stays was too restrictive, claiming that some of the best work of the Development Division up to that point had been done by means of secondment, notably in Iran. A happy balance, therefore, had to be struck between the two and this could best be done by limiting secondments to perhaps periods of six months. On the other hand, he adamantly rejected the idea of a more team-oriented approach and argued instead for flexibility and informality. Repeating arguments made previously during the OCI debate, he stressed that 'the Development Division was still dependent on requests from countries to visit them and if visits were over-organized, much of the personal contacts to which the Division's success was attributable would be lost'.[50]

What all saw the need for, however, was an increase in the BMEO's number of advisers – perhaps two for each field which would allow both the liaison and more prolonged work to go on at the same time. In a note to Bevin, Rapp warned that 'unless our efforts are much increased, it will not be possible for our position to be maintained'.[51] However, while a few small-scale changes to its makeup were made, namely the addition of two advisers in statistics and rural credit, no wholesale expansion of the BMEO was ever really contemplated. In fact, owing to yet another financial crisis in London, the proposal for expansion of the Development Division was abandoned before it ever reached the Treasury.[52] Moreover, as the 1950s progressed, this situation only worsened for while the Treasury continued to refuse to increase its size and budget, its regional mandate broadened. Ethiopia was now included in its rounds; the new government in Egypt seemed to be more amenable to British technical assistance, particularly in the fields of agriculture and cooperatives; as a result of increased oil revenues in Kuwait and the Buraimi crisis with Saudi Arabia, Britain took a renewed interest in the states of the Persian Gulf, prompting Crawford's first visit there in 1953;[53] and with the reinstatement of the Shah in Iran in 1953, an opportunity for the Development Division was now created to rekindle its influence there. After his first visit to Tehran in late 1954, for example, Crawford came back excited by the prospects and wishing that 'Dev.Div. had more resources, if only bodies'.[54] Finally, with the creation of the Economic Committee of the Baghdad Pact in 1955, advisers began to waste an increasing amount of time sitting around committee tables in Baghdad. However, despite the obvious need for more personnel, the Development Division actually saw the number of advisers at its disposal reduced in the 1950s prompting Crawford to comment that '[t]he Division is . . . a refutation of Parkinson's Law in that the more work it has been given to do, the more the staff has diminished'.[55] This trend started when the positions of health and entomology advisers were eliminated in 1952. This was somewhat compensated for by the creation of an *ad hoc* advisory fund[56] but this was not really enough. While Crawford never wanted to see a dramatic increase in its size, claiming that 'the Middle East is filled with deteriorating foreign experts who have not enough to do',[57] he nevertheless felt that he could have used 'with advantage' more, especially when the number of advisers diminished to five in the late 1950s.[58] He was particularly irked as the 1950s progressed with the disproportionate amount of support which London gave to the ETAP of the UN, a programme for which he had little regard. 'This seems amazing to me', wrote

Crawford, 'when I think of the difficulties Dev.Div. have in getting an extra adviser or in fact in getting anything at all.'[59]

Thus, of the three issues discussed at their in-house conferences, none were resolved in ways which, at that time, were felt necessary if the position of the Development Division in the Middle East was to be preserved. With the failure of efforts to coordinate technical assistance, the Development Division was left to maintain its regional position in a somewhat more free-wheeling and openly competitive atmosphere. To compete effectively, however, it was perfectly clear that they would need more finance, better systems of recruitment, and the expansion of the 'office' itself. None of these things, however, materialized and, thus, in light of the dire predictions of the Development Division's demise if the *status quo* was maintained, its future as it entered the turbulent decade of the 1950s in the Middle East did not look particularly rosy.

Finding its niche in the 1950s

Amidst all this worry, however, there emerged a new more optimistic train of thought which saw certain advantages in the way in which the Development Division was set up, ones which might compensate for the lack of resources. The more Point Four and the specialized agencies of the UN began to operate in the region, the more it became apparent that the mere addition of money and bodies into the technical assistance market was of debateable usefulness. What was important was the approach to the use of those resources. By comparing the Development Division to that of the other more well endowed agencies, it is hoped to give a more balanced appraisal of its position in the technical assistance field in the Middle East as it entered the more competitive days of the 1950s.

When the Americans announced their ambitious programme of technical assistance in the Middle East, not all viewed it as the same kind of threat to the Development Division as Threlkeld had nor did they look upon it as something to be emulated. While most were expressing concern for the effect which the 'invasion' of American technicians might have on the strength of British technical diplomacy, Bozman, the health adviser, downplayed the American proposals themselves as being badly thought out. They failed, for example, to consider the possible reactions of Arab governments, sensitive as they were to the threat of foreign interference, to the large influx of foreign technicians. More importantly, they were based on the misconception that 'experts' could somehow provide the missing link in the local development chain. When combined with the publicity and 'bally-hoo' which invariably accompanied American efforts in general,[60] the most likely and immediate effect of their presence would be the raising of expectations about the prospects for development beyond anything which could possibly be fulfilled. 'I hope I shall not be considered facetious', he thus wrote, 'when I record . . . a feeling of sympathy for the peoples of the Middle East since it would appear that in the near future there are going to be almost as many foreign "experts" . . . as local inhabitants! One begins to wonder if the approach of the Western Democratic powers to the Oriental problem is not wrongly conceived. Why should we think that by planting experts down in these countries we have any real hope of influencing local events to produce **within the time available** the results we want?'[61]

Apart from this general problem of over enthusiasm, early experience with the newly established agencies also revealed problems of administrative inflexibility. Point Four, for example, worked on the basis of both general country and specific project agreements, the two being necessary before work could begin on the ground. The General Agreement, however, appeared too much like a political alliance, something of course which it was meant to be, and made the acceptance of American aid more difficult than necessary. The Syrians, for example, who never accepted Point Four assistance, were very suspicious of American motives and believed that 'once you sign an agreement with the Americans, you are lost, overwhelmed with technicians, experts, programmes and overseers all with wives, children, cadillacs and diplomatic immunity; Arabism is at the mercy of the Jewish vote if not entirely lost in the American way of life'.[62] The problem, as this Point Four memo from Lebanon indicated where similar difficulties were being experienced, was that:

in the Arab states there is a great hesitancy in signing any kind of general accord, probably because of suspicion that we are trying to tie them up to some hypothetical future arrangement and possibly because they read into a general agreement the implications of a treaty alliance or other commitments which are not there and are not intended by us. The attitude seems to be 'We are friends. We can deal with every problem that comes up on an individual basis. Why do we need a general agreement?'[63]

Project agreements, which required that proposed schemes be rigorously laid out before aid would be offered, likewise proved administratively and politically awkward. To start with, as shown by the 'poor quality' of the proposals put forward to such bodies as the IBRD and the MEESM, Middle East bureaucracies were not yet in a position to make these kinds of specific preparations.[64] Given the budgetary necessity of these agencies to allocate funds for specific proposals or else lose the money, what too often happened as a result was that proposals were designed in Washington or New York and presented to the governments of the region lock, stock, and barrel with little to no room for negotiation.

This aroused the political sensibilities of Middle Eastern politicians who could not appear to be bowing to western pressure and resulted in delays, especially if the project in question had political ramifications. From a development point of view, it also led to the wholesale transplantation of ideas and projects without modification in light of local circumstances. This rigidity was reinforced by the tendency to send out technical teams which often harboured whole matrices of preconceived ideas. Similar criticisms were also being made of the specialized agencies of the United Nations. They sent out far too many experts with far too little experience of Middle East conditions and their approach tended to be more theoretical than practical. After attending a regional meeting of the FAO in Bludan, Syria, for example, Crawford reported that 'their heads are too much in the clouds and they do not seem to realize that before grandiose schemes for inter-regional cooperation can be put into effect, there is much on a lowly national level which must be done. This region is still in the stage where it is sensible to talk in terms of projects and unreal to talk of programmes and targets.' Crawford added that the most interesting discussion at the meeting concerned the necessity of introducing a cheap domestic stove into the region: 'To my mind this is indicative of Middle East needs which are small things and not over-ambitious long term planning.'[65]

The result of all this administrative inflexibility and over-ambitious thinking on the part of the new agencies was an immediate tarnishing of the lustre which had originally accompanied the announcements of greater technical aid to the region. As Windett concluded:

Largely due to the maladroitness with which UN agencies and even Pt IV are approaching the subject of technical assistance – for example, in the way in which they make their offers, in the conditions attached to the acceptance of their offers, and to the type of man who is sent out when they are accepted ... there is a developing resistance in the Middle East towards the employment of specialized agency advice.[66]

The Americans soon began to experience these sentiments at first hand with anti-Point Four demonstrations taking place in several Arab countries. This sparked some to rethink the American aid programme. Having previously disregarded the BMEO at their Istanbul conference, for example, the Americans were now giving it a second look with Hanson, the Deputy Head of TCA, expressing his envy 'at the simplicity of the BMEO approach which enabled our advisers to get on with the good work without awaiting the signing of formal bilateral agreements'.[67] In a subsequent meeting with the Head of the Near East Development Service of TCA, Hollis, the American admitted to being 'new to the Middle East game' and expressed interest in learning from

BMEO's more informal approach based on personal contacts.[68] In fact, so enamoured were they with the British set-up that they began to consider establishing their own American Middle East Office to complement the work done in individual countries.[69] As a first step, they set up a regional coordinating office in Beirut and appointed Edwin Locke Jr, a young, high-flying banker/bureaucrat who had been the chief American adviser to Chang Kai-Shek at the end of the war, as its head.[70] Unwilling to delegate authority to the field, however, the enthusiasm in Washington for the British approach stopped there and Locke's office was never supplemented with a team of technicians. Frustrated by Washington's inability to follow through on its original intentions and appalled by its more general approach to technical assistance – too many experts of poor quality, too many conditions, and not enough supporting finance – Locke eventually exploded publically in the Lebanese and American press at the end of 1952 in a tirade of vocal criticisms against Point Four. It proved to be both his demise and that of the regional office.[71]

This growing criticism of both Point Four and the agencies of the United Nations combined with the emergence of quiet interest in its own approach to technical assistance served to revive the regional standing of the Development Division. In a reappraisal of their situation by Windett, several factors were highlighted which helped to explain this reversal of fortunes.[72] A principle reason was its administrative style of operation – one that stood in stark contrast to that of the other agencies – which served to minimize and de-politicize the many obstacles to the successful introduction of foreign technicians in the Middle East. Its procedure was flexible, it did not operate on the basis of a contract, its advisers for the most part worked on a visiting basis and did not become permanent and politically sensitive house features, and it avoided publicity which too often operated in a manner which host governments found embarrassing. To the general public, therefore, advisers were invisible and could essentially slip in and out of each Arab capital without being noticed. While this way of operating seemed somewhat surreptitious and indeed led to accusations by some that the advisers were all spies,[73] on the whole, it was welcomed by those director-generals in the Middle East interested in British technical advice because they could now ask for it without arousing unnecessary political opposition. As this memo from the Development Division later explained:

We feel that one of the reasons why the Development Division is still able to function, in spite of its small budget and limited number of specialists is that it hides its light under a bushel. Thus, governments are able to take our specialists' advice without it generally being known that this advice has been given. In these days of intense national feeling, this seems to be the best way to work with the small resources at our disposal.[74]

Another and paradoxical advantage which the Development Division possessed over the other agencies in the region was its small size which allowed it to maintain the quality of both adviser and advice at a very high level. Its access to a growing number of highly experienced ex-Indian and ex-Sudanese colonial officials, legacies of a quickly dying imperial order, no doubt helped them, not only because the climatic conditions in both countries were similar to those in the Middle East but also because such officials had a great deal of experience working with local administrators given the indigenization of the colonial bureaucracies there.[75] The result was the assembling of a team in Cairo which stood up favourably to those from the United States and the United Nations. At one point, Crawford revealed that the Director-General of the FAO told him of his desire to take over 'the whole lot'.[76]

Enhancing this technical expertise and experience was its permanent location within the Middle East itself, a factor which facilitated the accumulation of a great deal of knowledge about regional conditions. This allowed advisers to get to work immediately upon visiting a country without wasting time on the 'preliminary study' stage which had become such a noted and criticized feature of visiting technicians at this time. Its location within the region also facilitated the system of repeat visits which Crawford felt was so important and helped build among officials of Middle East governments a sense that advisers maintained a continuing interest in the outcome of work done for them. The fact that many advisers stayed with the Development Division for a long time despite the lure of higher salaries from, what Crawford termed, the 'carpet-bagger' agencies of the United Nations only served to strengthen this sense of continuity. Among those with the longest tenure with the Development Division were Crawford (fourteen years), Porter (fourteen years), Mooney (ten years) and Eyre (seventeen years).[77]

Given its more informal way of operating, however, the success of the Development Division would ultimately depend upon the ability of its advisers to cultivate and maintain local contacts. After nearly five years in the region, it seemed to have accomplished this task with some success. The personalities of the advisers certainly played a part in this, Crawford's most of all. As this remark by a former member of the Development Division indicated:

[Crawford], with his impressive bearing and direct friendly manner together with his long experience of the ways of the Middle East . . . was able to form positive relationships with the Ministers and senior officials of the governments of the countries of the region and with senior British Foreign Service personnel stationed there. He was thus able to create opportunities for advisers to operate at the highest levels in their respective fields. [78]

. However, much can also be attributed to a unique *modus operandi* which was developed by the Development Division. Having taken the lead from the original London conference of 1945 which stressed the importance of local initiative, the task of advisers was first and foremost to make contact with like-minded local officials whom they could then befriend and support. Rather than being high-powered technical experts, Crawford was more apt to describe his advisers as a band of 'universal aunts'.[79] While direct advice was given and in some cases schemes set up and administered, this was only done for the most part by request and informally so that a local official could initiate and later take the credit for the scheme. It was a procedure which Paul Howell, Crawford's successor as head of the Development Division, described as the 'ventriloquization of aid'.[80] Though apparently *ad hoc*, it none the less became the rule of thumb in the Development Division and was communicated to all advisers upon the commencement of their duties. While perhaps not the most efficient way of giving advice, it is open to debate whether efficiency and development ever go hand in hand, this being especially true during the volatile days of the 1950s. As Crawford stated: 'In the Middle East, it takes a lot of time to do a very little and it requires repeated visits.'[81] In his mind, the great advantage of this more personal *modus operandi* was its emphasis on building up the confidence of local administrators upon whom the economic development of the region would ultimately depend while at the same time maintaining the influence of his own advisers and, thus, British prestige. The approach was not as tangible as one based on money and agreements, but as attested by the Development Division, it offered the best way of doing business in the Middle East and compared favourably with the approach of other agencies. As Rapp explained to London:

[T]he stiffer approach of many United Nations agencies, planning their work from a distance and anxious in too many cases to dress their own shop windows so as to perpetuate their own comfortable existences . . . is often in contrast to . . . our own approach [which] proceeds on a very human, informal basis – the emphasis being on friendly cooperation between equals, one of whom is able to lend a helping hand to the other.[82]

This approach was most successful and reaped tangible benefits for the Middle East in three fields of the BMEO's expertise: forestry, statistics, and rural credit. Forestry services, for example, which had been virtually non-existent before the war began to be organized in Iraq and Iran with

British forestry advisers being hired to run them. Much of this can be attributed to the prodding work of Maitland, the first forestry adviser of the Development Division and later that of Mooney. Both men, wrote Davidson, himself a forest adviser with the Development Division in the 1960s, 'were well versed in dealing harmoniously with local senior government officials . . . and particularly enjoyed travel in out of the way places far removed from the amenities of civilized life. They moved about the region in close proximity very often with district officials and the country people so they gained a first-hand knowledge of the many problems involved in finding ways of achieving forestry development.'[83] In Iran, it was in fact Maitland who was seconded as the Chief Forester for the Iranian Plan Organisation and Mooney was given the same post with the Iraq Development Board in 1951. They also managed to arouse preliminary interest in forestry development in Lebanon, Syria, and even Egypt where a report written by Maitland represented the first in any field given to that government by the Development Division.[84] Perhaps the most significant achievement in forestry, however, was the establishment of the sub-professional forestry training centre in Cyprus. It was originally a Colonial Office project but, due to the interest of Maitland and other British foresters in Cyprus, its scope was widened to include the Middle East, in the end, reserving fifteen of its places for candidates from the Arab world. The emphasis on 'sub'-professional forestry training is significant and is evidence of the more practical and cautious British approach to the promotion of development in the region as opposed to, for example, the French who had been keen to set up a high-level professionally oriented forestry research centre in the region. Though perhaps self-serving, Davidson went so far as to describe the creation of the training centre as 'the greatest boost to forestry development in the region' in the postwar period[85] and Chapman more generally claimed that 'forestry [is] beginning to come alive in the Middle East and without question [its] rebirth . . . [has] been solely the result of the influence and efforts of His Majesty's Government'.[86]

The Development Division also sparked significant progress in the statistical field. Central statistical bureaus were set up in Syria, Iraq, and Iran with British advisers being hired to direct two of them. In the case of both Iraq and Iran, Murray, the BMEO's statistical adviser, was seconded on a more permanent basis. As with forestry, this statistical work also culminated in the establishment of a regional training centre, the International Statistical Education Centre in Beirut (ISEC). This was a product of the joint efforts of the Ford Foundation, Professor Badre of the American University of Beirut, and the Development Division, namely the statistical advisers Murray, Windett, and Porter. When it opened in February

1953, Murray in fact was its co-director along with Faiz al-Khouri, a former director of the Statistical Department in Damascus.[87] As was the case with the Cyprus Forestry College, the ISEC was designed to train statisticians at the sub-professional level – to be statistical clerks rather than fully fledged professional statisticians. Porter used to give an annual set of lectures there until, by the end of the decade, the teaching medium became arabic in recognition of the larger pool of qualified Arab technicians.[88]

Though not until the 1950s, the Development Division also had ground-breaking influence in the field of cooperatives and rural credit in the Middle East. Largely still-born in the 1940s, efforts to stimulate interest in cooperatives took off in the next decade in line with the region's increasing preoccupation with the issue of land reform. It was the Development Division's unanimous opinion that land reform's success depended upon the provision of adequate credit facilities, particularly short-term cooperative credit. This required initiatives on the part of the state and, thus, much of the early advice in this field concentrated on setting up separate cooperative departments within the various ministries of agriculture, the passing of a basic law on cooperatives, and the training of local people to run schemes independently of foreign advisers. The success achieved by the cooperative advisors of the BMEO, Cheesman and Wordsworth, was fairly widespread. Cooperative laws were passed and departments set up in Jordan, Iraq, and Iran in large part due to pressure and advice from these two advisers – before the Suez crisis, there was also a great deal of activity in Egypt – and in many cases, foreign experts, Arab if possible, were brought in to get these departments started on the right foot.[89] To assist local personnel, training was given during the many repeat visits and in the case of Egypt and Jordan, handbooks were drawn up, the latter still being in use today.[90] Finally, as was the case with both forestry and statistics, efforts were made to establish a cooperative training centre in the region which culminated in a cooperative training course in Cyprus in 1952.

In at least three fields, therefore, the Development Division helped to stimulate interest in and lay the basis of a more solid state framework for future development. That this was accomplished in spite of the strong animosity which the Arab world held towards Britain and the limited – in some cases non-existent – technical interest in these issues was notable. They had begun their work in unchartered waters with virtually no precedents to look back on. It is true that none of this progress actually had any immediate and positive impact on the economic development of the region *per se*. It was all preparatory in nature, aimed at increasing the ability of states in the region to implement and administer policy in the future. There were certainly many failures and non-starters. Nonetheless, its work was pioneering and helped bring some states in the region to the point where, in certain fields, they could begin to realistically debate the more contentious issues of policy implementation.

With this reevaluation of BMEO's position in the Middle East following the introduction of technical assistance programmes from the Americans and United Nations, a reevaluation which highlighted several advantages to its own set-up – flexible administrative procedure, a high degree of technical competence, practical and long-serving experience with Middle East conditions, and a *modus operandi* which allowed its advisers to operate on the basis of personal rather than political criteria, the BMEO entered the 1950s with a greater sense of confidence than was at first apparent. One should not exaggerate the effect that this would have on its influence in the region. For the most part, its work would likely remain confined to those states pre-disposed to Britain. Moreover, much would depend upon the personalities and experience of the individual advisers. Not all would be a success. Finally, the degree to which it would be able to capitalize on its relative position of strength was limited. In no way could it displace other agencies. Nevertheless, despite the emergence of a highly competitive market for technical assistants in the 1950s, the BMEO's position remained secure. This was already evident by the resultant increase in its workload, a fact confirmed at a meeting of advisers in mid-1951.[91] This led Windett to conclude in the wake of the first meeting at Alexandria on the coordination of technical assistance in the region: 'I think it is fair to say that, if all attempts of such "co-ordination" break down and if an "advice-war" is unleashed, the position of BMEO's Development Division would not be seriously, if at all, affected.'[92]

What we now examine in greater detail are case studies of the actual work undertaken by the BMEO's Development Division in three Middle East countries: Iran, Iraq, and Jordan. In Iran, we will see the BMEO in its formative years operating in an environment of greater bureaucratic sophistication but also heightened political tensions. In Iraq, the BMEO takes a somewhat more backseat role though the reasons for this are quite interesting. In Jordan, the BMEO achieves its greatest successes and it is here that its distinctive approach to the promotion of development in the Middle East is most clearly seen.

4 The British Middle East Office and the politics of modernization in Iran, 1945 to 1951

Modernization and development have been an integral part of Iran's modern history. In the nineteenth century, Iran had been a weak and fragmented state over which a monarch reigned but in many ways did not rule. Saddled with divisions along geographic, ethnic, religious, and linguistic lines, Iran's rulers were never able to consolidate the power of the central state, let alone pursue a policy of integration and development. Neither were there strong westernizing influences from Europe to act as an imposed catalyst for change, certainly in comparison to the Ottoman Empire which found itself caught up in the whole Eastern Question. The result was the formation of a state in nineteenth-century Iran which has been described as 'pre-modern'.[1]

A change of dynasties after the First World War which brought Reza Shah Pahlavi to power ushered in a period of intense socio-economic and state-led reform that continued until the overthrow of the Pahlavi dynasty in the Iranian Revolution of 1979. The only notable exception to this general trend were the years between 1941 to 1953 which most concern us here. Mirroring the *étatist* policies of Ataturk in neighbouring Turkey, Reza Shah initiated a state-led modernization programme aimed at integrating the country through the establishment of a modernized military, an enlarged bureaucracy, an improved system of infrastructure, and an industrial base. By the outbreak of the Second World War, it appeared as though Iran had travelled a considerable distance down this road to modernity.

As was the case throughout the region, the Second World War revealed the shaky foundations on which Reza Shah's 'modern' Iran had been built. Despite attempts to strengthen its territorial integrity, Iran remained vulnerable to the machinations and interventions of foreign powers. In 1941, for example, the Allies forced the pro-Nazi Reza Shah to abdicate in favour of his son and subsequently proceeded to divide the country into spheres of influence with the Soviets occupying the north and the British occupying the south. This was joined by a drive to control Iran's economic resources, namely oil, symbolized by Soviet and

American efforts to balance off the British-owned oil concession with ones of their own. Foreign intervention also played a key role in the unravelling of Iran's facade of unity as region after region took advantage of the weakened centre by pushing for autonomy. This period of devolution reached a peak in the immediate postwar period with the creation of autonomous republics in Azerbaijan and Kurdistan and the outbreak of tribal revolts in the south which were clearly encouraged by the British.

Economically, Reza Shah's programme also proved to be shallow and uneven at best. The fruits of modernization were unequally distributed with Tehran benefitting at the expense of the regions and the Shah and his royal court benefitting at the expense of the wider population. Many of the industrial and public works projects were designed more often than not to benefit their own growing personal estates. Banani, in his study of Reza Shah's reform programme, described it as being 'beyond the bounds of economic rationale, not for the sake of efficiency and welfare but as a symbol of prestige and status'.[2] In the mean time, the vast majority of the population who continued to toil as peasants in the countryside benefitted little from the Shah's reforms and, in fact, saw their relative positions deteriorate with the imposition of a debilitating and regressive system of taxation.[3]

The weakest links in Reza Shah's modernization programme were political. Despite the existence of a Majlis and past movements towards constitutionalism, the political system in Iran continued to be very narrowly based. Few of the structural preconditions or political agents and institutions which characterize modern democratic systems of government existed. These had all been ignored by Reza Shah who concentrated instead on 'modernizing' a traditional form of patrimonial rule in which the Court prevailed over the Majlis and personalities over parties. New social groups such as workers and a nascent educated middle class that had emerged as a result of the Shah's reforms remained locked out of the political arena. With the removal of the strong patrimonial figure in 1941, however, Iran suddenly found itself sporting a parliamentary democracy in which a whole array of political forces emerged to vie for power: the Tudeh or Toilers Party on the left, the Society of Muslim Warriors led by the fiery cleric Ayatallah Kashani on the religious right, as well as the traditional political classes of royalists, tribal leaders, and landowners. Above these groups hovered the new Shah who never hid his contempt for Iranian democracy nor his strong desire to firmly reestablish the power of the Pahlavi dynasty. Confronted by the enormous problems of foreign occupation, national disintegration, and economic dislocation which many felt were laying the seeds for revolution, this competition for power in Iran's fledgling experiment in democracy often played itself out on the

streets and often with bloody results.[4] It is this political context, particularly the competition between the Shah and the Majlis for ultimate
control of Iranian politics, which sets the scene for our discussion of the
politics of development in Iran and Britain's role in that process.

Britain, Iran, and socio-economic reform

The political instability of postwar Iran was of tremendous concern to
British policy makers. At a time when British power in Iran was relatively,
if not absolutely, in decline, the threat to British interests there had never
been greater. Soviet activity in Azerbaijan and its support for the Tudeh
Party in Iran as a whole posed the dual threat of succession and possible
revolution and seemed to vindicate Bevin's worst fears about the negative
geostrategic effects of the emergence of power vacuums in the postwar
world.[5] These broad geopolitical concerns were combined with more
narrow economic ones – namely the protection of the Anglo-Iranian Oil
Company (AIOC), one of Britain's biggest overseas assets, a not insignificant source of taxation revenue for the British Government and, perhaps
most importantly, a dollar earner for the sterling area at a time when
dollars were dear. The granting of foreign concessions had always been
somewhat problematic in Iranian politics going back to the days of the
Tobacco Crisis in 1891–92. British control of Iran's oil reserves through
the AIOC provoked a similar response among a growing nationalist
movement in postwar Iran. The AIOC was accused of not contributing its
fair share to Iran's economic development, particularly with regard to
royalty payments which were smaller in fact than its taxation payments to
the British Government. It was also charged with failing to create enough
forward and backward linkages with the rest of the Iranian economy,
choosing instead to be dependent on Britain for supplying its needs, and
from excluding Iranians from access to senior management positions.
These latter grievances had led to a Tudeh-inspired strike in the AIOC oil
fields in Khuzistan in 1946. Although the AIOC was in fact a private corporation, it was seen, perhaps legitimately, in the eyes of Iranians as being
inextricably linked with Britain's imperial designs. The Shah eager for
western support in his struggle with the Majlis would try to diffuse these
sentiments by negotiating a Supplementary Agreement with the AIOC
that would have increased Iranian royalties. Caught up as it was in the
wider struggle for political power, this attempt would have little success as
the debates over the future of the AIOC increasingly came to dominate
the political arena in Iran and led eventually to the nationalization of the
AIOC in 1951, an unprecedented response from a Third World country
against the imperial domination of the West.

Britain reacted to these threats using a combination of classic gunboat diplomacy and more subtle political interference. For example, at the height of the Azerbaijan crisis in the summer of 1946 when it looked as though Soviet and Tudeh influence was reaching dangerous levels, Britain resorted to more direct ways of protecting her interests by reinforcing her base in Basra, preparing to send troops to Khuzistan, and anchoring two gunboats off the coast at Abadan. When the challenge was less immediate, Britain's main goal was to promote the kind of strong government in Tehran needed to deal with these enormous political problems. Until the emergence of the Shah as a more potent political force, this initially meant interfering in the day-to-day political process to promote the influence of politicians open to relations with Britain and able to sway the Majlis. By the beginning of 1948, however, with the Shah beginning to emerge as the 'central institution' in Iran, the British increasingly began to rely on him.[6]

Britain, of course, had floated the idea of a third approach to maintaining its influence in the region: the promotion of socio-economic reform. Iran, though it certainly had the socio-economic qualifications, was not originally included in Bevin's 'peasants, not pashas' policy which was designed more with the Levant and Egypt in mind. Its application in Iran, however, became increasingly attractive. It could be used to deflect attention away from the failings of the AIOC and, above all, it could prove a useful card in the emerging Cold War being played out in the north of the country.[7] Bevin, for example, had been very moved by the report of Maitland, the forestry adviser of the BMEO, made during a visit to a village near the Azerbaijani town of Astara on the Caspian Sea in which he had written that 'the state of this village and its people leaves one sick at heart, both for what man has made of man here and for the state of the administration which allows so little to be done for so many. We returned to the luxury hotel . . . but the stink and misery of that village haunted me for days.'[8] Azerbaijan was adjacent to the Soviet Union, 'on the front line – not only of Persia but of the world division' as Maitland wrote.[9] To do nothing about the situation was tantamount to inviting the Soviets to march on in. After reading Maitland's report, Bevin was more convinced than ever of the crucial importance of promoting socio-economic development in the region. Indeed, he scribbled in its margins that 'it is a disaster that Great Britain's influence has not been used before in these matters'.[10] Moreover, as Iran had an abundance of finance to allocate to development, Bevin's policy, based as it was on the provision of technical assistance, seemed to fit the Iranian context nicely.

If the promotion of socio-economic development was to become a cornerstone of British policy in Iran, the question remained as to how such assistance in the form of the BMEO should be introduced. At the 1945 Middle East conference, it had been generally accepted that the initiative for development planning had to come from the governments of the region themselves. To push a policy of technical assistance too vigorously would have raised skepticism about motive and tainted the BMEO as an instrument of British imperial policy in the region, something which of course it was. Nevertheless, as Bevin, wanted to give the appearance that it was an apolitical, technical instrument of British policy, it was decided that the BMEO should sit back and wait for the right opportunity.

In Iran, the wait was not long. Reform and development planning was very much on the postwar political agenda in Iran. In the spring of 1946, Qavam, the Iranian Prime Minister, formed a commission to draft a development plan which prompted London to instruct Le Rougetel, the British ambassador in Tehran, to start up a dialogue with Overton in Cairo about ways of getting the BMEO involved.[11] By all those concerned, this was recognized as a real breakthrough for the hitherto dormant BMEO.[12] By June, Qavam's commission had produced a five-year plan for agricultural development that included provisions for the distribution of Crown Lands to peasants; and by December 1946, he had added a Capital Development Commission whose purpose was to prepare a capital works programme based on proposals from interested ministries. These efforts culminated with Qavam's speech to the Majlis on the occasion of the Iranian New Year in March 1947, in which he announced his intentions of formulating a seven year programme for economic and social development. The scope of the programme was immense, prompting Le Rougetel to remark that 'in this remarkable statement, nothing has been forgotten from irrigation to lunatic asylums'. Estimated expenditure was to be in the neighbourhood of L 450 million or, as Le Rougetel skeptically pointed out, the equivalent of fourteen ordinary budgets in Iran.[13] Particular emphasis was placed on irrigation development in the southern provinces such as Khuzistan where the MESC had also shown some interest during the war. Qavam talked of 'reviving old glories' and of growing enough wheat to feed 50 million people.[14]

The British were fascinated by Qavam's vision for the south of Iran with Crawford calling it 'one of the big possible schemes of development in the Middle East'.[15] However, there remained reasons to be cautious. Qavam had a strong interest in reform but his political motives were at best unclear. His original foray into the reform business, for example, coincided with his move towards the left-wing Tudeh Party and the Soviet Union and a crackdown on pro-British politicians and businessmen, all of which was aimed at strengthening his position *vis-à-vis* the Shah by building up a social base of support. Reform-minded or not, however, this was not the kind of politics Britain was willing to support and thus no offer of assistance was made at this time. In fact, Britain worked to undermine the Qavam regime with its encouragement of tribal rebellion in the south and its buildup of troops near Abadan. Imperial interests would always precede those of the local population. What changed the British attitude towards Qavam was his dramatic about-face to the right in late 1946, in part brought about by British interference and gun-boat diplomacy, which left Qavam with little choice but to crack down on the Tudeh Party, cool relations with the Soviet Union and reassert central military control in the various run-away republics.[16] Now on the right side of the ideological divide, Qavam's reform programme looked much more attractive to the British. With his announcement of the Capital Works Commission at the end of 1946 and his request for access to the wartime files of the MESC on the Iranian economy, the British were once again talking of Iran as providing an 'excellent opening' for the BMEO.[17]

The entry of the BMEO into Iran was dependent on one further variable: the expected reaction of the Americans. Despite the traditional strength of British influence in Iran, it was the Americans who had provided the bulk of foreign advisers to the government typified by the Millspaugh missions to Iran in the 1920s and later in the 1940s, both designed to upgrade Iran's financial system.[18] This preference for American advisers emanated, in part, from Iran's desire to maintain 'positive neutrality' in foreign policy so as to avoid too close a dependence on Britain or the USSR as well as from the assumption that American participation might bring with it development capital, particularly from the newly formed IBRD. This explains Qavam's decision to hire Morrison-Knudson, an American consulting firm, to act as an adviser to the Capital Development Commission and it would later explain why Iran turned to another American consulting firm, Overseas Consultants Incorporated (OCI), to be official advisers to the Seven Year Plan. However, it was not only the Iranians who were suspicious of British designs in Iran. So too were the Americans eager to break down the Middle East as an exclusive British sphere of interest and capture some of the previously protected markets. In order to avoid arousing the suspicion of the Americans and perhaps setting off the kind of competition in the development field which the British could not hope to win, the decision was made to delay the inaugural visit of the BMEO's Crawford. 'We are naturally anxious', wrote Le Rougetel, 'that there should be no grounds for belief or mischievous propaganda that we were going behind the back of the Mission and the American Embassy here and trying to insinuate a rival British technical survey'.[19]

Not all in London were pleased with this decision. The Board of Trade, for example, had their own suspicions of the Morrison-Knudson mission and felt that the Iranians were handing over the job of providing a technical survey to a group 'whose opinions can hardly be considered unbiased'.[20] They believed that Morrison-Knudson which combined consultants with contractors would cater recommendations to the capabilities and specifications of American firms. This would not only adversely affect British trade with Iran but might also aggravate the dollar problem. Given the huge development expenditures that Iran seemed destined to make in the near future, it seemed logical to encourage some degree of competition with the Morrison-Knudson mission to ensure that British firms would get their fair share of the development pie:

[A]s Persia is not an unattractive market from the currency viewpoint and the longterm projects here discussed could provide useful jobs for our industries at a time when the immediate pressure on their books has slackened somewhat, I do feel that it would be a good move to put a spoke in the wheel if this is at all possible.[21]

However, as was a common theme throughout discussions of postwar British policy in the Middle East, all-out commercial competition with the Americans was not possible. This had already been proven to the Iranians by Britain's refusal, in August of 1946, to raise a loan on the London capital markets in order to finance the Lars Valley Dam scheme, even though it had been a British firm, Sir Alexander Gibb and Partners, who had done the initial survey work and who would have received the contract had the sterling financing come through. As justification for their refusal, the British had argued that the accumulated sterling balances in Iran could be used for such development projects.[22] The real crux of the situation was that the British could not even consider the export of sterling in the early postwar world as a means of facilitating British trade. Their only hope was either to encourage Iran to look to the IBRD or to cooperate with the Americans with the hope that an equitable division of contracts could be worked out. However, if such cooperation was to work, it was essential to overcome 'the longstanding American suspicion that we are always intriguing against any American enterprise'.[23] This meant that the BMEO would have to be cautious in how it promoted itself within Iran. While it was essential that BMEO participate in Iranian postwar development activities, such participation had to be low key and cooperative as far as the Americans are concerned. Part and parcel of this low key approach was the decision to delay Crawford's visit.

That visit finally came in March of 1947 and coincided with Qavam's New Year address to the Majlis and his announcement of Iran's first

Seven Year Plan for economic and social development. The visit seemed well timed. In his speech, Qavam had mentioned the AIOC as a source of finance for Iranian development plans which alarmed AIOC and Foreign Office officials alike. They feared that such an association would stretch royalty payments to the limit and arouse appetites for larger contributions while at the same time starve the working government budget of an important source of revenue. Politically, it was impossible to actually refuse AIOC participation in Iranian economic development. What was needed was an alternative offer of assistance to deflect attention away from the AIOC and this is where the BMEO came in. As the Foreign Office instructed Tehran:

If the Prime Minister shows any sign of wishing to identify the Anglo-Iranian Oil Company with his Seven Year Plan, you should inform him that the British Middle East Office in Cairo has been set up by His Majesty's Government and staffed with highly qualified experts precisely for the purpose of assisting Middle East Governments in their development projects, and in their endeavour to raise the standard of living of their people.[24]

It was in this manner, therefore, that the BMEO was introduced to Iran. It came as a technical organization designed to fulfil some rather weighty goals of British policy in the country. It was to be an instrument in the emerging Cold War, it was to ensure a commercial piece of the development pie, and it was to try and distract attention away from the AIOC. However, it would also have to overcome many obstacles in fulfilling this broad political mandate. It had to tread carefully with the Americans, it had to work with virtually no capital and it had to operate in an environment of extreme nationalist suspicion towards the British. This would make it very difficult for the BMEO, first, to get its foot in the door of Iranian development activities and, second, to translate any technical successes it might have into political ones.

Crawford's principal task during his first visit to Tehran in March 1947, was to open the way for working visits from his staff of advisers in Cairo. Given Qavam's greater willingness to cooperate with western powers, this task was much simplified but Crawford also seems to have had a special ability to open doors and make working contacts. In Tehran, his networking circuit included Prime Minister Qavam, Ebtehaj, at that time President of Bank Melli and later to become head of the Iranian Plan Organization in the 1950s,[25] Amir Ala, the Minister of Agriculture, and Dr Hassan Mosharef Naficy who became the Chairman of the Supreme Planning Board in late 1947 after the completion of the Morrison-Knudsen mission. Originally, Qavam had expressed doubts to Crawford about the adaptability of the BMEO's skills to the Iranian context, doubts which probably masked his broader political hesitancy to allow British

advisers into the country. Crawford tried to defuse his concerns by pointing out that Iran had similar conditions to India where most advisers had
gained their experience and he further stressed that British experience
with land settlement programmes could be very useful in carrying out
some of the proposed irrigation schemes in the south. No doubt relieved
by the quiet, low level approach of Crawford and the BMEO, Qavam
acquiesced to the visit of its advisers and, shortly thereafter, forwarded
invitations to four of them: Murray in statistics, Stewart in agriculture,
Maitland in forestry, and Fowler in animal husbandry.[26] This was the first
big breakthrough for the BMEO team in Cairo and gave these advisers an
important head start in their respective fields of activity.

The first visit was made by the agricultural adviser, Stewart, in June of
1947 and he concerned himself mainly with the proposed irrigation and
land settlement projects in Khuzistan. The main project in the area was
the Kuhrang Scheme, designed to supply water for the valley near
Isfahan by uniting the headwaters of the Karun River with those of the
Zayandeh-Rud River at Kuhrang.[27] Sir Alexander Gibb and Partners
were already active in surveying the technical potentials and feasibilities
of the scheme and Stewart was asked to assist. He was impressed by the
potentials of the scheme but, in much the same fashion that he would
later do in Iraq, cautioned against a 'delusive' emphasis on irrigation:
'The mere provision of more water is not in itself the sole cure for the
backward condition of agriculture.'[28] For example, he saw important
openings for work in crop husbandry in Khuzistan, commenting on the
'criminal' way in which weeds were allowed to run rampant on fallow
land.[29] In addition to irrigation and crop husbandry, Stewart followed
Crawford's lead in stressing the ultimate importance of carefully
planned land settlement schemes which were bound to be extremely
complicated given the semi-nomadic nature of the population. In discussions with the agricultural members of the Supreme Planning Board,
he reiterated the experience which the British had gained in this field in
areas such as the Sudan and Tanganika.[30]

The second major opening for BMEO expertise lay in forestry and soil
conservation. After a tour of the Caspian forests in May of 1948, BMEO
forestry advisor, Maitland, was taken aback, first, by the problems of soil
erosion which he described as being 'as acute in Iran as in any country on
earth' and second, by the rapid depletion of the magnificent forests of the
north.[31] He warned that without some drastic action by the Iranian
Government, these forests would become a thing of the past within one
generation. He was particularly taken aback by the alarming degree of
human poverty and deprivation and wrote at one point that in twenty-five
years of service in the Central Provinces in India, he had seen nothing

worse.[32] Part of the problem, Maitland admitted, had been caused by temporary factors such as the massive Soviet cutting in the Caspian region during the war. However, the root causes were more fundamental and had to do with the lack of government control and policy towards such issues as charcoal burning, felling, silviculture, and goat grazing, the latter being a regional problem of the Middle East in particular. To solve these problems of natural and human poverty, Maitland argued the need for more effective state control and recommended the establishment of a proper forestry service, integrated in such a way that it could also provide basic human needs such as health care for the more remote districts of the north, an idea carried over from his Indian experiences.[33]

Of the other advisers, Fowler examined the feasibility of expanding the Animal Husbandry Institute at Haiderabad and Murray, who had a wealth of experience in organizing statistical offices, visited the Central Statistical Bureau in Tehran. His visit was so successful that he ended up by being appointed its chief adviser in September 1948. However, one field of technical assistance did not look promising: that of health, though it was certainly not for lack of need. Pridie, the BMEO's health adviser, on his preliminary tour of Iran in July of 1947, commented, for example, that 'preventative medicine appeared to be conspicuous by its absence, and water supplies and sanitation in towns are a nightmare'.[34] Moreover, if irrigation schemes were going to be carried out, the health aspect of any subsequent settlement schemes were vital. As Le Rougetel emphasized:

When we are seeking to assist in raising the standard of life in Persia by promoting large-scale development schemes, it would be useless to proceed . . . and to render fertile a number of square miles of territory if at the same time the population is decimated by infant and maternal mortality and disease . . . [S]uch schemes can only be successful if at the same time considerable advance is made in Public Health.[35]

However, the BMEO was not able to make any inroads in this field of technical assistance in Iran. Sir Alexander Gibb and Partners did manage to win the Tehran Water Supply contract to be serviced by the proposed Lars Valley Dam project but on the whole, foreign influence in health matters, particularly French, was already extensive leading Pridie to conclude that 'it would be impossible to bring about a merging of British and Persian medicine as has been done in Egypt'.[36] To push for British involvement in matters of Iranian health, Pridie concluded, would only arouse suspicion. There was moreover a question of finance. Pridie, in fact, had been the first BMEO officer to visit Iran in the fall of 1946 to attend an anniversary celebration of the Pasteur Institute there. He made several comments and subsequent recommendations concerning Iranian

public health including a request for a malaria expert as well as an expert
to set up a nursing training school. Since the Iranian Government would
never pay for a high-priced British expert, however, Pridie pointed out
that financing would have to come from the British Government, a proposal to which London responded negatively.[37] Pridie's report was, therefore, never presented to the Iranians, Le Rougetel deciding that 'I regret
that I cannot for the time being see any advantage in proposing assistance
to the Persian Government.'[38] Waterlow of the MES was not happy with
this early defeat for the BMEO, commenting that 'if increased importance is to be attached to our economic work in the Middle East, then I
feel that we could and should put up a case . . . I suggest that we should
return to the charge'.[39] The end result of this 'charge' was Pridie's second
visit to Iran in July of 1947. That, however, was the last heard from the
BMEO in matters of Iranian public health.

More serious difficulties arose when in August 1948, the Iranians hired
the American consulting firm, OCI, to prepare the blue-print for the
Seven Year Plan. This meant the arrival in Iran of a whole new team of
competing technical advisors. The BMEO in Cairo was caught completely by surprise by the decision. While there had been some initial
contact between the Americans and the British with Lutz, OCI's head,
expressing interest in the work of the BMEO, in particular that of Murray,
during a stopover visit to London,[40] the British were concerned that OCI
were determined to 'run their own show' to the exclusion of the BMEO.[41]
There was particular concern about the neglect of Maitland despite the
fact that his report on forestry written during his first tour of Iran in the
spring of 1948 had resulted in Majlis legislation to set up an independent
Forestry Commission.

In Tehran, the embassy approached OCI about the matter but this
resulted in complaints from their project manager in Tehran that Le
Rougetel had been putting 'the heat' on him to use BMEO men.[42] With
direct pressure ruled out, the British turned to third parties such as Sir
Alexander Gibb and Partners for support. Maitland had described their
representative in Tehran as 'a most valuable link between BMEO experts
and the Americans'.[43] It was also hoped that the IBRD might help,
particularly since the representative in charge of Middle East loans was
Iliff, the former British Treasury attaché in the Middle East who had been
stationed with the BMEO team in Cairo when it was first established.
Finally, it was decided to approach State Department officials in
Washington who would be 'more likely than OCI to appreciate the political advantages of close Anglo-American cooperation in Persia'.[44]

In the end, two BMEO advisers were able to secure appointments with
OCI. Maitland salvaged his position during a visit to Tehran in March

1949, where he insinuated himself onto an OCI tour of the north and distinguished himself for reports on famine situations in the Moghan Plain in Azerbaijan and in Sistan Province.[45] For the latter, he received special thanks from the Governor General of the province.[46] He would later be appointed Chief Forestry Adviser to the Iranian Government. As for Murray, he had already been offered the position of Chief Statistical Adviser to the Iranian Government which, curiously enough, had raised some doubts within the BMEO as to whether he should in fact accept. These doubts were motivated by concern not to weaken the BMEO 'team'. Troutbeck spoke of Murray as a key man in the Development Division and worried about the loss of continuity in BMEO work if Murray were lost, particularly with respect to Iraq.[47] Trevelyan in Iraq seconded this concern.[48] With the announcement of OCI's visit, however, all doubts were pushed aside. As Le Rougetel wrote in a letter to Troutbeck: 'There can be no doubt that we shall need to muster . . . all the strength we can if we are not to be sidetracked by the Americans and relegated to the exclusive role of providing the wherewithal to get the plan started.'[49]

The one notable absence from the OCI team was Stewart. Maitland was disappointed by this result and thought it represented a fundamental failing of the BMEO in Iran. He was not impressed with the Americans who 'do not seem to be making any real progress with what are almost entirely administrative questions [and] are still struggling with Persian red tape which is a particularly bad variety'.[50] The real issue, he believed, lay with the organization of the BMEO itself. For an arm of the British Foreign Office, the BMEO worked in an extraordinarily unstructured and *ad hoc* fashion. There was very little control from the centre and very little overall planning. To some extent, this was a direct consequence of Crawford's more informal and personal approach towards the provision of technical assistance in the Middle East. As a consequence, the BMEO did not really work as a team and Maitland believed that this had hurt its ability to increase its influence in matters of Iranian development. 'I regard it as a pity', he wrote, 'that BMEO could not have put up a properly integrated land use team covering agriculture, irrigation, forests, pastures . . . This may be a pointer for future organization of BMEO.'[51] No doubt, Stewart's inability to be invited to participate with OCI can be partially attributed to this underlying factor.

The politics of Iranian Seven Year Plan organization

Before looking at the specific work of the BMEO advisors, it is necessary to set the stage for their activities. This requires an understanding of the

planning mechanisms created to implement the development programme and the political context in which those mechanisms operated.
The idea of planning in Iran was originally raised in the 1930s as a reaction to the corrupt and uncoordinated manner in which Reza Shah was
implementing his industrialization programme. After an initial attempt to
create an economic council in 1937, however, the issue was dropped probably because it meant an 'unacceptable limitation on the dictator's
whims'.[52] As we have seen, it was Qavam who revived the idea in the
postwar world. This had led, first, to the recreation of an economic
council in April 1946, and later to the establishment of a Supreme
Planning Board in November 1947. It was this body which was to prepare
a Seven Year Plan and make recommendations about the kind of administrative structures which would implement it.

The key question facing the Supreme Planning Board was the degree
to which any newly created planning organization would be politically
autonomous. Given that development planning was bound to be a major
issue in the power struggle between the Majlis and the Shah, the answer to
this question in many ways depended on which side of the political divide
one stood in postwar Iran. The Shah and his supporters, for example,
wanted to use the development issue as a way of bolstering their own position and power within government. They were particularly interested in a
development initiative which emphasized agricultural development and
land reform. With some of the worst poverty occurring in the remote
rural areas of the country, a rural-oriented development strategy might
ensure the support of those economically disaffected who were prime
targets for Soviet and Tudeh propaganda. Moreover, an effective agricultural development programme could also prove useful as a noose over the
heads of an equally dangerous opposition group: the nationalistic-
minded landowning élites. Thus, when the Seven Year Plan was eventually passed by the Majlis on 17 February 1949, one saw expenditure
directed towards the agricultural sector, 25 per cent in fact, as compared
to 14.3 per cent for industry.[53]

The landowning élites, however, were wary of a development programme which emphasized the agrarian sector, a wariness which helped
to foster an uneasy alliance with more left-wing groups who themselves
looked upon the agriculturally oriented plan as a way of perpetuating
Iran's dependence on the world economy and, in particular, on the capi-
talist and imperialist powers of Britain and the United States. A leftist
newspaper in Tehran wrote at this time:

The Seven Year Plan marks . . . [a] stage in the economic and political enslave-
ment of Iran by the ruling classes of America and Britain . . . The imperialists . . .
drafted this Plan with the object of stifling the industrial development of the

country and of converting it into an agrarian appendage . . . as a raw material base, and as a convenient market for the investment of capital, equipment and goods.[54]

They also portrayed the Shah as a client of the imperialists, sacrificing the national interest for his own. His dependence on western military aid during this time period seemed to add weight to their argument as did his favourable disposition towards the AIOC and the Supplementary Agreement. This portrayal of the Shah as a collaborator with imperialism became a powerful weapon in the hands of the opposition in the Majlis, particularly the National Front who were eventually able to challenge the Shah's authority and scuttle his development programme.

In light of this political opposition, the Shah and his supporters hoped to create a planning board somewhat removed from the political arena. The model that emerged was taken from a report completed by the Supreme Planning Board headed by Naficy and was based on four principles: (a) the board was to be independent of politics; (b) it was to have its own legal status and financial autonomy in the form of a bank account with Bank Melli and a proportion of the AIOC oil revenues; (c) it would execute projects as well as have broad powers as a planner; and (d) it would have its own staff and would be exempt from normal government rules regarding tendering and salaries. The executive structure of the board would consist of a Managing Director appointed by the Shah, a seven man technically oriented Supreme Council, and a six man Board of Control. The whole structure was to be called the Plan Organization. The formal influence of the Majlis would be limited to the appointment of the members of the Board of Control and the approval of its general operating programme.

The British and the BMEO supported these efforts to create a strong and autonomous development administration. Maitland, for example, after his first tour of Iran was struck by the feebleness of the Iranian bureaucracy, a feebleness which led him to conclude that:

whatever the theoretical constitutional disadvantages of such an "Imperium in Imperio" — *nothing else* short of a general upset will meet the present situation, restore respect for authority and provide a way out of the hopeless tangle of red tape, inefficiency, and corrupt bureaucracy which blocks development and creates the widespread sense of frustration and even despair among those who can see beyond their immediate horizon and who are not engaged in exploiting the situation for their own benefit.

After discussions with Naficy who stated that he would have nothing to do with the plan without the creation of a central and autonomous planning authority, Maitland concurred, writing that 'from what I have seen of the country, it would seem reasonable that a similar consideration should condition such Anglo-American aid as may be needed to implement it'.[55]

There was one major obstacle to overcome, however. The Seven Year Plan with its politically autonomous Plan Organization would have to be approved by the Majlis. Although the Majlis was by no means monolithically opposed to the Shah's development programme, it being filled with large numbers of royalists and independents, there was an inherent contradiction in the whole process of trying to obtain agreement among Iranian politicians of the day to limit their own influence over an area of policy which was highly political in itself and was bound to have a dramatic effect on the future direction of the country. In March of 1948, Le Rougetel reported that 'it is probable ... that the wide powers given to the Planning Organization ... will provoke ... controversy as it would enable the Organization to impose its policy on any department of the state'.[56] He went on to explain that 'some Ministers are jealous of the over-riding powers conferred upon the planning Authority and some of them are trying to persuade the Prime Minister to drop this part of the Bill altogether leaving the execution of the plan to the individual Ministries. If they succeed in this, the Plan will of course be a dead letter'.[57]

OCI who were lobbying heavily to become involved in the Seven Year Plan were worried by these developments. Max Thornburg, OCI's advocate in Iran, flew back to Tehran in mid-1948 to try and influence the Majlis debate on this issue. Like the British, he too insisted on the need for a central planning organization separate from everyday political life. To leave planning to the responsibility of the ministries would result in stagnation: 'Ministries ... have proven in the past not to have been able to carry out plans of even considerably smaller proportions ... [What was needed was] a central office where responsibility and authority remained continuously dedicated to the prosecution of the Plan.'[58] Thornburg tried to influence the debate further by predicting the refusal of financial assistance for development from the United States and the IBRD if the bill was not passed in its present form.[59]

These arguments and petitions had little impact. After the fall of the Qavam Government in December 1947, Iran was governed by a series of royally appointed weak prime ministers who were not able to control the Majlis nor influence the Shah. This resulted in a period of Iranian politics which Azimi has described as an 'exhaustive stalemate'.[60] The Seven Year Plan was a casualty of this stalemate and left many directly involved in its formulation extremely discouraged. Thornburg spoke of removing the Bill from the Majlis and waiting for a more propitious time; 'it would be better', wrote Thornburg, 'to have no plan at all than to submit its execution to constantly changing political agencies'.[61]

Another strategy considered was to abandon large-scale planning altogether and revert to a small-scale approach to development in Iran as a way of circumventing political obstacles. Crawford, who was already in sympathy with this approach from a professional point of view, agreed. 'From all that I heard in Tehran, I feel certain that the main thing is for the Persians to start in on a few small things, sort of pilot schemes, that can be built in later into bigger schemes.'[62] To this purpose, the American and British Embassies in Tehran met in June of 1948 to compile a shortlist of projects, indicating the urgent priority which both countries placed on the need for any kind of development initiative in Iran: 'It is vital to put some of these projects into effect . . . as otherwise the political and social climate may rapidly deteriorate.'[63]

Further complicating the political equation was the Shah's attempt to push a constitutional reform package through the Majlis which would have increased his powers considerably. At first, the British criticized this move as short-sighted but, as the political stalemate continued, Le Rougetel in particular began to question the logic of seeking economic solutions for political problems and suggested that constitutional reform, if it broke the political stalemate, might in fact be the best way to ensure progress on the economic front.[64] Some even began to suggest the idea of more forceful British interference but this was flatly rejected by Le Rougetel who emphasized that 'no good and much harm might come of applying pressure to the Government with regard to economic development while they are at loggerheads on the subject among themselves for those who are opposed to the bill would immediately accuse us of trying to foist this plan on them for our own nefarious purposes'.[65] The log-jam was finally broken in February 1949 after an assassination attempt on the Shah. Frightened, yet more determined than ever to strengthen his position, the Shah cracked down on political dissent and, under the threat of dissolution, forced the momentarily quiescent Majlis to ratify his political programme. Included was the Seven Year Plan which was passed by the Majlis on 17 February 1949. This made Iran the first country in the Third World to institute a planning process, pre-dating that passed by India in 1950.

However, the mere passage of the Seven Year Plan and the formal creation of the Plan Organization guaranteed little in terms of its effectiveness. From the start, there were numerous complaints about corruption and administrative inefficiencies, not surprising perhaps for a body which by 1951 had hired over 1,200 employees.[66] There was also an absence of any real accomplishments. Baldwin in his study of planning in Iran estimated that of the many recommendations put forward by OCI, less than a third were acted upon and less than a fifth were implemented.[67]

The major explanation for the ineffectiveness of the Plan Organization has to be political. Despite the attempt to create an autonomous development agency, politics intruded into all levels of the Plan Organization's work from the appointment of the Managing Director to the passage of its budget. Problems, for example, were created from the start with the appointment of Taqi Nasr as the Plan Organization's first Managing Director, a royalist with progressive leanings. The Shah had hoped that either Naficy or Ebtehaj would accept the position but both declined, Naficy 'unable to cope any longer with the delays and politiking' and Ebtehaj preferring to stay on in his position as Governor of Bank Melli.[68] When Nasr assumed the position, however, he chose to ignore the sectoral priorities desired by the Shah and proposed by OCI in favour of a more industrially oriented programme. In their interim report of May 1949, OCI recorded that while 14.3 per cent had been earmarked for industry, that sector had in fact received over 40 per cent of total outlays.[69] Immobilizing the bulk of this 40 per cent was the decision taken by the Plan Organization to assume all liabilities of the Industrial and Mining Bank. Maitland, in the midst of trying to organize a forestry service at this time, described this decision as 'a disaster as regards the first years work as the liabilities had swallowed up a large proportion of the funds'.[70] This decision was accompanied by another to create a Plan Bank to act in its place. With a further 40 per cent of the revenue of the Plan Organization being earmarked for the extension and completion of the Tabriz-Meshad railway, little money was left over for the remainder of the Seven Year Plan. As Lawford in the British Embassy in Tehran summarized, less than 20 per cent or little more than a half million pounds was left available for other vitally important activities such as agriculture, irrigation, and health.[71] It was originally hoped that the Seven Year Plan could find supplementary finance from the IBRD but the large sums involved together with the conservative lending policy of the bank forced the Iranians to concentrate on internal sources.

However, the government itself was having revenue problems brought about in part by Ebtehaj's war with the Majlis over the issue of currency cover and by the inability of the AIOC and the Iranians to come to an agreement over the issue of increased oil royalties. Starved for revenue, the Government eventually resorted to raiding some of the finances earmarked for the Plan Organization in order to finance the budget deficit.[72] All of this served to diminish the social and political visibility of development expenditure. As Shepherd, the new British Ambassador in Tehran, wrote, 'the Plan Organization ha[s] achieved little that was spectacular and likely to catch the imagination of the public'.[73] The British were now concerned that the Seven Year Plan, seen increasingly as the Shah's,

would begin to work against him politically and to the benefit of the opposition forces led by the National Front. That this dynamic was beginning
to play itself out was confirmed by Shepherd's despatch to London in
September 1950 which revealed that 'rumours have spread that the Plan
Organization is just another inefficient and corrupt Government body
and that its employees are busy lining their own pockets and buying themselves private cars with the money allotted for the Plan. The Organization
has done little to counter these rumours which were probably put about
in the first place by those who wished the Plan to fail.'[74]

To minimize the political damage, the Shah, concerned that Nasr's
political sympathies were moving away from his own, sacked him in
August 1949, and appointed Naficy in his place. That this decision was
merely an additional move in the on-going power struggle between the
Majlis and the Shah was obvious and even some of the more progressively
minded royalists saw the move as counterproductive. Prince Abdul Reza,
for example, who had been appointed as the Shah's special representative
on development issues, complained that 'the changes represented a
victory of "corrupt influences" over a group of young liberal-minded and
patriotic men. The [latter] had been represented to the shah as "left-
wing", "Tudeh" and the like and His Majesty had unfortunately been
receptive to these accusations.'[75]

Politics also intruded into the workings of the supposedly technically
oriented Supreme Council. This became particularly acute during the
short-lived premiership of Ali Mansur in the spring of 1950 with OCI
complaining bitterly about Mansur's political manipulation of the Seven
Year Plan. These accusations were confirmed by Lawford who reported
that:

it appears the Council, under the direction of Mansur, have accepted projects
submitted by Government Departments and by private interests without proper
examination and without proper references, on the one hand, to the recommendations of OCI and, on the other hand, to the financial resources likely to be
definitively available for economic development under the Plan . . . [T]heir adoption seems to have been largely determined by Ali Mansur's desire to seek political
patronage and personal profit.[76]

Under pressure from OCI, the Plan Organization established an executive coordinating committee consisting of the Managing Director and
four assistant managers with *de facto* representation by OCI. Its purpose
was to place executive control of the organization in this body and, thus,
check the excesses of the Supreme Council. It was hoped that 'the
Council would thus reassume the purely supervisory role for which it
was created under the Plan law'.[77] The intention was also to reinstate
the original priorities of the Seven Year Plan, shelve projects hurriedly

approved, and pass new ones which would coincide with the financial resources of the Plan Organization. Unfortunately for OCI and for those who wanted to minimize (or reverse) political interference, this committee was still-born and it was not long before Mansur used his 'influence' with Naficy to cease holding committee meetings.[78] By May of 1950, Thornburg was writing that 'the [Plan Organization] is so nearly completely dominated or victimized by either political or private interests that there . . . is little to choose between the Plan Organization and any government organization'. He went on to express pessimism at the ability to create development administrations divorced from the political arena: 'It does not seem realistic to expect more than a slight relief from political interference by giving such an organization statutory autonomy. The front is simply too long and too thinly protected to withstand rapacious invaders.'[79]

By the middle of 1950, the political stalemate in Iran was reaching dangerous proportions. The previously divided opposition in the Majlis began to coalesce in opposition to the Supplementary Agreement of the AIOC and the Shah and formed the National Front under the leadership of Mossadegh. This was paralleled by a growing public resentment against the Shah and his 'kleptocratic' court which led to the assassination of a leading royalist supporter, Hazhir, and the outbreak of numerous and violent demonstrations. Having been content with the appointment of a series of weak prime ministers, the Shah, fearing further instability and under pressure from the Americans and the British to get the Supplementary Agreement passed and behind him, made the decision to appoint General Ali Razmara to the premiership, the kind of strongman he had avoided appointing in the past. With his impressive military background and independent power base, Razmara was described as one of the most powerful men in the country.[80]

Razmara came into the premiership with very strong reformist credentials but his approach was much at odds with the original idea of central planning. Upon assuming the premiership, Razmara announced a broad programme of political and economic decentralization which included a reduction in the size and significance of the central Plan Organization and the creation of regional development organizations. Within less than six months, the staff of the Plan Organization shrunk from 1,200 to 540 and OCI had its contract terminated.[81] Even Murray who had spent most of his time trying to centralize statistical services in the country saw his work undone.[82] Despite its effects on Murray's work, the British were basically supportive of Razmara, particularly if he succeeded in passing the Supplementary Agreement through the Majlis. There was also the widely held belief with regard to the Seven Year Plan as it then stood that 'too much was attempted for Persian administrative capabilities both quanti-tatively and qualitatively' and that it would be much better to adopt a pro-gramme 'within the capacity of their administrative machine'.[83] This would have the added benefit of lowering the prospects for political inter-ference. As Shepherd remarked hopefully with regard to Razmara's reforms: '[they] should prove beneficial in getting rid of much deadwood and . . . allowing the Plan Organization to concentrate on constructive and practical planning without being shackled with the tortuous details and intrigues involved in the execution of projects in this country'.[84]

However, Razmara's new decentralized approach to development was never tested. After a promising start, Razmara's Government proved no better than the previous ones in breaking the political log-jam. Perceived as being the Shah's man if not a stooge of the foreign powers, the Majlis blocked all attempts at reform, so much so that Razmara even had trouble passing monthly budgets. What proved his downfall, however, was his support of the Supplementary Agreement. Attacked by the nationalists and without the full-fledged support of the Shah, Razmara's political vul-nerability eventually resulted in his assassination by a Muslim *fedayi* in March 1951. With the subsequent assumption of power by Mossadegh who proceeded to nationalize the AIOC, the Seven Year Plan lost all of its finances and momentum.

The BMEO, forestry, and the Seven Year Plan

With the passage of the Seven Year Plan in 1949, British and American technicians found themselves working together for the first time since the days of the MESC. However, much had changed since the cooperative days of the Second World War, changes reflected in the emergence of rivalries and resentment. Not surprisingly, for example, the British records are full of criticisms of the approach taken by the Americans under OCI, many of which revolved around their inability to work with the Iranian bureaucracy. Maitland, for example, questioned the attitude of American advisors and wrote that 'it is clear that the Americans need assistance on such matters as how to approach the Persians'.[85] American advisers were perceived as disrespectful and desirous of publicity, a trait which contrasted to that of the BMEO and, in Maitland's opinion, was to its advantage in that 'the effect of the typical American desire to be always in the limelight [may] actually [have] improved our standing'.[86] The fact that the profit motive behind OCI's work was never far from the surface did not help their credibility either and, as Maitland reported, 'it has been rather obvious to everyone, including the Persians, that the American business interests were closely linked up with the Plan'.[87]

By contrast, Maitland spoke of the British as having had an effect out of all proportion to their numbers and went on to add that 'the British contribution had probably prevented OCI from being a complete flop'.[88] Murray disagreed with the extremity of Maitland's conclusion singling out several American advisors like Thornburg as having begun some effective work. Nevertheless, there was never any disagreement with the substance of Maitland's remarks.[89] The British believed that their contribution to the Seven Year Plan, though piecemeal and shortlived, had been the most significant. After his tour of Iran in 1950, Crawford concluded: 'I was most impressed by what I saw of the work of the British experts in Persia . . . Their achievements stand out against the little that seems to have been achieved by the Americans in OCI.'[90] Thus, there is a question of 'style' which the British believed set their technical assistance programme in Iran apart from that of the Americans of OCI.

According to Maitland, however, the differences were more fundamental than ones of 'style'. The basic premise upon which the British technical assistance rested was completely different than that of the Americans and as Maitland described, 'OCI expresses that difference. The Americans consider private enterprise [to be] the best agency [of development] and the British think, in certain circumstances, the state.'[91] Thornburg, for example, set OCI up as being the 'Apostles of American Democracy'. They placed great emphasis on promoting private sector development and strongly advocated a policy of privatizing Iran's state-run industries left over from the days of Reza Shah.[92] In turn, they were very critical of the British approach to development for being too autocratic and top-down. For example, Thornburg wrote that while the British were good at building states with 'technically well equipped administrations', 'orderly procedures' and 'a line on the map delimiting its political jurisdiction', they were less successful at building nations with which the people identified. What prevented this transformation from state to nation, wrote Thornburg, was that 'the people . . . take little or no part in its development'. While the British hoped that the state would eventually 'grow down to meet them and become a part of their daily lives', Thornburg cautioned that '[t]his is a long process. Meanwhile, it invites such hostility from the masses who feel its discipline before they feel its benefits. And because those who exercise its authority look to an outside power for their support, rather than to the people, a vital quality of democracy is slow to grow, and may never be given the time for its maturity.'[93]

However, OCI's self-appointed role as 'Apostles of American Democracy' was not appreciated by Iranian officials who, at one point, warned Maitland that 'if the Americans persisted in imposing ideas which were too democratic, the plan would be a masquerade'.[94] These reactions tended to buttress the British sense, formed out of a curious blend of practical experience and orientalist discourse, that 'in Eastern countries, we cannot get away entirely from the state's control on account of traditional and special circumstances'.[95] A particularly strong case for the importance of the state was made in Maitland's report on the famine in Sistan province for which he had received so much praise. In response to the famine, the British Ambassador in Afghanistan, Sir Giles Squire, had written that the crisis in agricultural production in that region was unavoidable and part of a 'natural process of decay'. Maitland strongly objected to these remarks: 'Agriculture does not decay', he insisted, 'nor does the peasantry unless there is something rotten with the administrative methods and so on.' Citing Squire's remarks as 'characteristically Persian in their defeatism', Maitland added that 'if one accepts a "natural process of decay" in agriculture, one accepts the rest' including the famines which result in consequence. Maitland, for example, attributed the famine in the spring of 1949, which resulted in the death of over 100 people per day in the capital Zabul, not to a lack of food production but rather to the exploitation of food resources by powerful *sirdars* and merchants, a factor which also affected the distribution of emergency relief.[96] Characteristic of Maitland's emphasis on state control, he recommended, first and foremost, that martial law be declared in the region and that the government, with military assistance, prohibit the open market sale of grain and set up in its place distribution centres.[97] He made similar recommendations with respect to the problem of famine in the Moghan Plain in Azerbaijan, also in the spring of 1949.[98]

This emphasis on the state is even more apparent when one examines Maitland's reports and recommendations with regards to forestry reform in Iran and it is to these which we shall now turn. Maitland had come to Iran after years of service with the India Forest Service in the Central Provinces, having served as Chief Conservator there in 1946 to 1947. He was one of several BMEO experts who were casualties of the decolonization process. The lessons learnt in India were ones which revolved around the principle of maintaining order and an effective administration. After his preliminary tour of Iran in 1948, he was immediately struck by the contrast between the two countries: 'To one used to the organization built up . . . in India, it comes as a shock to see how far behind Persia lags and how little she has profited from the lessons to be learnt in that neighbouring country.'[99] The Iranians had established a Forestry Bureau in 1938 but its role had not been defined and it had little or no enforcement power. One of the basic tasks of any forestry organization was to determine the amount of state land which existed and over which one had

jurisdiction. At the time of Maitland's first report, he wrote in regard to
this issue that 'no one really knows. [I]n one place in the north I was told
that for one particular district all they know was that about 3 per cent of
the forests belonged to private owners and that the rest were all in
dispute'. With an acceleration of an 'already rapid process of reversion to
private ownership', the situation was fast deteriorating requiring, in
Maitland's opinion, immediate administrative action. 'There was never a
more urgent case', he wrote, 'for a delimitation commission and a final
settlement.'[100] The feebleness of forestry administration was further
revealed by its inability to enforce existing regulations. Maitland discov-
ered, for example, that only 500 offences at most were reported each year,
leading him to conclude that 'if any other proof were wanted of the complete inadequacy of control, here it is. Even in Syria, with a fraction of this
forest area and incomplete control, there are 20,000 cases a year.' It
seemed evident, therefore, that in Iran, 'the legal machinery to enforce
the law is *not* working'.[101]

This administrative ineffectiveness was attributed to many factors.
Officials of the Forest Bureau had no rural roots and 'know nothing about
the real needs of the forest sector. They spend their time in offices in
Tehran.' Of the 3,000 employees, 1,700 were working in Tehran leaving
less than a half to actually enforce policy in the field.[102] In addition, there
was a lack of a consistent and well-thought-out forest policy. Laws were
passed without thought to their effects in the field. Maitland, for example,
described a recent law making all forest land government-owned land as
ludicrous since 'without definition and delimitation, this will induce
forest owners to get rid of their forests as soon as possible'.[103]

Another major problem, according to Maitland, stemmed from the
placing of the Forest Bureau under the joint jurisdiction of the ministries
of Finance and Agriculture which meant the former since it controlled
the purse-strings. As a result, the Forest Bureau was treated as a revenue
maker only. Forest rangers were paid badly; little transportation or proper
housing was provided for them to facilitate the duties of patrol and
enforcement; and few resources were invested back into the forests.
Maitland estimated that on average over the years preceding his visit, the
Ministry of Finance had earned 20 million *rials* annually from the forests
while re-investing a meagre 4 million *rials*.[104] The role of the bureau was
confined to that of a 'permit issuing organization'. Given the effects that
this approach was having on the condition of the forests as well as that of
the inhabitants and given the perceived disadvantage of maintaining the
status quo, Maitland stressed the necessity of immediate reform.

Maitland made two principle recommendations for reform. He first
recommended the creation of a separate Ministry of Forestry with budg-

etary independence arguing that 'the ... scope of forestry work, the problems which it involves in land ownership, in private rights, and the relationship between the individual and the state are such that only when it is
centrally controlled from the highest level of the executive, able to give
considered, quick and firm decisions, can it effectively be carried on'.[105]
The second set of recommendations concerned the adoption of a forestry
policy based on the principle that community rights to forest resources
would take precedence over individual and commercial rights – 'permanent welfare was more important than temporary welfare'.[106] This meant
in practical terms that the number of charcoal burning kilns would have
to be limited and regulated, illegal felling curtailed and goat grazing
strictly controlled. In short, the emphasis would clearly be on protection
and conservation of resources.[107]

An American forestry expert who later worked with Point Four
described Maitland's approach to forestry as 'repressive', a 'stick without
a carrot' approach.[108] Maitland seemed to recognize this problem when
he wrote that any new forestry organization would have 'to deal with the
most truculent and difficult sections of the population ... Peasants, shep-
herds and tribesmen will not stand for even mildly repressive measures
unless something is done in the way of compensation.'[109] In his confidential note to London, he went so far as to say that 'a forest guard who in the
present conditions attempted to restrict abuses would probably get mur-
dered'[110] and this would have been a justified reaction since their lives
often depended on the resources of the forests. Thus, Maitland emphasized the need to achieve a wider public acceptance and understanding.
Forestry officials must not be seen to be 'unimaginative fanatics who considered vegetation of more importance than human beings.'[111] They must
show something of the 'missionary spirit' in order to tackle what are very
wide human problems. As a combined result of his experiences in India
and his observations of the impoverished conditions of the Caspian
region, Maitland was convinced that this 'missionary spirit' could best be
implemented by combining forestry work with basic health care.[112] After
witnessing the sufferings of a young girl in a village in the Ardebil Valley
near Astara, for example, Maitland wrote that '[i]f, as I imagine, this girl
is suffering from yaws – a disease of poverty and dirt, she could be cured
with a couple of injections. We wiped it out in forest tracts in the Central
Provinces in India by a simple campaign run by the Forest Department in
a few years.'[113]

It was these state-oriented ideas about reform in the forestry sector
along with his experience in working alongside indigenous bureaucracies
gained in India that Maitland brought to his work in Iran. The combination proved to be a successful one in that, until his untimely death in April

of 1950, Maitland's work in the field of forestry appears to have been the highlight of the Seven Year Plan. Certainly, he had a head start on the Americans and he was able to boast the creation of a Forest Department and the adoption of a forestry policy shortly after the Seven Year Plan was passed. Upon his return to Iran in the winter of 1950, Maitland was able to add some additional accomplishments to his name including an increase in the budget of the Forest Department from 1.5 million *rials* to 9 million *rials*, the provision of basic equipment such as maps, and the initiation of negotiations with both the Ministry of Finance and the Shah concerning the transfer of jurisdiction over land held by them to the Forest Department. He also managed to ensure that the Forest Department was properly paid which he described as 'quite an accomplishment'.[114] All in all, Maitland was pleased with his progress, writing to Troutbeck that while 'we are a fairly exasperated team . . . to be only fairly exasperated in this country with this administration is quite an achievement'. He added that the Americans were beginning to take notice of his work as a 'test case' of the possibility of executive action.[115]

One incident stands out as providing insight into the way in which Maitland succeeded in working with and activating the Iranian bureaucracy. In order to give the Forest Department a degree of financial autonomy, Maitland planned to establish a saw mill in the Caspian region and had suggested that the work be carried out by a British firm. However, this needed to be approved by the Plan Organization which had not yet approved any contracts. After delays of several months, Maitland resorted to a direct confrontation with Naficy who was now the Plan Organization's Managing Director. In that interview,

Dr Naficy enquired in a somewhat harassed fashion why the Forestry Organization always demanded instant action. I expressed the opinion that he should consider it fortunate that one section of the Seven Year Plan at least was endeavouring to save the Plan despite the Plan Organization itself. I indicated that he should be in a better position vis a vis the majlis if more heads of sections were to be concerned about their work as to risk his displeasure by pressing him for action. What the Plan had to fear from the newly appointed majlis was not so much a series of questions why certain commitments had been entered into but rather questions regarding the results, if any, which had been achieved by the Plan so far. Dr Naficy then agreed to sign the contract.[116]

This represented the first, if not the only, contract signed by the Plan Organization. Shortly thereafter, Maitland also reached an agreement with the Shah to place royal forest land under the jurisdiction of the Forest Department and succeeded in obtaining the additional agreement of the Iranian Government to hire two British forestry advisers. Therefore, though nothing had actually been accomplished on the ground, Maitland succeeded in establishing in the span of two years an administrative base on which future forestry work could be conducted. This initial success in policy implementation stood in contrast to the lack of progress in the rest of the Seven Year Plan. As Maitland stated: 'after wearying and protracted struggles with the Seven Year Plan purchasing organization which gave an almost perfect demonstration as to the clumsy and inefficient nature of the present set up, we have finally managed to overcome Persian delaying tactics and have revealed to the Americans even more clearly the inadequacy of paper planning in Persia'.[117]

Shortly after writing the above letter, Maitland died suddenly in the forests of northern Iran before he could pursue his work further. Perhaps the only bright spot in this tragedy was that Maitland never saw what became of his efforts. Maitland had tried to promote development in forestry in Iran by focusing on the administrative aspects and preconditions for development work, a premise which assumed a functioning state structure. After Maitland's death, however, that structure gradually became immobilized due to the political struggles which surrounded Razmara's assassination and Mossadegh's subsequent nationalization of the AIOC. All activity relating to the Plan Organization came to an abrupt halt and the contracts of the British timber firm along with that of the two British forestry advisors were terminated.[118] Maitland's work in forestry development in Iran, therefore, lay in ruins. His insistence on working with and improving the existing state structures had been the root cause of his initial success. His hope was that, once established, revamped administrative structures would be able to work independently of political upheavals. This desire to give bureaucratic structures in Iran a life of their own, however, was not given enough time in postwar Iran and it is highly questionable, given the more general political upheavals in the country, that such a strategy could really have met with much success.

This story of the BMEO's involvement in pre-1951 Iran provides the beginning of a more detailed picture of how it operated in its early years. It has highlighted its approach – both more low-key and state-oriented – by comparing its work to that of rival American technicians. This technique will be continued in the subsequent chapters on Iraq and Jordan. However, there is a distinct difference between what has been described here and what follows. In Iran, particularly in the work and reports of Maitland, there permeated a greater sense of optimism in the ability of the state to reform itself and to implement policy quickly and on a broad scale. Part of this was related to his experiences in India. Part of this no doubt was also related to the intense political struggle occurring in Iran at the time which must have lent development work a greater sense of urgency. However, it was also a reflection of Iran's greater bureaucratic sophistication, a legacy of Reza Shah's *étatist* days. This was distinct from both Iraq and Jordan where the bureaucracies were less developed, especially in those fields in which the BMEO specialized such as statistics, forestry, and cooperatives. Thus, while in the latter countries, it was forced to start from scratch, in Iran, with a bureaucracy – however corrupt and inefficient – already in place, there was more immediate emphasis on the actual implementation of policy. The combination of these factors meant that the cautiousness which characterized its later work in Iraq and Jordan was not exhibited in Iran. This case study on Iran, therefore, has been useful mainly as a way of emphasizing the BMEO's style of operation and its state-oriented approach. It is only in the subsequent chapters on Iraq and Jordan, however, that its more cautious views on economic development become more apparent. Indeed, the difficulties experienced in Iran may have been crucial in influencing the evolution of its subsequent approach.

5 The British Middle East Office and the politics of modernization in Iraq, 1945 to 1958

Iraq's modern history has revolved around attempts to integrate a diverse and fragmented country. Before its creation in 1921, Iraq had been a peripheral outpost of the Ottoman Empire consisting of three loosely administered *vilayets* each with its own distinct geographic, ethnic, and religious features. To a great extent, the desert ruled over the sown and the tribe ruled over the state. The integrating potential of the two great rivers of Iraq – the Tigris and Euphrates – that had once formed the basis of great civilizations in the past had been long neglected.

However, in the late nineteenth and early twentieth century, two factors emerged to push what was to become Iraq into the modern world of nation-states. The first was the implementation of the *tanzimat* reform programme designed to transform the loosely knit Ottoman Empire into a more efficient and centralized state. Aided by the penetration of European capital which served to integrate what had previously been a subsistence agricultural economy into the world markets, this had the dual effect of encouraging the settlement of the nomadic population while weakening the tribal fabric of society, all of which enhanced attempts by the Ottoman authorities in the nineteenth century to redress the imbalance of power between state and society.[1]

The second major development was the destruction of the Ottoman Empire and its replacement in Iraq with the British mandate in 1921. Iraq was given all the trappings of a modern state: boundaries, a constitution, a monarchy, a bicameral legislature, an administration staffed with British advisers, and a security apparatus. What it was not given, however, was a strong social base. Instead, the monarchy was awarded to an Hijazi, Prince Faisal who had collaborated with the British during the Arab Revolt, with more general power going to the mostly Sunni élite classes of merchants and tribal shaikhs – all of whom remained ultimately dependent on the British. By turning in particular to the tribal shaikhs for support, British policy had the added effect of reviving a traditional ruling class, giving them far more power than would normally have been their due. The result was the creation of a huge gap between those who ruled and those who were ruled. Much of the history of Iraq up to the revolution of 1958 can be understood as a series of attempts to bridge this gap and to create a truly 'national' state.[2]

Three specific weaknesses of the colonial and postcolonial state in Iraq are relevant to this discussion. To start with, its political legitimacy was coloured by its dependence on Britain. Formal Iraqi independence in 1932 made little real difference as evidenced by the terms of the Anglo-Iraqi Treaty of 1930 that replaced the mandate relationship.[3] This was made perfectly clear when Britain re-occupied the country in May 1941, ousting the pro-Nazi Rashid Ali government and replacing it with one dominated by the 'old gang' led by Nuri al-Said, an old sherifian officer during the days of Faisal's Arab Government in Damascus who subsequently emerged as Britain's arch collaborator in Iraq. In an attempt to re-establish their nationalist credentials, the 'old gang' in 1947 reopened negotiations in order to try and improve upon the terms of the Anglo-Iraqi Treaty. However, they severely underestimated the extent and depth of nationalist sentiment in the country, especially as it coincided with the deteriorating situation in Palestine. When details of the new treaty leaked out in January 1948, Baghdad erupted into some of the worst urban violence seen in the modern Middle East up until that point. Known as the *wathbah*, this widespread violence became a symbol both of the strength of Arab nationalist sentiment and of the ideological bankruptcy of Iraq's ruling élites.

The political system in Iraq failed to compensate for these ideological failings. No attempt was made by the ruling élites to broaden the basis of their power. Rather, politics remained élite-based and factionalized with deputies depending on local rather than national power bases. Given that the electoral system was indirect, subject to rigging, and heavily weighted in favour of rural areas, it became virtually impossible to challenge the establishment politicians. What existed in pre-revolutionary Iraq, therefore, was a classic case of what has been termed 'the politics of notables' of which Nuri al-Said was the master.[4] When placed in the context of a modernizing society in the throws of vast change, however, this system proved unable to adapt. Nuri, for example, was never able to grasp the potential usefulness of forming a political party to contain opposition nor the radio to counter the increasing amount of subversive propaganda which was seeping into Iraq in the 1950s, particularly via Nasser's Voice of the Arabs.[5] Rather than seek to mobilize in order to contain, Nuri merely quelled dissent.

The British had hoped that the monarchy in Iraq might develop some national roots independent of the ruling élites and, accordingly, had given the monarch broad constitutional powers.[6] However, Faisal's untimely death in 1933 followed by that of his son Ghazi in 1939 destroyed the continuity of the institution and left it in the hands of Ghazi's underage son Faisal and the Regent, Abd al-llah, whose cooperation with the British in 1941 severely damaged any popular base he might have had. Abd al-llah made his own attempts to improve his popular image by promoting a programme of political liberalization in late 1945. Rather than facilitate the entry of new social groups into the political process, however, the programme served to unleash a wave of verbal attacks in the press, protests and strikes all of which culminated in the *wathbah* of 1948. The liberalization programme was quickly scuttled and, with a few exceptions, politics returned to its normal pattern of intra-élite factionalism and extra-élite repression, the latter being particularly so during the 'iron fist' rule of Nuri al-Said.

The fundamental problems in Iraq, however, were structural. The political power of the tribal shaikhs and urban notables was rooted in their overwhelming control of Iraq's agricultural land. At the time of the revolution in 1958, 55 per cent of all cultivable land was controlled by 1 per cent of landowners leaving only 3.6 per cent of the land to be divided up between 64 per cent of all landowners.[7] Moreover, these figures omit the growing numbers of landless peasants, victims of the breakdown in tribal order, who were being pushed off the land and pulled into the squalid urban *sarifas* in search of a better life. In short, the socio-economic divisions in Iraqi society were tremendous.[8] Despite the brief foray of the Iraqi military, in alliance with the reformist-minded *al-Ahali* party, into politics in 1936, there were no real attempts to use the state to transform the socio-economic structure of the country as had occurred in Turkey and Iran. Aided by the absence of effective political pressure to change, certainly in comparison to Iran where the voices of discontent were more organized,[9] the élites continued to use the state to consolidate their economic power based on the land rather than on transforming that economic power through a programme of socio-economic and industrial reform. Denied access to the political arena, those interested in structural reform turned to more violent and radical means of transforming the system. As Batatu commented in his monumental work on Iraqi politics: 'In the late forties and fifties outbursts bore a hitherto unfamiliar stamp. The discontent, up until then political, now became social. It was no longer directed in the first place at a particular Cabinet, or at the manner of government, but at the order of society.'[10]

This continued rise in political and social tension in postwar Iraq ultimately forced the élites to take another look at the idea of promoting social and economic development. This was facilitated by the dramatic rise in Iraqi oil revenue from a 1948 total of L2 million to a 1958 total of

L79.9 million which meant that the élites could promote development without having to make any economic or political sacrifices. Having failed to create a social base of support through modified foreign policy stances or political liberalization, they now turned to development as a way of reinjecting some legitimacy into their ideologically bankrupt rule. Symbolized by the *Miri Sirf* Land Development (MSLD) Programme which was designed to settle peasants on newly created land, the goal was to promote a more equitable socio-economic climate gradually without making any sudden alterations to the socio-economic structure of the country. Whether development without structural reform was possible is a question that has been much debated.[11] The answer depends in large part on whether one thinks individuals, policy, and even technology can make a difference in history or whether structure determines all. Certainly, these very same issues were being debated in Iraq in the 1950s and it is in the context both of these debates and of the wider and growing socio-political tensions in Iraq that an examination of Britain's efforts to promote socio-economic reform must be placed.

Britain, Iraq, and socio-economic reform

Britain had always had a strong position in Iraq dating back to the beginning of the mandate in 1921. Formal Iraqi independence in 1932 only saw its perpetuation by more subtle means through political, military, and economic agreements backed up behind the scenes by the ultimate sanction of force, a sanction actually used against the Rashid Ali government in 1941. While the key to this influence was found in the two British air bases at Habbaniyya and Shaiba in Iraq which formed a vital part of Britain's air defence strategy for the Persian Gulf, the strength of this influence was nowhere more marked than in the economic sphere. The Iraqi *dinar* was linked to sterling and its supply was regulated by a currency board in London; major sectors of the economy were controlled by private British business concerns, be it in oil with her 23.5 per cent interest in the Iraqi Petroleum Company (IPC), railroads or banking; and, most importantly with regards to the issue of economic policy, government departments were staffed by a large number of British technicians and administrators. In fact, according to the Anglo-Iraqi Treaty of 1930 whose provisions were set to run until 1957, all experts hired by the Iraqi Government had to receive the prior approval of the British. The Iraqi Government were still able to remove foreign experts and, in fact, there was a decrease in the number of British officials in the Iraqi administration in the 1930s. This, however, did not diminish their overall impact guaranteed by their strategic placement within the bureaucracy.

Moreover, with the advent of the Second World War and the influence of the MESC, their numbers once again shot upwards. Thus, long before Bevin initiated his policy towards the Middle East in 1945, there was an established and dominant policy of British technical assistance in Iraq.[12]

In the past, this considerable influence had been used to protect British interests: order remained the first priority. In the postwar world, this approach no longer seemed adequate. Anti-British sentiment was on the rise, engendered by the British intervention in 1941 and the subsequent imposition of wartime MESC controls. In postwar Iraq, the situation was exacerbated by grain shortages caused by drought and locusts and by the general postwar inflationary trend which left the incomes of workers, *sarifa* dwellers, and civil servants on fixed salaries grossly inadequate. In 1948, for example, the year of the *wathbah*, Batatu calculated that real incomes were less than half of their pre-war value.[13]

What concerned the British in the postwar world was that these sources of discontent were beginning to organize themselves on both the extreme right and the extreme left. The nationalists represented by the *Istiqlal* Party posed a constant ideological threat to the pro-British élites but, in many ways, the more dangerous one came from the Iraqi Communist Party (ICP) which had adopted a more revolutionary platform after the Second World War and had begun to implement a strategy of infiltrating certain key institutions such as schools and major British installations in the country – namely the railroads, the port at Basra and the oil fields at Kirkuk which was referred to by the ICP as 'the mother monopoly of imperialism in Iraq'.[14] By mid-1946, workers in the Kirkuk oil fields, encouraged by infiltrators from the ICP, staged a strike in demand of more wages. The government's response was brutal, killing ten workers in what became known as 'the Kirkuk massacre'. For all the talk of liberalization and the promotion of social justice, it was clear that the British, foreshadowing their approach to the Tudeh-inspired strikes in the oil fields at Khuzistan just a few months later, had encouraged this course of action.[15]

Bevin, however, saw the need to move past mere repression. In separate meetings in London in mid-to-late 1946 with both Abd al-llah and Fadhil al-Jamali, the Iraqi Foreign Minister, he recommended dealing with the opposition by using both the carrot and the stick.[16] While not on 'the front line of the world division' as was Iran, the British and the Iraqi élites clearly perceived Iraq to be threatened by the spread of communism and it was Bevin's constant theme that such threats could best be countered in the long term by the promotion of socio-economic reform. Aware that 'with the old gang in power, this country cannot hope to progress very far', the British talked a great deal about the promotion of more progressive elements to power.[17] Such talk should not be confused, as Louis points out, with the underlying sympathy which the British had for the old gang; they certainly wanted reform but they would not go so far as to alienate their collaborators to get it.[18] What was needed, therefore, was to transform the old gang into 'peasant-minded' pashas. In short, Britain was interested in promoting socio-economic development without structural reform.

How to make practical headway in the matter remained the problem. There was some very early optimism in the Foreign Office when, in May 1945, the Iraqi prime minister of the time, Hamdi al-Pachachi spoke of recruiting a commission headed by a world-class engineer to undertake a long-term economic survey of the country with special emphasis on irrigation and agriculture.[19] Lord Altrincham was clearly excited about this early opportunity to get involved in such an 'unimperialistic activity' and Stonehewer Bird urged haste lest the Iraqis turned to the Americans.[20] By February 1946, the British had recommended Haigh, a former member of the Indian Service of Engineers, whom the Iraqis subsequently hired. However, Haigh's appointment was quickly forgotten in the struggles which followed Abd al-llah's announcement of a liberalization programme. In fact, Abd al-llah's new Prime Minister, Tawfiq al-Suwaidi, confessed to knowing nothing about the appointment.[21] In the mean time, Haigh, instead of heading up a wide economic commission, eventually found himself in the Irrigation Department which was already being administered by another British adviser, Atkinson. Not surprisingly, considerable confusion and tension developed between the two men, all of which Greenhill described as 'unfortunate', particularly the loss of the economic commission.[22]

Nevertheless, Haigh made the best of his situation by setting up what was to become the Irrigation Development Commission staffed by a newly recruited team of engineers and surveyors. By October 1946, he was ready to release an 'Interim Report on Irrigation and Flood Control in Iraq'. Largely forgotten by both the Iraqis and the British, Haigh now made an impact. Bevin was especially encouraged by the report and, in subsequent meetings with the Americans, described Haigh's proposals as being 'the most promising in the Middle East'.[23] This enthusiasm led to an escalation of expectations about what Haigh's proposal would actually be able to achieve. One memo from the MES talked of the Iraqi economy being 'revolutionized'[24] and the Ministry of Food talked of the emergence of Iraq as a 'Middle East Granary'. Haigh's proposals also seemed to offer a solution to the politically sensitive problem of land reform through the introduction of more democratic systems of land tenure.[25] There was even talk of solving Egypt's population problem through the transfer of

Egyptian peasants to Iraq's newly irrigated lands and, later, the idea of settling Palestinian refugees was added.[26]

It was at this point that the BMEO became involved. Copies of Haigh's report were sent to Cairo for comments and by November 1946, a series of reports had been prepared whose tone was practical and served as a brake on the vast theorizing of the Foreign Office and the Iraqi Government who, for political reasons, wanted quick and dramatic results. Crawford, for example, expressed the concern that Haigh's report was principally concerned with flood control and had neglected important productive issues such as what type of crops would be grown, how would newly created state domain be organized, and what provision was being made for drainage.[27] Stewart concurred with Crawford on the need for a wider perspective towards irrigation development and suggested that the Iraqis make provisions for the hiring of soil chemists and agriculturalists as well as for the establishment of agricultural experimental stations.[28] Pridie criticized Haigh's proposals for neglecting the health problems associated with irrigation, namely bilharzia.[29] Finally, the Head of the BMEO, Sir A. Overton, recommended the establishment of a comprehensive Iraqi planning committee with which he hoped the BMEO would be associated.[30] This last proposal was, in effect, a revival of al-Pachachi's original suggestion for a separate and broad planning commission made in 1945.

The question remained, however, as to whether the élites would be able to focus their energies on a more broadly based development programme. Like in Iran, the idea of development planning went back a long way. Between 1927 and 1939, Iraq had no less than eight different development plans.[31] Based on the original Willcocks report of 1911, this had resulted in the construction of several irrigation and flood control projects including the Hindiyya Barrage in 1913, the Abu-Ghraib Canal in 1935, the Deyala Weir and the Kut Barrage in 1939, and the Hawija Irrigation Project in 1940.[32] In postwar Iraq, this was followed by al-Pachachi's call for an economic commission, Abd al-llah's call for economic and political reforms and, when the authoritarian Urshad al-Umari replaced the more liberal al-Suwaydi as prime minister in June 1946, his own call for a 'Ten Year Plan' for political and economic reform. This last appeal, coinciding as it did with his brutal repression of the strike in Kirkuk, had little credibility and, according to British evaluations, was unworkable anyway.[33] The real problem facing those interested in socio-economic reform in Iraq was to convince the élites to broaden the scope of their proposals and inject some political will into their declarations. Bevin, for example, expressed strong concern that 'the immense accretion of cultivable land which the scheme . . . will bring about shall not fall into the hands of a few privileged landlords and pashas but should be made available on a wide democratic basis to the people in general on proper terms of land tenure and security'.[34]

Hopes were raised with the elevation of Salih Jabr to the premiership in March 1947. Jabr was a Shi'ite of humble origins who had worked his way up the establishment ladder. He was relatively young at the age of forty-seven, had a forceful and able character and, as a former member of the *al-Ahali* group, was an advocate of social and economic reform. He seemed to be just the kind of 'progressive' candidate for which the British were looking. To capitalize on the moment, the British immediately organized a series of meetings with Jabr in April 1947 at the British embassy in Baghdad to which Crawford and representatives from Sir Alexander Gibb and Partners were invited. The discussions revolved around the idea of setting up a development board: why it was needed, whether it should be politically autonomous, and who should sit on it. Jabr, declaring that his government would end the hitherto piecemeal approach to development in Iraq, was receptive to the idea of wide economic planning, especially in the agricultural sector which, he said, must 'go parallel with the development of irrigation'. He thus agreed in principle to the establishment of a development board and accepted British offers of assistance from the BMEO and Sir Alexander Gibb and Partners to prepare a report on how the proposed Iraqi Development Board should proceed. All in all, the British left the meetings extremely encouraged with Stonehewer Bird reporting to Bevin that, if the discussions are properly followed up, they should result in 'something like the complete reorganization of the planning of the Iraqi Government'.[35]

Jabr's premiership proved to be an extreme disappointment lasting only ten months and ending in the Portsmouth disaster and the *wathbah*. His Shi'a roots and his more progressive reputation proved to be of little political value and as Batatu stated, 'it [all] meant nothing to the workers without bread, the lawyers without lawsuits, the forgotten clerks, the students clandestinely propagandized and the parties held in leash'.[36] Moreover, his political failures were matched by a surprising degree of repressiveness shown towards the opposition forces.[37] Jabr, therefore, did not turn out to be Britain's new 'progressive' man in Iraq. With British hands already scorched by Portsmouth and with the Palestine crisis looming in the background, the time was not propitious for pushing the idea of a development board and it quickly got lost in the larger political battles. As with treaty revision, Bevin chose to 'stiffen his imperial lip' and wait for a more suitable opportunity.

Paradoxically, the heightened political tensions in Iraq created an opening for the BMEO to get more involved in Iraq's development activities. Before his initial visit to Iraq as head of the BMEO in 1947, Troutbeck had been skeptical as to whether it could be of much use there, particularly given the host of British experts in Iraq at the time. By the end of his visit, he was convinced of their utility if only to act as a source of encouragement to those experts already in place.[38] With the idea of a development board shelved for the moment, the BMEO also offered an alternative mechanism with which to counter the narrow scope of the Irrigation Development Commission. It might provide that catalyst for change from outside the country which seemed to be lacking from within. Accordingly, the visits of BMEO advisers picked up and by the middle of 1948, Troutbeck reported to Bevin that, despite the Iraqi preoccupation with political questions, the BMEO was busy working behind the scenes on a 'personal relation basis'.[39]

One of the most active fields of technical assistance for the BMEO was in statistics. In fact, Murray had already completed a three-month mission to Iraq in 1947 aimed at strengthening the Principal Bureau of Statistics (PBS). His work had culminated in an extensive report recommending a thorough reorganization of statistical services in the government.[40] Released during Jabr's term as Premier, however, it fell victim to the political turmoil of early 1948 and was not passed until the spring of 1949. Efforts to recruit young Iraqis to the proposed PBS were also hampered by the financial crisis of 1948-49 which eventually led to a ban on all government hiring. Faced with enormous problems of procuring even the simplest of equipment, Murray remarked that his function throughout this unsettled time became 'more diplomatic than technical'.[41] Eventually, however, Murray was able to convince the Iraqis to hire a more permanent British statistician, Fenelon, to head up the PBS in 1951. He stayed in Baghdad right up to the revolution of 1958 and succeeded in aiding the transformation of Iraq's statistical services into some of the strongest in the Middle East at this time.[42]

The second major preoccupation of the BMEO in Iraq before the creation of the Iraqi Development Board was to monitor the work of the Irrigation Development Commission directed by Haigh. The bulk of this task fell to Maitland who was worried about the continued neglect of the ecological dangers that large-scale irrigation works posed. Despite Iraq's severe problems of soil erosion and deforestation, Haigh seemed to be completely ignoring the importance of land-use considerations when undertaking vast irrigation works and, in fact, at one point, absolved himself of responsibility to do so.[43] This infuriated Maitland who retorted: 'Haigh should inspect some of the "lunar scenery" . . . in the head water areas of the Tigris. That should convince anyone that correct land use is a combined operation.'[44] In order to come to grips with

complex planning which irrigation development required, Maitland recommended that the Iraqis start with a small pilot project, a recommendation echoed by Stewart and Crawford.[45]

It should be apparent by now that there are major differences between
the context for development planning described in Iran and that which
prevailed in Iraq in the postwar period. The first major difference was that
the British in the days preceding the Iraqi Development Board faced no
competitors in Iraq as they did in Iran. In fact, American policy in Iraq
was for the most part aimed at buttressing Britain's position.[46] The
second major difference, one lamented by Maitland in particular who
seemed to relish his experiences in Persia, was that Iraq lacked a strongman like an Ataturk or even an emerging Shah who could forcefully push
through a broad-based development programme.[47] In the absence of
strong internal leadership, the best that could be hoped for was that
outside pressure on Iraqi politicians would move policy in the right direction. This certainly overestimated the influence which any one technical
adviser could have in a structural context like that of pre-1958 Iraq.
Perhaps it was not so unrealistic, however, as hoping that the agents of
that structure would readily reform themselves. This was implicitly recognized in a remark by Walker of the British Embassy in Baghdad – made in
reaction to some of Maitland's more grandiose hopes – in which he cautioned:

> I think . . . that we shall very soon have to accept the fact that development in Iraq
> is *not* going to be coordinated and . . . that it will continue to be piece-meal. In
> these circumstances, it will be for the Embassy and the BMEO to try and secure
> adequate allotments of funds for the projects such as forestry and land settlement
> which we consider to be of fundamental importance.[48]

Two factors at this point emerged to revive British hopes that the Iraqis
would agree to the creation of a development board. The first was the
expectation of much increased oil revenues; the second was the possibility
of a loan from the IBRD to complete the Wadi Tharthar and Habbaniya
Lake projects, a loan which was made conditional on the establishment of
a development board. By spring of 1949, the Iraqis had responded by circulating a draft development board law to the IBRD and the British for
comments.[49] One year later, a six-man Iraqi Development Board complete with four technical divisions to serve as an administrative backdrop
was officially established culminating a process that had started with al-
Pachachi's call for the creation of an economic commission in 1945. In the
context of both the postwar Middle East and of the Third World in
general, two aspects of the new Iraqi Development Board stand out as
truly remarkable. The first was the decision to allot two seats to foreign

advisers, one British and one American, although this stipulation did not go uncontested and remained a controversial feature of the board until the very end.[50] The second was the decision to place all of Iraq's oil revenues under the board's jurisdiction. Designed to isolate Iraq's emerging wealth from the political process, this decision would in many ways come to symbolize how removed Iraq's ruling élites really were from the realities of Iraqi society in the 1950s. Nevertheless, the British were delighted by the outcome and began to look at Iraq's development programme as the 'model' to be followed in the rest of the Middle East.[51]

The politics of the Iraqi Development Board

The Iraqi Development Board was a pioneering institution in the Middle East and in the emerging Third World. Its programme was particularly interesting because it paid almost exclusive attention to increasing the long-run potential of the agricultural sector. While this was appropriate for a country with two great rivers running down its centre, it flew in the face of what was to become conventional wisdom in the developing world in the 1950s: that industrialization and the pursuit of national self-sufficiency were the best strategies to follow. None the less, in seeking to enhance Iraq's 'comparative advantage', the board's accomplishments were impressive. It oversaw a fourfold increase in Iraqi public expenditure; it administered a programme of capital works improvement which, with the completion of the Wadi Tharthar and Habbaniya Lake projects in 1956 as well as numerous dam projects in the north, eliminated the previously constant and devastating threat of floods and provided the possibility of considerably extending Iraq's agricultural potential; and it laid an impressive foundation of roads and bridges throughout the country, particularly in Baghdad. This was all done despite the numerous internal and regional political upheavals, highlighting perhaps the greatest accomplishment of the board – its continuity of effort and policy. This was facilitated by what seemed to be a unique system of having six full-time members who devoted their entire time to running the board's programme.

However, this efficiency in spending oil revenue failed to solve some of the fundamental development problems facing the country. Despite the completion of several water storage and irrigation projects by the mid-1950s, Michael Ionides, the British member of the Iraqi Development Board from 1955 to 1958, doubted whether the productivity of Iraq's agricultural sector had actually been improved and complained that during the seven years of the board's life, it had not put 'a single drop' of new irrigation water onto the land.[52] Its emphasis had been on building dams and storage basins without any consideration of where to put the water saved. The Government talked about creating new settlements, a goal which also attracted the attention of many foreign advisers who saw in them an opportunity to develop the country through the application of new technology. This was by and large a socially motivated policy, 'à la Warriner' as Ionides called it, whose economic impact he profoundly questioned: 'We shall have storage capacity . . . to supply an extra summer supply of many hundreds of cubic metres per second – four or five hundred or more – say ten Greater Mussayib canals – and no where to put it except the Persian Gulf. It would take half a century or more to absorb all that in new canal systems.'[53]

Apart from their limited economic potential, these schemes were also very hard to implement. A major problem was simply their size and number. An employee of Point Four, which was put in charge of the MSLD programme in 1953, described their magnitude as 'staggering', being equivalent to that achieved by the United States' Bureau of Reclamation during the entire fifty years of its existence.[54] This had the added effect of diverting human and financial resources away from more productive applications, especially the existing irrigation systems which were being ignored. The result was unsettling for Ionides: 'We are neglecting what we possess and making new projects which we can't operate properly. If we carry on like this, the net usage of irrigation water will decrease, for the loss of usage through silting and deterioration of existing systems will never be balanced by the rate of opening of new canals.'[55] While supportive of these projects in principle, Ionides was deeply critical, from an economic point of view, of the priority which they received. This led him to conclude that 'in cold fact, if we *don't* abandon this policy of putting new water only onto new *Miri Sirf* projects, it will take decades before there is any appreciable increase in agricultural production arising out of extra water'.[56]

A further problem with the board's programme was its neglect of the less glamorous but vitally important administrative aspects of development. Part of this stemmed from its extreme autonomy which had the effect of isolating the development programme from the everyday problems of administration, in much the same way that capital works projects had been before the creation of the board. Rather than oversee an integrated approach to the development of the country, the board increasingly acted like a mere construction agency. This, in Ionides' mind, was simply not real development:

A *fellah* will not become a good mixed farmer overnight just because he is given a plot of land on an up-to-date irrigation system; the experience and skill needed for managing and operating intricate industrial processes is not created automatically by the act of installing a factory; legislation and administrative structures for manning, operating and maintaining all these new works cannot be conjured up just by calling in contractors to construct them. As the works are constructed, they present the challenge.[57]

One way to improve the situation would have been to give government departments more responsibility in the running of the development programme. As it stood, however, they found it difficult to pick up the slack, particularly as they had no access to the vast majority of the oil wealth. As happened in Iran during the Seven Year Plan, considerable tension began to develop between the board and the regular administration with the latter accusing the former of building up a parallel organization and leaving them out of the picture.[58]

The situation was made worse by the dictatorial methods of Urshad al-Umari, architect of the Kirkuk massacre and the board's first chairman. There was a revealing meeting in November 1951, for example, between al-Umari and Mooney, Maitland's replacement in the BMEO, who had been appointed Forestry Adviser to the Iraqi Development Board. Mooney, formerly of the Indian Forestry Service where he had gained extensive experience and a renowned reputation, had not been impressed with what he had seen by way of a forestry service in Iraq. Reports by one of his predecessors had revealed similar problems to that which had existed in Iran: no clear demarcation of state ownership of land except for a law codified in 1867 which was described as being 'almost a dead letter'; no separate Forestry Department; only a tiny coterie of officials most of whom worked in Baghdad; and an exclusive emphasis on the revenue making duties of licensing of coal and charcoal burners and controlling the transport of forest products.[59] Given this grossly inadequate administrative capacity, Mooney, therefore, made it his first priority to strengthen the regular forestry service and, as a result, spent most of his time giving administrative rather than technical advice. Mooney wrote:

The stage has not been reached where [technical matters] can be applied. The foundations on which the future Iraqi Forest Service must be built have not yet been fully dug, let alone laid; hence the present needs of the case are elemental, and it would be unwise to confuse the issue and perhaps baffle and discourage the Iraqis by introducing subjects which they did not understand or as of yet appreciate the need for.[60]

Al-Umari, however, was interested in large-scale forestry work and wanted to set up his own parallel forestry organization within the board itself. Mooney felt that this was an 'absurd' suggestion both because of the growing sense of resentment within the regular administration and, more fundamentally, because spectacular, large-scale projects in the field of forestry were simply 'out of the question' in the absence of a full-time regular forestry service.[61] When al-Umari continued to speak 'dogmatically' about complete afforestation projects in the catchments of the Bekme, Dokar, and Darbendi Khan dams within five years, however, Mooney retorted: 'Clearly he does not fully appreciate the magnitude of the task he proposes to undertake or the fact that he has no efficient instrument . . . to carry it out . . . He has not read my report of May 1951 . . . I doubt if he will read it. He is not interested to hear anyone's opinion . . . He is a self-important little cocksparrow . . . completely carried away by his own enthusiasm and by the sound of his own voice.' He ultimately concluded that 'the Pasha *does not want* advice'.[62] In the end, neither man seems to have gotten his way. The board never did become involved with afforestation projects and, while the Forest Division had its status raised to that of a department and oversaw the creation of a forest service in the Arbil region of the north, it never tackled its own administrative problems to the extent that it could begin to implement any significant afforestation programmes.[63]

As typified by the experience in forestry, the administrative aspects of development remained a neglected feature of the Iraqi development programme to the end. Some improvements had been attempted in the early 1950s when a decision was made to release 30 per cent of the oil revenues to the ordinary government budget, revenues which had vastly increased as a result of a new profit-sharing agreement with the IPC. This was followed by the creation of a Ministry of Development in 1953 whose main responsibility was to improve the coordination between the board and the administration as well as to deal with the smaller projects directly related to the board's programme.[64] However, by the mid-1950s, the multiplying effect of the board's programme on the activities of the administration had reached a state of overload and civil service salaries remained appallingly low which made it difficult to attract trained personnel. A case in point was the Irrigation Department which bore the brunt of the board's programme of building of dams, barrages, canals, and drains. Despite its increased workload, Ionides remarked that 'for several years, no new professionally qualified young Iraqis had joined the Department; they found more agreeable and better paid jobs with contractors, consultants, or in business working for the Development Board. What was worse, several of the senior Iraqi engineers had left the Irrigation Department for similar reasons.'[65] Additional finance would have helped but, not only were all attempts to increase the normal revenue of the government through taxation reform resisted; the government was also barred access to the mounting surpluses of the board itself. The result was administrative deterioration which led one member of the BMEO to describe the state of Iraq's civil service in the late 1950s as 'deplorably squalid'.[66]

The main criticism of the board's programme, however, was its neglect of the social aspects of development. Out of a list of projects carried out by the board in its early days, ones which included new houses of parliament, a new royal palace, and a new public library and museum, all were targeted at the urban population and only one – a housing programme for the Tel Mohammad district of Baghdad – was targeted at the poor.[67] Moreover, this list largely ignored the lot of the majority of Iraq's rural population. Their plight was made dependent on the success of the long-range programme of irrigation development and distribution of state land under the MSDL programme). Meeting in the *sarifas* that had begun to surround the outskirts of Baghdad, these two neglected groups began to wonder on what all the new-found oil wealth was being spent. While the economic situation had improved somewhat from the austere days of the *wathbah*, the large-scale expenditure of oil wealth created its own distortions and paradoxes. As Troutbeck reported to Eden in 1953, 'the increase in material wealth and the inflation of the prices of the staple articles of diet and clothing has benefitted the landlord and the merchant . . . [whereas] with a large and unskilled labour force, the labourer's wage has lagged noticeably behind. Therefore, for example, although electricity may be plentiful . . . the majority of the population cannot afford it.'[68]

The dissatisfaction which resulted was inevitably directed at the board. The Iraqi press, for example, pointing to the representation of foreigners and the award of the Wadi Tharthar contract to the British-owned Balfour Beatty and Co and not the Arab-owned Contracting and Trading Company, accused the board of being a tool of the British and their Iraqi clients. Some even went so far as to accuse the board's programme of reinforcing Britain's military position in Iraq through the improvement of transportation and communications.[69] Symptoms of a greater malaise, this tension finally broke out into the *intifada* riots in November of 1952 to which the Iraqi Government responded with characteristic repression. The basic calculation was to suppress all social discontent until the long-run effects of the development programme would begin to have effect.

Some efforts were taken to improve the board's public image. The board started a publicity campaign in 1953 and this was followed by the invitation in early 1954 of Francis Williams to Baghdad, a well-known British publicist, who recommended the creation of an Information Section for the board.[70] The most serious effort to improve the board's standing, however, was the appointment in that same year of Lord Salter, formerly a Governor of the Bank of England, to undertake a reappraisal of the entire development programme; to write a 'report to end all reports' as he put it. A great concern of his was the absence of short term, visible, and socially oriented projects: '[W]hat was needed if the country was to be reconciled with Nuri's dictatorial political methods', reported Salter, 'was a programme of conspicuous and immediate improvement in conditions of life for the working classes.'[71] In his report published in 1955, he made a strong appeal for an extensive urban housing programme and, more generally, argued that the board should pursue 'more limited and quickly attainable goals'.[72]

However, while there was some improvement in the social expenditure of the board in its later years, its fundamental priorities remained the same. Much of this can be directly attributed to the influence of Nuri al-Said who was reappointed prime minister in the summer of 1954 and ruled over Iraq with an 'iron fist' for the next three years. In many ways, Iraq had found its strong man that the British had felt was so important. That Nuri might channel this political power towards restructuring the development programme along less top-heavy and more practical, coordinated lines, however, was quickly ruled out. Nuri was no Ataturk and, as one member of the British Embassy in Baghdad commented: '[His] interest is always so absorbed in *haute politique* and his desire to master the 'tedia' of economic and administrative problems is so spasmodic that I fear there is little hope of him doing anything very serious unless he is strongly pushed.'[73]

It was not that Nuri lacked interest in development. Ionides described him as 'never flagging in his pressure to get on with the job'.[74] He attended every weekly meeting of the board during his time as prime minister and received for his efforts the nickname of Iraq's 'father of development' in some circles.[75] The problem, however, lay with his conception of what 'development' meant, a conception much different than that presented by the likes of Salter and Ionides, let alone the more radical left-wing groups in the country. To Nuri, the development programme was simply part of a wider policy to preserve the immediate stability of the Iraqi state. This strategy depended on physical results which meant completed projects of all kinds, especially the spectacular ones which could be officially opened during the annual 'Development Week', a ribbon-cutting gala first held in the spring of 1956.[76] This 'capital works' approach to development offered Nuri several political advantages. It laid the infrastructural foundations for long-term growth which he hoped would 'trickle down' to the rest of the population; it provided him in the short term with much political capital, though not as much as he hoped; and, finally, it did all this without disrupting the political status quo in

Iraq. Nuri basically used the development programme to buy off political discontent in the most painless way possible through the spending of oil revenues. Rather than being concerned with 'development', Nuri's main preoccupation has been more appropriately described as being with 'distribution'.[77] While it left an infrastructural legacy for the Iraqi economy, its social, economic, and administrative achievements fell far short of the mark.

This discussion of Nuri's approach to Iraqi development reveals the underlying problem from which emanated all the above social, economic, and administrative criticisms of Iraq's development programme; it had to operate within restrictive political parameters. Whether separated or integrated into the government machinery, any policy adopted by the board ultimately depended upon the cooperation of the ruling élites for its implementation. That cooperation, for the most part, was not forthcoming. Examples are numerous. Henry Wiens, for example, Director of TCA-Iraq in the mid-1950s, attributed the lack of success with the MSLD programme to 'political resistance and inertia'.[78] The American team of technicians had clearly not been happy with Iraqi policy in this field, one American technician labelling the MSLD programme as mere land distribution and not true land reform.[79] For political reasons, distribution had been going ahead far too quickly before community support services were being established and was being distributed to those with political influence and not to those in need. One British Embassy official noted, for example, with respect to land settlement in the Greater Mussayib Canal area that 'this is about the most attractive area not already settled and has been for years the subject of intrigue . . . The Mutasarrif of Hilla has told me that he does not think there is a single influential person in Baghdad who is not trying to get hold of it, usually through some bogus client'.[80] However, for the Americans to try openly to make it anything more than land distribution was bound to arouse political suspicion, as this internal TCA-Iraq memorandum made clear:

I believe that any action taken by TCA should be carefully considered and the words 'Land Reform' should not be used too freely in official Iraqi circles as they naturally resent foreign interference in a typically internal problem. Adverse publicity about the TCA meddling in "Land Reform" in Iraq could jeopardize American participation in the MSLD Program.[81]

Attempts to push development policy along the economic lines desired by Ionides – by concentrating on the enhancement of existing rather than on new lands – faced even greater political constraints. Ionides' proposal was straightforward enough calling for the release of the stored water in the summer time when land usually lay fallow. The problem was that, according to Ionides' plan, the landowners would be required to foot the bill, highly unlikely given the postwar politics of Iraq.[82] Attempts had already been made by the more socially conscious government of al-Jamali in 1954 to replace the regressive *istihlak* or consumption tax with a land tax. The bill, however, met with very active protesting, a 'storm of indignation' as Troutbeck put it, from the landed shaikhs. This opposition was spearheaded by Nuri who consistently refused to consider any policy which might break up their authority.[83] As a forerunner of things to come, this did not bode well for any future attempts to include the landowners in any schemes of social and economic reform, particularly along the lines suggested above by Ionides. As Troutbeck remarked in early 1954: 'If these proposals . . . [which] were relatively unimportant . . . encountered such firm opposition, prospects were not good for the Government's plans to exact payment from the Shaikhs for the benefit that would accrue to their land as a result of new irrigation schemes.[84]

This political situation made it very difficult for British diplomats and technicians in Iraq to pressure for reform. Eddington Miller, as secretary-general and later as financial adviser to the board until 1955, made no attempt to influence board priorities and concentrated entirely on ensuring its administrative efficiency. This earned him the criticism of many who felt he blindly backed every decision of the 'erratic' Urshad al-Umari and failed to do his part in encouraging the board to produce a clear and integrated economic plan instead of a list of projects.[85] On the wider political level, Troutbeck tried to fill this gap by making a concerted effort to promote wider social and economic reforms. His proposals were by no means radical and he shared the landed élites' aversion towards structural reform. However, he pushed hard for such economic reforms as the land tax and used what influence he had in Baghdad to facilitate the coming to power of more progressive-minded politicians with similar ideas. With the accession to power of Nuri in May of 1954, however, who tolerated no concessions in this area, Troutbeck's 'campaign' was defeated and, soon after, he was removed from Baghdad.[86]

The next effort to redirect Iraq's development programme was led by Lord Salter and followed up by Ionides. Salter's report had much to say on a wide range of issues but the real challenge would be implementing these ideas. There was concern, for example, that if he simply presented the report to the Iraqi Government and, then, left the country, it would most likely suffer the fate of most other foreign reports and be pigeon-holed. His first strategy, therefore, was to delay its presentation in order to give him time to encourage the adoption of his ideas.[87] This seemed to have an initial payoff in so far as some of his ideas on social reform such as a beefed up housing programme were subsequently incorporated into the

Six Year Development Plan passed by the Iraqi Parliament in 1955.[88] Nonetheless, more fundamental changes recommended by Salter such as a greater emphasis on improving existing cultivable lands were left unadopted by the government.

Ionides picked up the mantle of Salter's report and continued to push it from inside the Development Board. Nuri's policy of tightly controlling the press and squashing any type of political dissent, however, made it difficult for Ionides to directly confront the development priorities of the government without destroying what influence he had. To get around this problem, Ionides established contact with Elizabeth Monroe of *The Economist* and used her as a spokesperson for his ideas. What resulted was the publication of the article, 'Development in Iraq',[89] which prompted Ionides to remark that 'it is remarkable how *The Economist* fills the gap caused by the lack of corresponding media here'.[90] Ionides' 'big push' came after Nuri's government was replaced by that of the more progressive-minded al-Jawdat in mid-1957. With the relaxation of press censorship laws, Ionides published an article entitled 'Summer Water' in the *Iraqi Times* in which he promoted his ideas about agricultural development and the use of stored water, an action which he described as being a 'landmark' in the political context of late 1950s Iraq.[91] He encouraged Monroe to pick up on this particular theme in order to add to the momentum of the moment, though he warned her not to give the impression that there was a 'plot between us'.[92] With his position on the board up for renewal in mid-1958, Ionides had decided to go all out in plugging the theme of summer water, a 'make-or-break' strategy as he labelled it, using the renewal of his contract as an indication of the success of his campaign: 'If, with the policy before the Board in my name, I get a renewal of contract, then in my last two years here, with Wilson and Vernon and the Irrigation Dept. with me, I think I can transform the picture. If it doesn't come off, then it will be better for me to leave anyway.'[93]

The 'going public' of Ionides' ideas coincided with al-Jawdat's announcement of a rural development programme which was a concerted effort to break the political deadlock over the issue of development policy. However, even as Ionides was embarking on his campaign, it was obvious that it would not 'come off'. Al-Jawdat's government resigned in late 1957, eventually to be replaced by Nuri al-Said. The rural development initiative was abandoned and, not surprisingly, Ionides' contract with the Development Board was not renewed. The political deadlock in Iraq continued, only to be broken by the revolution in July of 1958 which brutally swept away the power of the old regime.

The BMEO, Point Four, and land settlement programmes

One of the great hopes of the old regime before its demise in 1958 had been the *Miri Sirf* Land Development (MSLD) Programme. As Louis wrote, the idea of creating new lands in order to circumvent the need for structural reform became the 'the shibboleth of the Nuri regime' and 'the supreme test of the development program'.[94] Yet, early experiences with the MSLD programme – particularly at Dujaila in the southern Kut province – had proved extremely disappointing. A cooperative set up for the provision of mechanized equipment to the new settlers had been legally foreclosed by the Agricultural Bank for its failure to pay back a loan. This not only affected farmers at the Dujaila settlement but, as one expert from Point Four stated, 'heralded right across the country' and made it extremely difficult for settlers anywhere to procure the needed credit. At the Hawija project, for example, it was reported that farmers were being forced to sell their livestock to survive.[95] The success of the MSLD programme, however, with its promise of transforming Iraq's socio-economic structure gradually without disrupting the country's political and collaborative equation was of vital importance to western political interests. Moreover, seeing in the schemes the chance to apply the magic of modern technology, foreign technical assistance felt it had something to offer and, thus, sought to become actively involved in the programme.

However, the record of western involvement in the MSLD programme was little better than that of the Iraqis and, in trying to come to grips with the reasons for this failure, it is worth concentrating on the ideas of Michael Ionides who, as we have already seen, was the British member on the Iraqi Development Board. Ionides was a water engineer by training who had accumulated extensive experience in the Middle East first in Iraq in the 1920s and later, in Transjordan in the late 1930s where he assumed the position of Director of Development. In an article published one month after the revolution in Iraq, Ionides made some sweeping criticisms, not of the internal or structural problems which impeded development in the Third World which one might have expected, but of the whole manner in which the problems of development were being approached by the West. Mirroring earlier points made by Maitland concerning the approach of OCI in Iran, these criticisms revolved around questions of both substance and style and were directed, primarily, at Point Four's work with the MSLD programme.

Ionides considered the western approach to economic and technical aid to have been too political, too theoretical, and too laden with assumptions about the West's superiority. It seemed to have been founded on the basic principle of 'conceive things as you think they ought to be and plan as if they were' rather than on the more down-to-earth approach of 'see and study things as they are and then find practical ways to make them better'. In Iraq, for example, foreign technicians seemed to make plans under the automatic assumption that Iraq had an administrative capacity. Thus, programmes were technically based, founded on the belief that 'Western arts and science were going to the help of countries who were too backward to help themselves . . . [T]he more spectacular the works, the more clearly the purpose . . . could be demonstrated.'[96] The end result was a greater strain on Iraq's nascent administrative capacity than was necessary. Ionides, for example, was very critical of Point Four's technical work on the MSLD programme which he felt had been 'planned and designed as if the farmers, supervisors and engineers were up to Californian standards and thick enough on the ground – which they aren't. [It] has no flexibility . . . [and] presupposes a body of people to run it and people it with a skill and experience we just don't possess.'[97] While there were certainly Iraqi technicians capable of handling the complexities of these plans, the essential point with regards development was that these 'higher standards at the top must rest on a pyramid of higher standards all the way down the scale, technically, and administratively, down to the farmer or the *fellah*, the artisan or the workman. To push in higher technical standards at the top at too high pressure tends to jam the works and defeat the object.'[98] Similar to the ideas expressed by Mooney and to the more general approach of the BMEO in general, what Ionides would have preferred to have seen was a more practical, less theoretical, and less spectacular emphasis on smaller works:

Let us first devise an administrative structure, operating on the basis of devolution of initiative and responsibility, with which we can do the very simplest and most easily defined of practical things in the villages . . . When you've worked that out, then it will be time enough to start talking about . . . vague but excellent abstractions like raising the standard of agriculture, health, inculcating a sense of civic duty . . . and the like.[99]

Point Four's organizational structure also became the focus of much criticism. The programme was very centralized, high profile, and based on a lot of publicity and a large number of technicians, most of whom were based in Baghdad. It was also very formal in its approach and required agreements at every step of the way before work could proceed. Crocker, the ambassador in Baghdad in the early 1950s warned Washington of the dangers of its high-profile approach arguing that while there was a 'sound basis for real service' in Iraq and 'a great opportunity to show Point IV operating at its best', 'it must be a low pressure program here with our works speaking rather than our words . . . It must not (repeat not) be a big splash.'[100]

Nonetheless the Americans were clearly excited about what they termed the 'gargantuan' prospects of this programme and looked upon it as their number one technical assistance priority in Iraq. They wanted to send a team of technical assistants who would be involved in *all* stages of planning. However, Point Four's guidelines stipulated that this be formally agreed to by the Iraqi Government before any work could start. Negotiations soon started on the MSLD Project Agreement but after over one year of effort, little was accomplished. Progress was in part delayed by successive changes in governments. The most serious delays, however, were caused by the reticence of Iraqi politicians to publicly accept such extensive foreign assistance in this politically sensitive area of reform, a reticence shown by the repeated attempts of the Iraqi Minister of Agriculture, al-Chalabi, to question the need for an agreement at all: 'Why should not the Iraqi Government just ask for the specialists involved?'[101] Similar sentiments were expressed by Haidari, the Director-General of Agriculture, when he explained that any formal agreement between his ministry and Point Four would be 'seized upon immediately' by the local press and result in accusations against both the government and the ministry itself that they were 'selling their birthrights' to the Americans.[102]

This lack of an agreement began to have practical consequences on the ground. With or without the participation of the Americans, the land distribution began to accelerate at alarming rates in the early 1950s and, as Haidari explained, was becoming the government's 'chief propaganda tool'.[103] In July of 1952, for example, the Iraqi Government distributed over 2,000 plots, more than had been distributed in total up to that point. Yet, it was being done without setting up any of the proper facilities. At Sinjar where 1,500 plots were distributed, little more had been done than to mark the plots on the ground by plowed furrows. No project facilities had been constructed, no wells had been dug and there was no sign that water exploration had even begun. Similar stories were being heard from the projects at Latifiya, Shahrazoor, Hawija, and Dujaila.[104] Given the obvious inability of Iraqi Government machinery – the MSLD Committee in the Ministry of Agriculture headed by Mohammad Hassan Ali – to deal with these issues, it was felt essential that Point Four's Land Settlement Team directed by J.D. Hancock be put to work immediately. It was also a question of reputation since Iraqis associated Point Four with these projects, whether a programme agreement was signed or not.[105]

The wrangling over Point Four's involvement in the MSLD programme, however, went on for another year, in part, delayed by the outbreak of the *intifada* which had resulted in various demonstrations against Point IV's 'new imperialism by cowboys'.[106] When agreement was eventually reached on a 'recast' MSLD programme in April 1953, it was done only after a severe reduction of the scope of the proposed Point Four Land Settlement Team. Hancock felt this was disastrous for the MSLD programme and became further concerned by Iraqi talk of revising MSLD legislation. When he approached the Minister of Agriculture about it, however, he was flatly told to stick to 'technical matters'.[107] Rather than blame the Iraqis for the situation, however, Hancock was more critical of the Point Four programme itself. In March 1953, for example, Hancock threatened to resign complaining about 'the entire confused travesty of programming' required by Washington.[108] By June of that year, he had followed through on that threat. In a later interview with Belgrave of the British Embassy in Baghdad, he outlined his reasons for resigning in more detail:

The fundamental mistake of the Point IV idea was that it was controlled and planned by people in Washington who, although sincere in their motives, had no practical knowledge of the varying problems of foreign countries, and who thought that, because a particular kind of programme was 'fundamentally right', it could automatically be applied to all underdeveloped areas. This attitude, combined with the constitutional necessity for drawing up programmes some 18 months in advance in order to obtain money from Congress, led the Point IV authorities in Washington to draw up programmes of action which, when it came to the point, were quite impractical and were frequently also unacceptable to the local authorities.[109]

Hancock's views are interesting because they have direct bearing on our discussion of the BMEO's Development Division. He was impressed by the procedural style of British technical assistance and felt that it directly and favourably contrasted with that which had been set up by the Americans. He told Belgrave that, while he was moving over to the private firm of consulting engineers, Knappen, Tippetts and Abbott who were also doing work in Iraq, he nonetheless hoped to exercise some influence over the future nature of American technical assistance policy. In doing so, he stated his intention 'to press for more practical assistance on the lines pressed for many years by the British, and in particular for the setting up of an organization similar to our Development Division which would work closely with the latter, and for continued provision of a small number of first class experts to do practical work within Iraqi Departments'.[110]

The BMEO's first involvement with the MSLD programme had been indirect and related to the more specialized issue of cooperatives. As we have seen, the failure of the cooperative at Dujaila had severely impaired the development of a viable cooperative movement in Iraq. Wordsworth, the BMEO's cooperative adviser in the mid-1950s, attributed this failure in part to the weakness of the supporting administration in Baghdad. A

Department of Cooperatives had been set up in the Ministry of Economics but was given little support. Qualified personnel either left or were not offered employment in the first place, leaving the department with a 'bitter discouraged feeling'.[111] Hope that the appointment in 1952 of Haig, a cooperative specialist with the FAO, would bring 'order and progress out of chaos and stagnation' did not pan out. His organization of six paper cooperatives on the Hawija Project had proved to be complete failures and he had personal difficulty in getting his advice across at higher levels of government.[112] Letters to Nuri went unanswered and he was unable to prevent the Minister of Economics from drastically reducing the number of travelling superintendents.[113] All this was particularly unfortunate for the BMEO who had hoped that Haig might prove to be a useful contact for them. As Wordsworth stated with respect to Haig: 'He has a good theoretical knowledge of cooperatives and a fairly long experience in Africa, but he does not get on well with Arabs and is far too pedantic . . . I don't think much will be done while he remains, and it is difficult for me to do anything with him there.'[114]

An equally serious obstacle preventing the initial entry of the BMEO into the field of short-term agricultural credit in Iraq was the intense competition from other foreign technical assistance agencies. Formal American involvement in the MSLD programme along with similar work being done by the Ford Foundation and by Haig made it extremely difficult for Wordsworth to get involved in any aspect of land settlement. Unfortunately for Iraq, none of this advice was having any immediate effect and, in fact, it seemed to provide 'an example of technical assistance making confusion worse . . . all advising the Iraqis to do something different and none telling the other what he is up to. The first need seems to be for someone to knock the foreigners heads together.'[115] The situation was particularly bad given what was perceived as Point Four's protective attitude. They did not coordinate their activities with Haig and concentrated on 'supervised' as opposed to 'cooperative' credit for the MSLD projects. Nor were they forthcoming with information about their activities. Finally, they were not pleased with the appointment of a British agricultural expert, Guest, to the MSLD Committee and reacted suspiciously to rumours about a possible visit by a 'BMEO credit specialist' in 1954.[116] Crawford was 'very worried' about this confused situation particularly with land distribution about to start on the biggest and most important Miri Sirf project at Mussayyib. Without provision for credit, Crawford warned that within two years farmers there would be 'sunk' in debt, creating 'appalling complications' for any future scheme of cooperative and short term credit.[117]

The BMEO's breakthrough came in 1955. At the invitation of Haig, Wordsworth came to Baghdad several times to discuss the issue of cooperatives. This initiative received explicit support from Salter who was impressed with the work of the Development Division in the development of cooperatives in Jordan.[118] With Haig's appointment terminating in April of 1955, Wordsworth hoped to take advantage of the opportunity to get in a new and more effective foreign expert for a year or two to set up the department. 'I shall be wasting my time', wrote Wordsworth, 'if I tried to do much in Iraq until a small cooperative department had been trained and this can only be done by an outsider with experience. We must get such a man there and then support him.'[119] A candidate, Yusef Brair, at that time with UNRWA and formerly of the Palestine Cooperative Department, had been selected by Wordsworth and Haig but his appointment was proving difficult. The government was ambivalent about promoting any kind of 'association' – political or economic – which left the future of the Cooperative Department of the Ministry of Economics uncertain[120] and there was talk of transferring it to another ministry or of abolishing it altogether.[121] By November, however, Wordsworth's influence seemed to have been on the upswing. Brair was indeed appointed as adviser to the Cooperative Department and Wordsworth was asked by the Minister of Economics in October 1955, to write a comprehensive report on the problems of cooperative development in Iraq.

Drawing on his experience elsewhere in the Middle East, Wordsworth's main recommendations were based on the 'statist' assumption that cooperation must first be compulsory and controlled, something which he felt Haig had neglected. This would necessitate changes in the law to allow the Cooperative Department to play a more active part in the development of cooperatives. Crucial in this regard would be a Cooperative Bank which could provide cooperatives with both the finance and supervision. As distinct from the emphasis of both Haig and the Americans, Wordsworth felt that the goal should be eventual but not immediate self-help.[122] With the creation of the Cooperative Bank by the Ministry of Economics in 1956, it seems that Wordsworth's advice was accepted.[123]

However, the BMEO's main concern in Iraq was the MSLD programme over which the more long-term advice of Wordsworth on the development of cooperatives would have little effect. As Wordsworth himself stressed to Iraqi officials, 'the Miri Sirf failure is not simply a failure of cooperatives but of the whole plan of settlement, and I do not think any large scale success can be achieved through cooperatives, supervised credit or any other support programme unless the management of the scheme is completely overhauled'.[124] While the Americans were making significant contributions to the MSLD programme, their 'technical' approach was simply not dealing with the more fundamental development issues. 'The basic problem', as Wordsworth pointed out, '[was] how to build up an administration service for these schemes which will perform efficiently and/or induce the settlers to carry out the agricultural plan laid down.'[125] Consistent with their approach towards cooperative development, what the Development Division, and in particular Wordsworth and Crawford, wanted to see was greater emphasis on the 'compulsion' and 'controlling' of settlers' activities by a management board at the local level who would in turn be supervised and supported by a more effective inter-ministerial committee in Baghdad. Given the *Miri Sirf* Law as it stood, however, 'compulsion' was impossible which meant that the exploitation contract issued to each new settler could be and usually was flouted. Moreover, given the *tapu* clause, any power which a management board might have had was lost after ten years. Wordsworth concluded that 'it would be quite impossible to run a scheme . . . on these terms, and a complete change would be necessary. Many of us have felt that this was true for a long time and I think the failure at Dujaila and Hawija must by now have caused the government to realize that all is not well with the basic policy.'[126]

This type of 'top-down' initiated scheme had been a consistent theme of the BMEO going back to the days of MESC and Keen's report on agricultural development in the region. It was, as Crawford admitted when he suggested this approach towards land settlement to the Iraqis in the early 1950s, 'pure Sudan-Jezira and Agricultural Board stuff. [Eddington] Miller [who had been an expert for the Gezira Scheme in the Sudan] will, of course, spot it at once.'[127] However, to convince the Iraqis to adopt this approach would be a difficult task indeed. The 'Gezira Scheme' conjured up all sorts of notions of colonial exploitation, notions which were reinforced by the outright opposition of the Americans to anything which 'smacked' of its more state-oriented approach.[128] In technical assistance terms, what one saw emerging over MSLD policy in Iraq was a conflict between the state-oriented advice of Wordsworth and the Development Division which was based upon British experience with similar types of schemes in the Middle East versus the more theoretical and political opposition of the Iraqis and the Americans.

With the progressive failure of the MSLD programme, however, Wordsworth's advice began to look more attractive to the Iraqis. Salter had started the ball rolling on a rethink of MSLD policy by recommending the reformation of the MSLD Committee in Baghdad along inter-departmental lines.[129] Already in town advising on cooperatives, Wordsworth used this favourable atmosphere to plug his ideas on land settlement. Interest began to be shown by Mohammad Hassan Ali whom

Crawford stated wanted to run the new Mussayyib project on Gezira lines 'and be done with it'. In fact, he had taken the initiative of sending an assistant of his stationed at Hawija to the Sudan to investigate.[130] A more significant step forward was a request from an Iraqi member of the Development Board, al-Jalali, for Wordsworth's comments on a 'Greater Mussayyib Extension Project' report.[131]

This flurry of activity in Baghdad over the future of MSLD policy generated thought in the Embassy and in London as to where to go next. Crawford wanted the Iraqis to hire, either directly or through the FAO, an expert from the Gezira Scheme to advise on policy for the Mussayyib project.[132] London piped in with an alternative suggestion, no doubt motivated by a desire to gain commercially, of hiring a team of development consultants to actually run it.[133] This, however, was rejected in characteristic style by Ionides: 'The general need is not now for firms of advisers with offices in London or Bombay, but . . . [for] men such as those who used to run our own Empire, who also know and are prepared to teach the people how to apply and administer the technical plant they construct, relating their works to the social conditions of the people.' Rather than turn to outside advisers, Ionides thought the best plan was to keep the Iraqis interested in Wordsworth;[134] his advice was sound, he was good at targeting small groups of 'keen and influential' Iraqis, and his whole emphasis was on having the Iraqis carry out their own projects, something which Ionides saw as particularly important.[135] In the end, London deferred to Ionides' better judgement and adopted a policy of 'masterly inactivity'. With Wordsworth seemingly having the initiative in Iraq with regards to this 'altogether knotty problem' of MSLD policy at this time, it was felt best to let Wordsworth 'imbue the more influential Iraqis with the right ideas . . . so that they may more readily plug them as their own'.[136]

At this point, the record of Wordsworth's involvement in Iraq's MSLD programme was seriously curtailed and this was no doubt due to the Suez Invasion. In fact, Wordsworth was in Iraq during a repeat visit in late 1956 when the Suez invasion was launched and was asked to leave.[137] This was unfortunate since there had been signs that the implementation of policy was improving. A conference of MSLD estate managers was held in Baghdad for the first time in April 1956 in order to discuss budgets for the upcoming year. On the ground improvements were also noticed, particularly at Hawija, where normally intransigent settlers were now showing signs of cooperating with the manager in the implementation of the 'usufruct contract'. There were even signs that interest in the dormant cooperative societies originally set up by Haig was beginning to revive.[138]

Improvements, however, were piecemeal at best. There were no dramatic changes made to Baghdad's basic policy. The real problem, of course, was the absence of political support in Baghdad for the MSLD programme. Changes of the kind recommended by Wordsworth which involved a delegation of power from Baghdad, first, to the MSLD Committee in Baghdad itself and, more importantly, to the managerial units which actually ran the various MSLD estates, required a degree of political commitment which was not there. It had been the theoretical intention of the programme to both provide services and enforce a sort of discipline 'which agriculture by irrigation demands' but that intention was never realized. There were recurrent complaints from the managers of the schemes visited by Wordsworth in 1956 of the lack of support from Baghdad, either from the MSLD Committee itself or from the various ministries: they had no independent budget, logistic support was non-existent, and their reports were never read. They were unanimous in their complaint that they 'badly needed someone in authority to persuade the government departments to give them the services which ought to be available' and, thus, were very supportive of Wordsworth's suggestion for the creation of stronger local committees.[139] That they did not receive such recommended support from the centre was the prime reason for the overall failure of the MSLD programme, a failure which, ultimately, foreign technical assistance could do nothing about. Wrote Wordsworth: 'The MSLD Committee has never been given the staff, money or authority to make a real success of its schemes . . . Mr Hassan Mohammad Ali . . . has [therefore] been obliged to steer a careful and at times tortuous course, avoiding clashes and only putting into effect those parts of the law and the contract which were easy.'[140] Therefore, although Wordsworth, with his low-key style and practical approach, may have in the mid-1950s gained the initiative in the efforts of foreign technical assistants to advise the Iraqi Government on the MSLD programme, his advice was unable to overcome the unsympathetic political atmosphere in Baghdad which surrounded the whole project. Whether his advice was heeded by those responsible for land reform in Iraq after 1958 would be interesting to know. It is of note, however, that the only request made by the post-revolutionary government in Baghdad to the Development Division was for a return visit by Wordsworth in 1960.[141]

The influence of the BMEO in Iraq's development programme in the 1950s was not very great and was overshadowed by the hoards of private British consultants, experts, and contractors already in the country and later by the influx of technicians from the American and the United Nations' technical assistance programmes. Neither did the advisory work it did manage to perform have any direct bearing on the actual improvement of conditions for the poor. However, it is precisely in the BMEO's failure to get their ideas across that one sees the historical significance of its work. There was a clash of approaches to the question of economic development in Iraq, a clash which took on a two-fold dimension. The 'Anglo-American' clash, so to speak, was an implicit one revolving around the former's criticism, as represented by the views of the BMEO advisers like Crawford as well as Ionides, of the latter's excessive and ultimately counter-productive emphasis on technically perfect and over-sophisticated projects. The other clash, shall we call it the 'Anglo-Iraqi' one, was based on the former's efforts to get the latter to think about development less from a political and more from a practical point of view. That the British won neither battle was indicative of the fact that the tide of the times, which placed great hope in large-scale technologically driven development, was running in the opposite direction. Thus, efforts by Wordsworth and Ionides to get the Iraqis to focus more on the administrative problems of development, minimizing them both by a decentralization of effort and the utilization of administrative and technical expertise which already existed, proved futile. So too did the unspectacular, sober and realistic advice of Mooney with regards to the development of Iraqi forests. No doubt, the political and strategic games which Britain continued to play in the region in the 1950s did not help their situation. When it comes down to it, however, it was not only the 'Britishness' of the advice which hindered its success. It was also, if not primarily, the heightened and urgent atmosphere of the postwar world in the Middle East which forced policy makers in Baghdad, as well as in Washington, to devise programmes with their political utility in mind. From that standpoint, the kind of advice offered by the BMEO was simply not attractive and, consequently, one saw a decline in its influence.

6   The British Middle East Office and the politics of modernization in Jordan, 1951 to 1958

Transjordan was the most artificial of the states created in the wake of the First World War. Born out of a temporary agreement between Amir Abdullah and Britain in 1921, it has proved resilient in the face of the various domestic and regional tensions that have threatened its existence. In part, this was due to Abdullah's ability to establish a viable form of patrimonial rule based on a series of alliances with Sharifian, Palestinian, Syrian, and Circassian expatriate élites which gave him some degree of independence from the indigenous social, mainly tribal, forces of the region. Ultimately, however, Transjordan (or Jordan as it became in 1945 after the signing of the Anglo-Jordanian Treaty which established Jordan's independence) owed its existence to the financial, military, and diplomatic support of Britain. As Mary Wilson has written, 'it had no reason to be a state on its own . . . except that it better served Britain's interests to be so'.[1]

This tenuous viability, however, was increasingly threatened in the volatile postwar world of the Middle East. The regional prestige and influence of Britain, Jordan's long-time patron, was beginning its precipitous decline, symbolized most dramatically by its decision to withdraw from Palestine in 1947, though this paradoxically resulted in an increase in the relative importance of Jordan in British strategic thinking. More serious for Jordan, however, was the disastrous outcome of the war in Palestine which resulted, among other things, in the tripling of Jordan's population due to the influx of Palestinian refugees and the incorporation of West Bank Palestinians into the country in 1950. This significantly altered Jordan's political equation by 'superimpos[ing] a society with a comparatively well-developed middle class and a relatively high rate of urbanization on a predominantly rural-nomadic society of Transjordan'.[2] While many of the better-educated and well-off Palestinians emigrated to other Arab capitals in search of a better future than Jordan could offer, Jordan nonetheless found itself with a more politically aware population that would challenge the patrimonial and élite-based politics of the mandate period. All this provided the backdrop for the rise of more radical political movements and parties which began to emerge in Jordan as in the rest of the Middle East in the 1950s, groups such as the Ba'athists, the Communists, and National Socialists. This widening of the field of power in Jordan to include 'commoners as well as kings' was accelerated by the assassination of Abdullah in 1951. This left a vacuum at the very pinnacle of power in Jordan and resulted in what Robert Satloff has described as the country's 'lone period of weak monarchy' in which the young and inexperienced King Hussein tried to strike a balance between the emerging nationalist forces and the old political élites.[3] Only in the spring of 1957 did Hussein, bolstered by a large influx of American aid, defeat the nationalist challenge and reassert political control at the top.

This political fragmentation was compounded by the economic effects of the Palestine war. Jordan's economic viability had always been an open question. The resource base was very limited and revolved around a precarious agricultural sector plagued by periodic drought, pervasive deforestation, and soil erosion. Outside agriculture, there were no modern industries, few mineral resources, and no readily available sources of energy. During the mandate period, the state did play a limited role in improving these conditions. With the help of a few strategically placed British advisers, it embarked on land registration programmes, established seed distribution schemes and experimental farms, and promoted the development of small-scale irrigation facilities. This latter work was aided by the creation of the Department of Development in 1937, headed by none other than Michael Ionides, who carried out an extensive survey of irrigation possibilities using water from the Yarmouk and Jordan rivers.[4] More indirectly, the significantly larger amounts of finance allocated towards the Arab Legion, Jordan's British-commanded military, also seems to have had some positive effect on the socio-economic development of Transjordan by integrating some of the dislocated tribal elements into the socio-economic fabric of the new state and by providing it with some basic infrastructure such as roads.[5]

However, all of this proved inadequate in the face of the challenges posed by the creation of Israel. Established trading patterns were completely disrupted forcing a costly realignment of commercial activity in the direction of either the port of Aqaba to the south or the more circuitous route of Damascus-Beirut to the north. Moreover, this adjustment had to be carried out while looking after an additional population of approximately 800,000, over half of whom were refugees and most of whom were crowded onto the least viable remaining land of Palestine – the West Bank. Some emergency assistance was initially forthcoming from private volunteer agencies. This was later followed by a £1 million loan from Britain in 1949 and relief assistance from the UNRWA estab-

lished in 1950. However, the transfer of resources in and of themselves
was not enough. Jordan also needed to develop an apparatus to administer funds and implement projects. With the exception of a few rudimentary departments staffed by British advisers, these institutional
prerequisites for a more concerted attack on Jordan's socio-economic
problems were entirely lacking. Clearly, if Jordan was going to absorb all
of the changes brought on by the Palestine war in 1948, it was going to
have to formulate a more concerted programme of socio-economic modernization.

Britain and the politics of the Jordan Development Board

The élite politicians in Jordan looked to Britain to shoulder the main
responsibility for modernizing the Jordanian economy; after all, it had
been Britain's neglect of Transjordan during the mandate period that had
left the country totally unprepared to deal with the effects of the Arab
defeat in Palestine, itself a British responsibility. The British, however,
were more than a little wary of becoming the financiers for an expanded
programme of development in Jordan. When Bevin had devised his
'peasants, not pashas' policy in 1945, he had done so with the more politically significant states of Egypt and Iraq in mind, not tiny Jordan. Initially,
Jordan was not even included on the list of destinations of the peripatetic
advisers of the BMEO. Certainly, postwar events in the Middle East saw a
relative increase in the strategic importance of Jordan for Britain.
Moreover, as Elizabeth Monroe has written, if any state was within the
financial capabilities of Britain, it was Jordan.[6] But, as we have seen when
examining Britain's response to the dramatic depletion in Jordan's sterling balances in 1948–1949, this did not immediately translate into
greater financial commitments, at least in the economic field. Only after a
series of impassioned pleas for more relief and development assistance
from Alec Kirkbride, the British Resident in Amman, did Britain offer a L
1 million loan and it was not until the spring of 1951 that Britain began to
consider financing a more concerted programme of economic and social
development. At that point, the BMEO were instructed to incorporate
Amman into its tours of duties and, shortly thereafter, its advisers began
to descend upon Amman to scout out potential development projects. By
the fall of 1951, they had formulated a series of proposals to be used as the
basis for discussion at the annual Anglo-Jordanian financial talks in
London.

Not all were pleased with the growing role of Britain in the economic
affairs of Jordan. As we shall see, the Americans represented by the US

Point Four programme were wary of British motives in the development field and would play an ambivalent role *vis-à-vis* their British colleagues. Even more significant, however, was the attitude of certain Jordanian politicians and bureaucrats. We are not referring here to 'the king's men' whose commitment to economic progress was lukewarm at best, especially when placed beside the issue of political survival. Rather, the principle challenge to British involvement in the field of development in Jordan came from the nascent but growing nationalist camp. Among its political spokesmen were Khalusi al-Kheiri, a former Ba'athist, and Anwar al-Khatib, both West Bank politicians who held respectively the post of Minister of Economy for much of the 1950s. Its symbolic leader, however, was Hamid al-Farhan who, as permanent undersecretary in the Ministry of Economy from 1951 to 1957, wielded considerable influence in the development field. Farhan was an ardent nationalist and held the British and their Hashemite collaborators in contempt for what he judged to be their economic neglect of Jordan during the mandate period. As we shall see, he wanted to replace their minimalist agenda with a more extensive and state-led programme of modernization. He was also an able administrator, a valuable commodity in a country with limited administrative capacity. Before his transfer to the newly formed Ministry of Economy in 1951, he had spent two years building up the Department of Statistics from scratch into a reasonably effective organization.[7] He would do similar things with the Ministry of Economy. This effectiveness combined with his more radical ideas made Farhan an influential force in Jordanian development politics. In fact, his transfer from the Statistics Department to the non-existent Ministry of Economy in 1951 was a blatant attempt by the political élites to bury his influence;[8] the British and later the Americans would also take their own measures to minimize Farhan's influence. Of obvious importance to this study, Farhan was described by the British in the following manner:

He is undoubtedly one of the most able, intelligent and industrious of Jordanian civil servants; he is personally honest in financial matters, but unscrupulous to the point of dishonesty in professional matters; he is a potent source of political embarrassment to the Jordanian Government as he commands support from the leftist-nationalist students and young professional element and nearly all Ministers dislike and fear him; and he is himself of course very much the Arab nationalist and xenophobe.[9]

It should be apparent by now that the setting for a discussion of the politics of development in Jordan differs substantially from that of other Middle East countries. This was so for two reasons. On the one hand, Jordan's economic dependence automatically gave foreign donors greater leverage in determining the parameters of development activities. This was especially so given the weakness of the political centre in Jordan, characterized by the emergence of uncertainty in the relationship between the young and inexperienced King Hussein and the old political élites of his grandfather. This not only made it impossible for the Jordanians to determine the objectives of their own development programme, it also made it difficult for them to coordinate the activities of the various foreign donors active in the country. On the other hand, this political weakness gave individuals such as Farhan an opportunity to promote their own nationalist agenda more freely than might normally have been the case. The result was a myriad of actors in the development field in Jordan in the 1950s, all of whom competed for hegemony and none of whom achieved it. Before looking at the BMEO's role in the development of Jordan in the 1950s, we first turn to an examination of this fragmented context for development planning. The story revolves around British attempts to centralize all development activities within the Jordan Development Board (JDB).

As we have seen with respect to Iraq, the British were strong advocates of development boards. They provided Britain with local institutions through which its assistance could be channelled and, thus, they helped to reconcile the seemingly intractable differences between nationalism and imperialism. They also provided the country in question with a permanent institution in which development policy could be planned, coordinated, and supervised. In Jordan, however, the British also saw a development board as providing them with a way of safeguarding any investments they might make. This was important to the British for two reasons. First, the British had been very dissatisfied with the inefficient manner in which its initial loan to Jordan in 1949 had been administered. They had initially called for the creation of a development board at that time but, after only one meeting, its activities fell into abeyance. The British then made attempts to supervise its expenditure more directly but there still seems to have been a considerable amount of wastage, especially with regards the capital spent on road building.[10]

Moreover, there was concern to curb what were seen as Jordanian excesses with regards to development planning. When the Jordanian delegation arrived in London in the fall of 1951 to discuss the parameters of the future development programme, they made an initial request for a loan of over L 14 million, most of which was to be channelled towards a series of state-run mining and industrial studies and projects. The proposal had the mark of Farhan on it who had already emerged as a consistent advocate of large-scale state-led planning. His ultimate goal was to exploit Jordan's phosphate reserves to the point that it could become a major supplier of fertilizer on world markets, a goal which would entail the development of phosphate and potash mines, the construction of an oil refinery to provide a steady source of fuel, and the expansion of the transportation network including the port facilities at Aqaba. In short, it was a far-reaching proposal which fell within the main stream of much 'big push' thinking on development that was beginning to prevail in the emerging Third World. In similar fashion, Farhan would later advocate large-scale agricultural projects such as the development of the oasis at Azraq and irrigation development in the Jordan Valley.[11]

The British negotiators, however, rejected these proposals out of hand, describing them as little more than a series of 'shot in the dark' projects, and reduced the offer to L 1.5 million – less than one-tenth of the original loan request and much reduced from even recommendations made by the BMEO.[12] This was to be channelled towards a more gradual invest-ment programme aimed at developing infrastructure and agriculture.[13] The mastermind behind these British counter-proposals was Crawford and, as this statement by Rapp suggests, his views stood in direct contrast to those of Farhan.

He has turned a deaf ear to suggestions of larger and as yet unproven projects. What Crawford will back will be a series of small schemes which . . . can be effi-ciently carried out with the available administrative and technical resources (a serious limiting factor) and which will make a definite if small contribution to the Jordanian economy.[14]

In order both to ensure the faithful execution of these plans and to prevent further 'unrealistic' planning by the Jordanians, the British insisted on making the loan conditional on the creation of a develop-ment board. The proposed board would be made up of nine members, six of whom would be Jordanian with three positions being reserved for a British Secretary-General who would be responsible for all matters of administration, a representative from Point Four, and a representative from UNRWA. It was a similar but much reduced version of the devel-opment board in Iraq. Despite the initial agreement of Tawfiq Abu'l Huda, the Jordanian Prime Minister, at the financial negotiations in the fall of 1951, the Jordanians balked at the condition, largely due to pres-sure from the nationalist politicians like al-Kheiri, and set up their own development committee. It was only after some additional pressure from Britain that the Jordanians finally agreed to establish a develop-ment board, sparking one official in London to remark that 'we have in fact got away with it'.[15] The board was created in May 1952, and Crawford was appointed as its first interim Secretary-General. From the British perspective, he did a admirable job in facilitating the smooth expenditure of the loan, so much so that Jordan was forwarded an additional L 500,000 at the next set of financial talks in London in February 1953.[16]

However, the British were not able to maintain the JDB as the main focus of development planning and implementation in the country. Interestingly enough, the first challenge to its role came from the Americans and, in particular, from Tracy Welling, the first director of Point Four in Jordan. At the first meeting of the JDB, Welling refused to recognize its right to coordinate development activities on the grounds that it was merely an extension of British imperial control. When the JDB subsequently created a sub-committee to study a British proposal for the development of irrigation facilities on the Yarmouk river and appointed Miles Bunger, the Point Four irrigation engineer, to sit on it, Welling vigorously opposed the idea and had the sub-committee struck down. This was in part because the Americans had their own more grandiose ideas about how the Yarmouk should be developed, ones which differed substantially from a more modest 'pilot project' being proposed by the British. It was also, however, a product of Welling's more generally held suspicion, if not paranoia, of British imperial motives in Jordan. Exacerbating these tensions was the appointment of Arthur Edgecombe to replace Crawford as Secretary-General of the JDB. Edgecombe was a former engineer in India who quickly rubbed several Jordanian administrators the wrong way by his tendency to treat them as if they were 'subordinate native officials'.[17] When Joseph Green, the American Ambassador in Jordan, attempted to calm Welling down, suggesting that 'Edgecombe could no more control the operations of Point IV than I could . . . the operations of the Arab Legion', Welling replied that 'the UK now controls the country's currency, export-import trade and Army. This is deeply resented by the Jordanians everywhere . . . Shall the UK further dominate the Jordan economy through the strengthening . . . of the Development Board? Jordan officials privately but vigorously oppose this assumption.'[18] In the end, Welling succeeded in his actions, a success which he described as having 'tripped the UK boys and broke the stranglehold they were getting on running the Point IV program'.[19]

The spring of 1953 saw further challenges to the British-designed development programme. The timing is significant, coinciding as it did with the accession to the throne of the young King Hussein and the appointment of Fawsi al-Mulqi to the premiership. While hardly known to the public, Hussein's crowning was described as having 'electrified the rather staid government of the day' and al-Mulqi's appointment, the first East Banker to hold the office of prime minister, added to that sense of enthusiasm and change. Al-Mulqi was known as a reformer with a particular desire to include the younger generation in the building of a modern Jordan, an interest which no doubt went back to his days as a teacher in the secondary school in Salt where many of the young East Bank technocrats like Farhan were first educated. In the first few months of al-Mulqi's premiership, his more liberal inclinations exemplified by greater freedom for the press and the release of political prisoners provided the window of opportunity for those groups that wished to challenge the prevailing political order in the country. The resultant increase in expressed nationalist fervour by the opposition was epitomized by the growing campaign to eliminate British control of the Arab Legion, exercised both financially and administratively through its British-born head, Glubb Pasha, and the volatile parliamentary debates over the government's decision to accept a British grant-in-aid of L 750,000 to cover a budgetary shortfall.[20]

On the development side, they were reflected by efforts to increase Jordanian control over the JDB. The process began when the JDB passed some small amendments to the British loan agreement in May 1953. This was followed by a decision to transfer responsibility for the most promising British project in the country, the Village Loans Scheme (which will be discussed later), from the JDB to the Jordanian Agricultural Bank, a decision which the British labelled 'a radical departure in principle'.[21] Edgecombe, spurred on by treasury officials in London, tried to get the decision overturned but was greeted with the response that he had no right to interfere with the expenditures of a loan for which the Jordanian Government was responsible.[22] The British Ambassador in Jordan, Geoffrey Furlonge, who in the past had taken a more conciliatory line towards the Jordanians and whose diplomatic abilities were more generally described as 'ineffectual',[23] was now put in the position of having to consider more heavy-handed action. 'We and Edgecombe', wrote Furlonge,

are now in a difficult position in regard to the Development Board as the new Ministers as well as the Undersecretaries who sit on it are more or less nationalistically minded and are highly critical of any attempt on our part to dictate to them . . . Theoretically, they should of course be grateful for all we have done and are doing to help Jordan economically and should, therefore, be willing to accept our advice and guidance on how the loan money should be spent. Unfortunately however, their national pride makes them even more difficult to deal with than if they were not completely dependent on us. We can obviously get our way by using the big stick . . . [but] I have hitherto tried to avoid this . . . [Now] I fear I may have to have a showdown with the Jordan Government on the question of principle as a lesser evil than having our money wasted.[24]

At the same time that British control over the JDB was being challenged, there were also moves to create alternative development institutions. In June of 1953, al-Mulqi suggested setting up a Higher Economic Council to be responsible for all matters of aid coordination, thus bypassing the JDB altogether, although this was offered more as a compromise solution to the differences that had emerged between the British and the Americans.[25] Farhan, meanwhile, had quietly been making his own efforts to establish an independent economic planning unit. Initially, he had not been opposed to letting the British, particularly the more development-minded BMEO, in on the planning process since they were the main suppliers of capital to Jordan. In fact, he had asked the BMEO's statistical adviser, Bob Porter, to prepare a development plan for the country with the hope that it might be used to pressure the British at the annual round of financial negotiations.[26] London, however, already wary of Farhan's agenda, refused to allow Porter to participate on that basis and began to contemplate taking further steps to tighten up on the planning process within the country. Following a decision by the Ministry of Economy to launch the Jordan Industrial Corporation in order to try and attract private capital in a series of joint ventures, for example, Furlonge suggested that the JDB should have more formalized control over such decisions.[27] He claimed that the JDB was performing a planning function anyway, drawing up what he described as 'a sort of Five Year Development Plan' for use at the February financial negotiations.[28] However, when Edgecombe tried to act on that suggestion by claiming jurisdiction over Farhan's proposed planning unit, the Jordanians supported by Welling balked and proposed instead that it be located within the Ministry of Economy.[29]

Farhan, with the help of John Lindberg, an economist from the United Nations Technical Assistance Administration (UNTAA), now attempted to build the economic planning unit into what the British referred to as 'a private empire of their own'.[30] Progress, however, was exceedingly slow. Anwar Nashashibi, a lawyer and not an economist by training, was appointed as the unit's first head testifying to the difficulty in staffing the new administration with appropriately trained personnel. Neither was there any clear idea about what the unit should be doing. During its first six months, it seemed it did nothing at all.[31] Moreover, the existence of the planning unit encountered strong opposition from a variety of sources. The governing élites, for example, were not eager to enhance either Farhan's influence or that of his economic agenda. Much controversy had already been raised, for example, over the cabinet's rejection of the proposal to create an oil refinery with one former official in the Ministry of Economy going so far as to accuse the cabinet of bowing to merchant interests.[32] Their opposition was surpassed by that of the British who were unimpressed with Lindberg. He was described as being 'virulently anti-imperialist' and 'likely to encourage the excesses of Jordanian nationalism with his poisonous talk' and he also held 'grandiose' ideas about development, similar to Farhan's, which were likely to produce nothing better than 'a mass of half baked and impractical schemes'.[33] As a result, they made several attempts, all unsuccessful, to have the planning unit transferred back to the JDB. As a stop-gap measure, Edgecombe was instructed to continue the *de facto* planning activities of the JDB by circulating departments in order to get advance notice of their plans.[34] As much opposition also came from Welling who was described as having fought the thing all along on the theory that it was 'a diabolical device to give the British control of Point IV funds', Furlonge also had several discussions on the matter with Green.[35]

In early 1954, tension over the economic planning unit broke open when the UNTAA informed Farhan that its financial support for the unit would be reduced. Coinciding as it did with American delays over the Yarmouk scheme and increased tension on the frontier with Israel, Farhan interpreted the reduction in UNTAA support as being orchestrated by the West in order to decrease the influence of his economic nationalism. He responded by threatening to expel UNTAA from the country if they could not produce more substantial budgetary support. He played his trump card when he spoke of 'an already worked out plan' to replace UNTAA contributions for the planning unit with those from Arab states and to create an all-Arab technical assistance board.[36] This coincided with a similar campaign being waged by Anwar al-Khatib, the Minister of Economy, and Farhan against foreign assistance in general.[37] In the end, Farhan's suggestion of an all-Arab plan was merely a bluff and he was forced to back down. Nevertheless, after a problematic beginning, the economic planning unit eventually began the kind of work Farhan had intended for it. This was facilitated by additional support from UNRWA and continued support from UNTAA which supplied it with a new economic adviser. One of its first substantial tasks was the collection and evaluation of statistics on small industry in Jordan.[38] From that point, it went on to become a central component of an increasingly dynamic Ministry of Economy.[39]

Up until the mid-1950s, therefore, the British were thwarted in their attempts to establish the JDB as the premier development institution in the country. Its power to plan was opposed by Farhan who wanted the freedom to promote his own development agenda for the country; and its power to coordinate the work of the various foreign agencies was curtailed by the unwillingness of Point Four to even discuss its work at the level of the JDB.[40] Its activities, therefore, remained confined to administering the projects and studies funded by British loan capital. When this function too was threatened, the British momentarily flirted with the idea of placing the British loans under the same degree of control as the Arab Legion although this was eventually rejected on the grounds that it might spark a nationalist backlash.[41] All this was resulting in serious problems of coordination. A report by al-Gritli, the new UNTAA economic adviser and Lindberg's replacement in the Ministry of Economy, criticized the development effort in the country for being too scattered and project-oriented. This criticism was echoed by the survey mission of the World Bank that visited Jordan in 1955.[42] To minimize duplication and fragmentation of effort, it recommended a strengthening of the JDB by appointing a permanent director and by separating its budget from that of the regular administration, as had been the case in Iraq.

The Jordanians were delighted with the recommendations. At the Anglo-Jordanian financial negotiations in London in December 1955, Farhan, arguing that the Jordanians had gained enough experience over the first few years of the development programme to efficiently administer a more powerful JDB, asked for British support in implementing them. To Farhan's surprise, he found the British, on the whole, forthcoming with their support. They had already considered the idea of scrapping the stipulation that the Secretary-General had to be British and had made their own attempts to increase the power of the JDB by convincing al-Kheiri to allow it to sign its own contracts with consultants.[43] Thus, when the World Bank interim report was released, the British found that it contained many of the ideas which they had already been promoting. As Russell Edmunds wrote:

We are all agreed that the Board needed to be reshaped in order to conform with what had always been our views. A sound central body is required which would initiate and coordinate all economic planning in Jordan and would also implement these plans through a balanced programme culminating in the execution of all development projects under the Board's supervision and control. The functions as now framed go a long way to meeting this end.[44]

It is difficult to answer exactly why the British were more willing to delegate authority to a revamped JDB, particularly given that the Jordanian request was made in the midst of the crisis over Jordan's accession to the Baghdad Pact and was followed soon after by Glubb's ouster from the country on 1 March 1956.[45] Certainly, the presence of BMEO advisers on the ground helped to assure British officials of the safety of their investments. This most certainly was joined by a sense that the administrative capacity of the Jordanian government had improved as argued by Farhan in support of the World Bank's recommendations.[46] Finally, there were also signs of a convergence of opinion between the British and Farhan over certain aspects of the development programme brought about by the increased interest of the British in surveying possibilities of mineral development and in enhancing the country's infrastructure by expanding the facilities at Aqaba and building a desert highway to connect it with Amman. As the 1950s progressed, the JDB became almost exclusively concerned with these matters.

The most interesting reaction to the World Bank's proposal to strengthen the JDB was the complete objection of the Americans whose political capital was already at a low ebb as a result of their politicking with the Yarmouk and Jordan Valley plans and the more general rise in nationalist tension. The Americans had built up a very large development presence in Jordan, particularly after the expansion of the Point Four programme in 1954. This made them especially wary of delegating too much authority to the Jordanian government whose institutional capacity let alone political direction they strongly questioned.[47] The proposal to create a permanent JDB director, for example, was interpreted as a means by which Farhan, who 'evidently pictures himself as the logical candidate', could secure a more prominent position from which to push his economic and political platform and, thus, pursue objectives contrary to American interests.[48] Like the British before them, the Americans too tried to isolate and minimize Farhan's influence. Moreover, there was a concern that the Jordanian administration was just not up to the task. 'Centralized planning and direction of development efforts has an attractive ring', wrote Duncan, but 'it assumes a competence in administration and a command of economic theory and practice that does not exist in Jordanian circles.'[49]

When the Nabulsi Government came to power in the fall of 1956, it tried to renegotiate the terms and increase the scope of the Point Four Agreement by bringing it more in line with the recommendations of the World Bank. Workinger, Point Four's new director in Jordan, however, refused to cooperate unless an increase in the JDB's powers was paralleled by a substantial increase in the powers of its foreign members. This was too high a price to pay for a more coordinated development effort. What angered the Jordanian negotiators, although they recognized that they had no real power to finesse such a request, was the complete disinterest of the Americans in maintaining even a facade of a mutual and cooperative relationship. Then a young lawyer, Amin al-Hassan remembers bringing a copy of the Anglo-Jordanian Treaty of 1946 to Workinger as an example of the kind of wording he was looking for in the new Point Four agreement but to no avail.[50] No doubt, the American stance was, in large part, determined by their disinterest in cooperating with Nabulsi. However, the nature of the American development programme, with its high degree of centralized power in Washington, also made it difficult under any political circumstances to delegate much real authority to the field. This, in fact, may provide an important insight into why the British, with their more decentralized system of the regionally based BMEO, were more willing and able to consult with if not delegate power to local authorities and institutions.

The end result was a highly fragmented development effort in Jordan. The JDB, by and large, continued to be solely concerned with the expenditure of the British loan throughout the 1950s. Point Four's operations remained completely separate from the regular Jordanian administration. And, UNRWA which has not been discussed here has been described as having formed its own 'blue state' within Jordan. Farhan and his growing team within the Ministry of Economy made some attempts to impose some rationale on the development effort in the country. But, as the numerous reports and surveys on economic development in Jordan indicate, those efforts were largely unsuccessful.[51] Farhan's influence, while significant, was ultimately inhibited by his own dependence on the élite-controlled state which he was trying to challenge. In short, no actor in the development field was able to impose its own priorities. This left the field open for the testing of a wide variety of approaches. More than anywhere else in the Middle East, Jordan became the scene for an 'advice war'. It is to the BMEO's role in the 'war', highlighting its involvement in the fields of forestry, irrigation development and rural credit, that we turn now.

Debating approaches to forestry development

In the nineteenth century, much of the northwestern areas of Jordan were covered by forests of Mediterranean oak and pine. However, by the middle of the twentieth century, hard hit by the effects of Turkish felling during the construction of the Hijaz Railway and the First World War, forests covered little more than 3 per cent of the country. This was exacerbated by the unrestricted grazing of goats and sheep which tended to kill seedlings before they had a chance to grow. During the mandate period, efforts were made to reverse the situation. Land settlement and demarcation was undertaken in order to determine which land was owned by the state; a forest division was created in the Department of Lands and Surveys; staff were hired and trained at a forestry college in Cyprus, including Yacoub Salti who was appointed as the division's head;[52] and several limited measures were implemented including the creation of village fuel areas, the establishment of several small enclosures to prevent the encroachment of goats, the creation of several nurseries, and the inauguration of Arbour Day on 15 January 1949. The cumulative effect of these measures prompted the BMEO's forest adviser, Chapman, to conclude that 'Jordan may claim the honour of being the most advanced [in] forest development of all the Arab countries'.[53]

The challenges facing Jordan's small forest division after the Palestine War, however, dwarfed these previous accomplishments. 'There is no commoner sight along the roads of Arab Palestine', wrote Mooney, 'than parties of women on droves of donkeys carrying bundles of . . . shrubs . . . picked by their roots . . . to provide fuel for cooking and heating the numerous refugee camps.' Given the intense demand and 'spirit of lawlessness' which prevailed, Mooney was predicting the 'complete obliteration' of forests on the West Bank unless the limited capacity of the new Forestry Department could be upgraded.[54] How best to revitalize forestry on the East and West Banks now became a topic of much debate. Given the lack of financial resources to which Salti had access domestically, it was a debate whose outcome was determined by the Forest Department's foreign patrons. At the beginning of the 1950s, British views, in particular those of Mooney which were backed up by allocations from the development loan, tended to have the upper hand.

As was his approach in Iraq, Mooney advocated a gradual approach to forestry development, characterized by an emphasis on training, the establishment of a legal and administrative framework for forestry work and, finally, the execution of some limited afforestation projects. He was critical of large-scale approaches to forestry and responded to an ambitious twenty-year forestry plan devised by a UN expert in 1951 by describing it as 'out of all proportion' to the size and resources of the country:

I can see all the possibilities open to forestry and forest development in Jordan and nobody could be more keen to see the work pushed on; but I do deprecate excessive speed or too harsh expenditure. This might eventually result in the building up of an unwieldy organization which the country could not subsequently afford to maintain. It could easily lead to superficial and unsatisfactory work which could do nothing but harm to the advancement of forestry. I believe in 'hastening slowly' so as to ensure a steady expansion closely linked with the current financial resources of the state.[55]

However, Mooney's approach to forestry development in Jordan was seriously challenged by that of Point Four. Before examining the disputes which followed, it is first important to understand the nature of Point Four's operations in the country. As in the case of Iraq, Point Four looked upon the introduction of technology as being crucial in sparking the development process in the Third World. To this effect, it concentrated on building laboratories, hospitals and on importing new agricultural technologies such as water spreading that would make 'the desert bloom'.

While the immediate effects were often spectacular, particularly with regards to water spreading in Jordan, the long term sustainability of these projects was more problematic. Projects with a high technological content were often expensive to administer, and required a technical sophistication that simply did not exist. Given their role as financiers of the Jordanian deficit, the British were particularly sensitive to these concerns but had difficulty getting their views across to the more optimistic Americans. As one British official wrote: 'We will continue to plug the thesis that Jordan's absorptive capacity for the newest technical apparatus ... is strictly limited ... I am afraid that in doing so we shall inevitably incur the accusation that we are dragging our feet.'[56]

Point Four's administrative set-up created similar types of burdens for the nascent Jordanian bureaucracy. The basis of their operation was the 'cooperative department' which, in theory suggested a sensitivity to the need to build up Jordanian institutional capacity. In practice, however, Point Four's cooperative departments tended to grow in leaps and bounds, facilitated by the higher salaries they were offering in comparison to their so-called Jordanian partners. This was particularly so after the expansion of Point Four's operations in Jordan in 1954 which saw the number of Jordanians employed in Point Four's elaborate apparatus jump to over 1,500. As Edgecombe observed, this had the effect of 'weakening the departments of the government rather than strengthening them towards self-sufficiency'.[57] In fact, there was some concern that whole sections of the Jordanian bureaucracy such as the Division of Irrigation in the Department of Lands and Surveys were in danger of being 'swallowed up' altogether.[58] Lester Mallory, Green's replacement in Amman, recognized the problem and warned Washington that

[t]he sky is not the limit on technical assistance. There are strict limits to the carrying capacity of the Jordan Government. [We] cannot build up the amount of services they are to furnish the public or the amount of people they carry on the payroll very far without doing them a dis-service rather than a service. Psychologically, they are willing to get along at present far more than is indicated for their own good. It is up to Point IV to exercise some constraint.[59]

If American activity in the field of forestry is any indication, however, it seems that Mallory's concerns went unheeded. Point Four involvement in forestry in Jordan came on the heels of the expansion of its programme in the country in 1954. They immediately proceeded to propose a more grandiose programme than that which had been funded by British loan capital and did so without even consulting Salti whom they presumed was merely a 'British-boy'. Predictably, Mooney was quick to criticize the American actions on the grounds that 'it would be better to build up a responsible Jordanian Forestry Department slowly rather than put in a number of foreign technicians who will carry out the work for a few years and then leave the Jordanians with insufficient experience to carry on effectively'.[60] Joining in on the criticism of Point Four was Salti. In an unusually candid annual report on the activities of the Forestry Department for 1954, Salti complained that despite the 'enormous funds' made available for afforestation and the protection of soil and pastures by Point Four, most of the money was spent on 'huge salaries for a large number of employees' with no benefit accruing to the Forestry Department itself. Of the afforestation and nursery projects started by Point Four, all were 'excessively expensive', most were unsuccessful, and all ignored the more modest projects already being carried out by the Forestry Department. In fact, under the pressure of the agenda set by the Americans, it seemed that much of the Forestry Department's own work had to be abandoned.[61] Moreover, when American assistance was suddenly reduced in 1956 and 1957, the Forestry Department found itself unable to deal with the numerous technical assistance projects which had been left behind and this was a scenario which repeated itself in many other fields of Point Four activity.[62] In 1955, al-Kheiri felt the situation serious enough to write a formal letter of complaint to Nelson, Point Four's Director in Jordan at the time.[63] By July 1956, al-Kheiri was demanding that all administrative and executive functions of Point Four be handed over to Jordanian ministries, a request which of course the Americans refused.[64] The result of all this was an administrative and development mess. As Donald Davidson, a forestry adviser with the BMEO in the 1960s, stated in examining the legacy of the confusion in the field of forestry development: 'I cannot help remarking on the relatively unproductive effect of all the money and expert advice which has been expended in the past. . . One cannot avoid the conclusion that if half the money which has already been made available for technical assistance in land use development had been provided over a much longer period of time . . . more success would have been achieved.'[65]

Debating approaches to irrigation development

The sensitivity of the British to the institutional aspects of the development process is also evident with regards to their views on the promotion of irrigation development in the Jordan Valley. The barriers to the development of irrigation there were perhaps greater than those experienced in Iraq. No finance was available, making Jordan completely dependent on the contributions of outside governments and agencies. Neither was there much in the way of an administration to run such facilities when completed. During a visit to Jordan in 1949, Waterer, the Conservateur of Forests in Cyprus, after expressing his surprise that irrigation development was not more extensive in the country so blessed with many small streams, went on to comment that

an explanation was provided in the Wadi Hasa, where a tiny plot of cereal had been irrigated to produce a good crop. The owner squatted patiently at the edge of his crop. Enquiry elucidated that from the time the crop was sown till it was harvested its owner had to keep guard day and night to save [it] from destruction by the herds. So the everlasting conflict between the cultivator and the herdsman still goes on just as it did thousands of years ago. But, in Jordan, it is still the herdsman who is in control and so valuable water supplies flow idly to waste to the detriment of the community.[66]

The small Irrigation Division in the Department of Lands and Surveys had made some progress towards controlling the seasonal flow of water from the nine *wadis* which flowed down the east *ghor* into the Jordan river. Started in 1945, this work was highlighted by the opening of a small dam on Wadi Arab in 1949.[67] However, this work had only been able to intensify cultivation, not extend it and was certainly not significant enough to contribute towards the resettlement of Palestinian refugees, something which would require irrigation development on a much larger scale.

Perhaps the greatest obstacles to the large-scale development of irrigation in the Jordan Valley were political – namely the sticky question of land and water rights. Other countries in the region had circumvented these problems by targeting peasant resettlement on state-owned land. The distribution of crown land in Iran and Egypt and the *Miri Sirf* Land Development scheme in Iraq are noted examples. In Jordan, however, the amount of state land was limited which made similar resettlement schemes dependent on the expropriation of land from large landowners – something which would be very difficult in a small state to a large extent dependent on those same landowners. In conversations with one Jordanian landowner, for example, Crawford reported warnings of a 'revolution' if the Government tried to expropriate land: 'My impression', wrote Crawford, 'is that his attitude to refugees is "Je m'en fiche".'[68]

The final difficulty surrounding any major scheme of irrigation development in the Jordan Valley centred around the need for an international agreement on the division of riparian claims. Complicated in any case, a solution was rendered virtually impossible by the necessity of convincing the relevant Arab states – Jordan, Syria, and Lebanon – to sit around the same negotiating table with Israel. If any agreement was going to be reached, it certainly would not come quickly. Yet, the plight of the refugees and of the Jordanian economy demanded quick action. As the only hope for any dramatic improvement in the situation lay in the Jordan Valley, the challenge which faced foreign technicians in Jordan was to design a scheme which minimized all of the above constraints, allowing for the speediest expedition of work on the ground.

The British technicians in the field saw the answer to this challenge in what became known as the Yarmouk pilot project. This was an offshoot of a study by Sir Murdock MacDonald and Partners in July 1951 financed by the first British development loan. It recommended a four stage plan culminating in irrigation canals on both the east and west *ghors* fed by a storage.basin in Lake Tiberius.[69]

The first stage called for the construction of a canal on the east *ghor*. It is this first stage onto which the British policy-makers latched. During informal discussions in London in the fall of 1951 between Walpole, Ionides, and Sir Murdock MacDonald, a decision was taken to push for the implementation of a scaled-down version of stage one, aimed at irrigating 25,000 *dunums* through the construction of a pump-fed canal from the Yarmouk River to Wadi Arab. It was this project which was presented to the Jordanian Minister of Finance in October 1951.

There was a threefold logic behind the scaled-down proposal. Financially, such a pilot project was within the means of the Jordan Government and, if successfully completed, would provide a firm basis for raising funds for stage one in its entirety. It would also provide practical experience for politicians, landowners and administrators in solving the questions of resettlement, water, and land rights, experience which, as Ionides stressed, would greatly facilitate the planning of a bigger project and allow the Arabs to use their own labour and supervisory skill, thus minimizing the call on western experts.[70] As there would be no need for a prior international agreement, the pilot project could also be implemented quickly.

However, the head of the Water Resources Cooperative Department of Point Four, Miles Bunger, developed his own plan for exploiting the water resources of the Yarmouk river through the construction of a dam at Maqarin. A technical controversy erupted between the British and the Americans over the perceived advantages of each scheme and, ultimately over control of policy, one which, as has been shown, was reflected over the controversy surrounding the Yarmouk Policy Committee of the Development Board in 1952. The British objected to Bunger's plan on several grounds. In part, they believed that problems of soil salinity would arise in much of the *ghor* land south of Wadi Zerqa. However, they were equally concerned with the cost and technical sophistication of the proposal. It was based on something called a 'unified development concept' which Ionides had been very quick to criticize when it had first appeared in the Jordan Valley section of the Middle East Economic Survey Mission's Report (the Clapp Report) in 1949.

> In this ... country, my candid opinion is that this sort of doctrinaire project is just sheer nonsense. You do not want 'concepts of unification' or any other kind of dogmatic abstraction. You want to start getting water on to the land where it can be done cheapest, so that people can start straight away and grow things to eat, on a subsistence basis. When you have done that, it will be time enough to start lecturing the Ghoranis about 'unified development concepts'.[71]

What the British wanted was a scheme which could be started immediately and would give the Jordanian technicians the kind of experience which they would eventually need if they were to be able to run any bigger schemes. The Bunger plan moved away from this goal and would make Jordan far more dependent on western finance and expert advice while doing nothing in the meantime to ease the plight of the refugees. As Ionides wrote: 'It would provide a lot of employment for ... planners and experts with bigger desks to work at and more committee tables to sit around. If the refugees could eat paper and drink ink, they would be very well off.'[72]

The British, however, failed to regain the initiative. The Americans were more and more convinced of the economic marginality of the pilot project and were being pushed by both Blandford, UNRWA's Director, and Locke, Point Four's regional Ambassador, to support the larger scheme. As it was UNRWA and the Americans who were putting up the money for whatever project was chosen, the British had no choice but to adopt a more cooperative attitude. In the long run, it was hoped that as the political complications that went along with the larger scheme became more apparent to the Americans, one might see them 'swing back' to the idea of a small introductory scheme.[73] However, it took the Americans six years to swing back to the idea of a pilot project on the Yarmouk River. Rather than being scaled down, American plans for irrigation in the Jordan Valley were described as 'increasing steadily in grandeur'.[74] With the support of Green, Bunger had tried hard to stop this upward spiral by getting Washington to commit itself firmly to his own plan. However, it became increasingly apparent that the practical recommendations of men on the spot were being pre-empted by political and technical debates over the issue going on in Washington.[75] Green was infuriated by the 'academic manner' in which the department was treating the issue, 'just as if it were some theoretical problem to be dealt with by committees *ad infinitum*'[76] and Bunger, frustrated by delays and politicking in Washington, threatened to resign several times. Much of the delay in Washington seemed to emanate from the Bureau of Reclamation, a body which Green claimed was 'riddled with Zionist tendencies'.[77]

Bunger tried to circumvent the Department of State's obstructionism by renegotiating the Yarmouk-Jordan Valley project agreement in July 1953 without reference to Washington or the relevant British counterparts in Jordan, thus presenting them, in the words of one American diplomat in the region, with a '*fait accompli*'.[78] However, in light of the withdrawal of State Department funding for the Bunger plan, this attempt at pre-emptive action proved ineffective. This left Green, who was interestingly enough recalled from Amman shortly thereafter, with a strong sense of disappointment: 'I have utterly failed to impress [upon] the Department . . . the necessity of transferring the Yarmouk Project from the realm of academic discussion to the realm of practical politics and practical economics.'[79]

Bunger, however, had really been the architect of his own defeat, having designed a scheme which was bound to activate those who were politically interested in its demise. In these circumstances, a 'marginal' pilot project would have been better than one which, although technically designed to give greater economic results, omitted to take into account political factors which would make a larger project a non-starter. This was as much as admitted by Lynch, a US diplomat in Amman at that time, when he described his government's policy as running up 'a blind alley': 'Economic rationality', he added, 'means nothing in the face of political problems.'[80]

UNRWA attempted to salvage the situation by commissioning the Tennessee Valley Authority (TVA) to undertake a desk study in November 1952. The response was symptomatic of the American tendency to turn to the technician to find solutions which were by their nature more practical and political and prompted criticisms such as this one from the BMEO's Murray that the decision would shed no new light on the problem but was merely a 'shocking waste of money'.[81] Indeed, when released in September 1953, the desk study merely confirmed conclusions reached by Ionides fifteen years earlier: that water from the Yarmouk was Jordan's resource, not to be divided, and that the most immediate work should begin on the construction of a diversion weir – in other words, the pilot project. This brought a very sarcastic and embittered response from Ionides. There had been eight reports on the development possibilities of the Jordan Valley since his of 1938 yet at the end of it all, 'it [was] left to Charles T. Main Inc sitting at a desk six thousand miles away in Boston, Mass., to discover that we were right in 1938'.[82] While noting that his report had been written on a shoestring budget of L 15,000 with six Arab assistants and one British driller, the Americans, he stressed, with all their technicians and money had contributed 'not one jot' to the furtherance of the scheme. This led him to label the American claim to efficiency and productivity as nothing more than a 'popular myth' when placed in the context of the Middle East: 'When it comes to tackling facts and getting results in the Middle East at this sort of thing, the Americans just don't know what productivity and economy and speed mean.'[83]

To get work on the ground started, Furlonge with the support of the BMEO suggested that London assume both the financial and technical responsibility for the Yarmouk scheme.[84] However, such recommendations of British officials in the field were sacrificed for the wider British need to cooperate with the United States on higher political issues. The issue continued to be in American hands who escalated the scope of the scheme even further by latching on to the overall emphasis of the TVA report on regional coordination of water resources. The subsequent story of Johnston's ill-fated negotiations in the Middle East are well known and do not have to be recounted here. What is interesting is the consistency of British technical opinion on the matter which continued to push for a step-by-step, 'piecemeal approach' to the development of the Jordan Valley.[85] The Americans, however, politically concerned about Israeli reactions and technically worried about the difficulty of fitting a smaller scheme into the larger regional one, continued to reject British suggestions.[86]

It was not until late 1955 that serious planning for the construction of an irrigation canal down the east *ghor* of the Jordan river was revived, this being at the initiative of the Jordanians who dropped out of the Johnston Plan negotiations which had been taking place in Cairo. Farhan made the first move, reintroducing the proposal at a meeting of the JDB on 16 November 1955 in order to try and gain British financial support for the project.[87] While no loan finance was immediately forthcoming, the Jordanians persisted by setting up a technical team in the joint Jordan-Syria Yarmouk Committee, recruiting Simanski, at that time with the FAO, as its head.[88] By the middle of 1956, he had prepared three potential pilot schemes.[89] With these in hand, Farhan reopened the question of financial assistance from Britain for the project in a series of talks with Crawford.

Crawford hoped that this revived interest in a pilot project in the Jordan Valley would not be dismissed outright. He reminded London, for example, that 'we have more than once told the Jordanians that they must do something to stake a claim on the Jordan and the Yarmouk water. Trefor Evans, Ionides and myself have always been insistent on this. [Thus], it would be illogical to turn down the pilot scheme out of hand'.[90] Moreover, from the point of view of developing Jordan, Crawford was encouraged by what he considered to be a return to reality. 'It is a pity', he wrote, 'that all of us should have been put out of stride by the visionary Bunger and Johnston plans.'[91] For Crawford, the smaller schemes had always been the way to go in Jordan. Perhaps the best example of that was the inconspicuous work to control the flow of water from the *wadis* which Walpole had initiated in 1945. It had gone ahead regardless such that by the mid-1950s, work had been completed on all but the southernmost Wadi Sha'ib. Assisted by the British sponsored agricultural research farm at Deir Alla, these works had resulted in a tremendous increase in the amount of irrigated land in the Jordan Valley.[92] Crawford, in fact, described them as one of the 'outstanding successes of the Middle East' and added that 'with little money and with next to no Government help, [Walpole and his team of Jordanian irrigation experts] did more for the Jordan Valley than anyone has ever done. The proof is in the large areas under bananas, oranges, wheat, tomatoes, and marrows, and the large number of houses that are seen all along the valley road. In this year of drought, the Jordan Valley must be by far the richest place in Jordan.'[93] He therefore hoped that London would seriously consider financially supporting more small-scale irrigation work, if not a canal on the east *ghor*, then at least the improvement of the *wadi* control schemes through the lining of the irrigation canals.[94]

London, however, reticent to cross the Americans who still had their sights set on the Johnston Plan and under attack from Jordanian nationalists, were in no mood to accept financial responsibility for this still 'politically explosive' project.[95] Therefore, the Jordanians were left to finance and administer the preliminary stages of the project themselves. Interestingly, the JDB attempted unsuccessfully to bring Ionides back at this time as head of all water development in the country, including the Jordan Valley.[96] This coincided with the transfer of, what was now called, the East Ghor Canal Technical Team to the JDB in 1957 and the grant of JD 100,000 from the Nabulsi government.[97] By the end of that year, most of the preliminary studies were completed and actual excavation work on the canal begun.

However, it was not until mid-1957 that the Jordanians received commitments for the kind of financial support needed to fully implement the scheme. This, surprisingly, came from the Americans though only after the fall of the Nabulsi Government. Formal American participation was agreed to with the signing of the East Ghor Canal Project Agreement on 31 May 1958.[98] To Crawford, who had always looked upon the East Ghor Canal Project as a 'British baby',[99] this eventual American acceptance of the pilot project, a full seven years after it had been proposed first by British technicians, engendered a strong sense of satisfaction and provided a degree of vindication for his

Bill Crawford, Head of the British Middle East Office, in front
of the newly opened East Ghor Canal in Jordan, 1958.

long-standing emphasis on the importance of starting with small-scale
development schemes in Jordan.

The BMEO and rural development in Jordan

In all the work which has been described above, be it in Jordan, Iran, or
Iraq, little of it actually resulted in any development *per se* in the sense that
it had a direct and positive effect on the lives of poor people. For the most
part, advisers were concerned with the general and pre-policy questions
such as how to set up schemes and departments. The reason for highlighting this work has been mainly to emphasize the uniqueness of its
approach to economic development in the 1950s, more sensitive as it was
to the institutional preconditions for development success and to the possible negative consequences of aid which neglected those preconditions.
In Jordan, however, there was one field of activity in which the BMEO
had a direct and positive bearing on the lives of its poor – that of rural
credit.

Jordan was a country in extreme need of assistance in the field of rural
credit. About 75 per cent of the indigenous population made their living
on the land. In contrast with most of the other countries in the region, the
majority of land holdings in Jordan were small. In fact, it was estimated
that approximately 82 per cent were valued at less than JD 100.[100] While
this lessened the political problems associated with land concentration, it
presented special ones in relation to rural credit. In seeking both short-

and medium-term credit, smallholders rarely had enough collateral and were often unable to adequately document their title to the land. They were, therefore, a high risk option for commercial and private money lenders, particularly given the unstable natural conditions which prevailed in Jordan. Smallholders were, consequently, faced with extremely high rates of interest, varying according to one report between 20 per cent and 60 per cent in the 1950s.[101] The inevitable result was a rise in the level of rural indebtedness, near to JD 3 million in 1954,[102] and the return of sharecropping on a large scale. Wrote the BMEO's first cooperative adviser, W. Cheesman, '[e]verything points to conditions of lending which will lead to the loss of land by small farmers and an accumulation of large holdings by a few wealthy lenders of money'.[103]

Exacerbating the problem of rural credit in Jordan in the early 1950s was the adoption of a law in 1947 prohibiting the seizure of mortgaged agricultural land.[104] Prompted by a wave of foreclosures which had occurred during that year of drought, the law resulted in a decline in private rural lending. Deprived of their ultimate sanction, lenders channelled their capital into urban areas and debtors, no longer feeling the urgency to honour their commitments, were delinquent in paying back outstanding debts.[105] With 77 per cent of its capital tied up in outstanding loans in 1952, even the state-run Agricultural Bank was suffering at the hands of the moratorium.[106] To break the deadlock, it was obvious that some government-led initiative was necessary in the fields of both short- and medium-term agricultural lending.

That initiative came from the BMEO who were to carve for themselves a dominant position among foreign technical assistants in the field of rural credit in Jordan in the 1950s. The first basis of that success was in cooperative development. Cooperatives were not an entirely new phenomenon for Jordan. There had been a history of cooperatives in the West Bank with their number, at one time, exceeding 240.[107] In 1952, sixty of them had expressed an interest in being revived.[108] With many former employees of the Cooperative Department in the Mandatory Government still around, there was also a legacy of indigenous expertise which could be put to good use. To both revive the dormant cooperatives as well as to set up new ones, Cheesman, during his first visit, worked to establish the legal and administrative framework upon which future cooperative development would depend. In 1952, he drew up a cooperative law which was duly passed by the Council of Ministers and, in the spring of 1953, he returned to organize a Cooperative Department within the Ministry of Reconstruction and Development. This, in fact, was done in consultation with the JDB where a Cooperative Sub-Committee had been set up.[109] Finally, staff were recruited composed of a registrar, an assistant registrar and four field organizers. Emphasizing the importance of recruiting indigenous rather than foreign experts,[110] Cheesman brought in Amin al-Husseini, formerly of the Cooperative Department in Palestine and, at that time, under Wordsworth's direction in the Sudan, as registrar where he stayed until 1967.[111] In addition, four Jordanians were sent to Cyprus for technical training in 1954.[112] Finally, Britain agreed, on the advice of Cheesman, to allocate L 50,000 from British loan capital towards the cooperative movement.

The Jordan Government, however, remained unimpressed with the idea that cooperatives were the best way to tackle problems of short term debt. They refused, for example, to finance the costs of establishing the proposed department and it was only after a plea by Crawford that London agreed to assume the costs herself.[113] Later, they began to consider an alternative idea of liquidating debts by transferring them to the Government.[114] This counter-proposal worried Cheesman. He did not consider such handouts to be 'development' and, when applied in other countries, it had been disastrous.[115] Most seriously, however, it was proposed at a time when the Jordan Government, as part of the loan agreement with London, was supposed to be assuming financial responsibility for the new Cooperative Department itself and seemed to reinforce his concerns about their weak commitment toward it. '[A]t present, I have a feeling that most of them regard the Department as unnecessary. They agreed to it because the Development Board paid. I anticipate difficulty when the next budget has to be met by the Government.'[116] It was only after strong pressure from the department itself with behind the scenes support from Cheesman that the government decided to honour its commitments. While difficulties continued to be experienced at the level of the JDB, the department's position was for the time being more secure. As Rapp stated, the ball was now in the other court. 'It is now for the Jordanians to make the best efforts to operate the machinery which has with considerable care been devised for the betterment of the conditions of the most depressed region of the country.'[117]

Considerable and immediate progress was made. By the end of 1953, Cheesman was able to report that twenty-two new societies had been created, eleven each on the East and West Bank, and twenty-six old ones revived. They had received 1,644 disbursements totalling L 37,054.[118] By 1954, the number of societies had increased to fifty and there was tremendous demand for more.[119] Brair, UNRWA's cooperative advisor who had been temporary registrar in Jordan pending the arrival of al-Husseini, was impressed with these beginnings;[120] so too was the IBRD mission who concluded in their 1957 report that 'the establishment and revival of cooperative societies are viewed by [us] . . . as one of the most significant recent developments towards a constructive solution of the credit problem facing the farming community'.[121]

With the cooperative movement successfully launched, Cheesman's main concern was to strengthen its administrative foundation. This meant limiting the proliferation of cooperatives to a programme based on existing administrative capacity, an approach which the department seems 'wisely' to have adopted.[122] It also meant planning for future expansion through the coordinated use of all foreign assistance which by the mid-1950s also included the Society of Friends and the Ford Foundation.[123] Finally, it meant 'weaning' the cooperative movement away from direct government support. While assistance from the state was necessary in the early stages of development, cooperation in the long run had to be based on the principle of self-help; it had to do 'as much as possible to help itself'.[124] This was all the more important in a state with limited resources like Jordan whose commitment to the support of co-operatives might weaken if faced with increasing demands for credit and field workers.[125] To promote 'self-help', Cheesman recommended 'co-operation among cooperatives' in the form of a union which would take over some of the functions performed by the department's field workers allowing that organization to transform itself into a small and efficient advisory service. The union would be financed from the difference between the 7 per cent rate of interest charged its members and the 3 per cent which each society is allowed to keep.[126] This last recommendation was fulfilled during Cheesman's return to Jordan in 1958, this time as an advisor for the FAO under the Expanded Technical Assistance Program (ETAP). On that visit which lasted for a year, Cheesman supervised the creation of what was called the Jordan Cooperative Credit Union Ltd which centralized under the direction of the cooperatives themselves the service side of the cooperative movement. This was opened by King Hussein on the 7th February 1959.[127]

By the end of the 1950s, therefore, Jordan had managed to establish with financial and technical assistance from Britain and the BMEO a viable cooperative movement. It did not solve the problem of short-term agricultural debt. Money lenders still held a significant if not dominant position in the rural economy. What it did do was diversify the credit options for farmers and, thus, lessen their dependence on crippling sources of finance. The growth of private savings within the cooperative societies themselves, estimated at JD 200,000 in 1959, testified to this fact.[128] With over 246 cooperatives by 1959, 176 being of the credit and thrift variety, Cheesman was able to conclude that these developments represented 'a significant step forward' for Jordan's economy.[129] From the point of view of foreign technical assistance, it stands out as particularly successful since, while help had been received from the outside, for the most part, that 'step' had been taken by the Jordanians themselves.

However, while the promotion of a cooperative movement helped farmers with their seasonal problems of agricultural credit, dramatic increases in the productivity of Jordanian agriculture would depend upon the ability of farmers to make capital improvements to their land. This was particularly important in the West Bank where much of the most productive land had been lost to Israel in the 1948 war. Due to the debt moratorium and the resultant immobilization of agricultural credit, however, farmers had few means to make such improvements. As a result of a direct initiative by the agricultural advisor of the BMEO in the 1950s, Jack Eyre, a scheme was initiated designed to assist those whose livelihoods had been disrupted as a result of the Palestine war.[130] It made available medium-term loans to assist farmers who were interested in making capital improvements in their remaining lands. In contrast to the other development schemes started by the British, this one was administered by the JDB directly and not integrated into the regular Jordanian bureaucracy. In part, this was because of the weakness of the existing machinery, the Agricultural Bank, whose funds were frozen as a result of the debt moratorium. Mainly, it was done in order to allow for maximum supervision of the large amount of capital which would be needed. Loan offices of the JDB were established in Jerusalem and later in Amman when the scheme was extended to the East Bank in 1953 with Jordanian heads being appointed by the board for each, Ibrahim Kaibni in Jerusalem and Farah Abu Jabber in Amman.[131] While the offices themselves were responsible for all matters of administration, it was a sub-committee of the JDB which made all final decisions on allocations.

What became known as the Village Loans Scheme was based on a very grass-roots style with minimal expenditure on administration. Loans under JD 1,000 were not secured on a mortgage as was the case with private lending but depended on a high degree of supervision, this being carried out for the most part by Eyre himself. Payments were made in instalments depending on the progress of the work. Thus, there was a great deal of contact between donors and recipients. This was enhanced by the fact that all cheques were delivered by Kaibni or Abu Jabber in person and at the village level; farmers were not forced to go to either Jerusalem or Amman. It was Eyre's belief that the scheme's success would depend upon this local field and supervisory work.[132] For example, during Abu Jabber's first visit to Kerak for the purpose of distributing cheques to the shaikhs of the al-Majalli tribe, he spoke of meeting initial opposition on the grounds that the money was from the *majlis al-isti'mar*, the imperialism board. As Abu Jabber himself stated, it was certainly well known by 'every peasant in the country' that the loan money came from Britain.[133] However, when they saw that Abu Jabber was its representative, they accepted the money.[134]

With access to cultivators assured, Eyre was able to have more influence over the development of agriculture in the country than might normally have been the case under a more directly administered British scheme. As early as the autumn of 1952, Rapp was reporting that the scheme had caught the public imagination.[135] Within two years of its inception, terracing began to proliferate on the West Bank and there was evidence of increased awareness of the need to combat problems of soil erosion.[136] Two years later, Eyre was able to report that an additional 94,000 *dunums* of land had been brought back into cultivation, leaving little doubt in his mind as to the scheme's beneficial impact on the development of Jordan's economy.[137] By the end of the 1950s, the scheme was being showered with praise. The IBRD report of 1957, for example, concluded that:

this scheme has been an outstanding success . . . It is possible to see villagers literally creating soil out of what appears to the uninformed observer to be barren hillsides . . . As more and more of the hills are being terraced, and as irrigated orchards have been developed on land that was formerly unproductive . . . the aspect of the countryside in some areas of West Jordan . . . has been completely changed.[138]

Even more revealing of the scheme's success were the figures on agricultural production in Jordan for the 1950s. In part due to a series of bad harvests, general agricultural output in the 1950s had been on a trend downwards.[139] There was one exception to this trend, however, in the land serviced by Eyre's scheme. As Porter noted in his evaluation of the effectiveness of foreign aid in Jordan in the 1950s: 'One encouraging feature of an otherwise bleak situation has been the increased production of fruits and vegetables mainly under irrigation . . . [This] can be attributed in large measure to the effects of the United Kingdom loans which went to the "Village Loans Scheme" of the Development Board. This is one of the few cases where the effects of development assistance are clearly visible.'[140]

However, economic nationalists in Jordan did not share similar opinions about the significance of the Village Loans Scheme. In part because its effects were scattered, small-scale and agriculturally oriented, Farhan did not consider it to be 'true development' and made several attempts to gain more direct control over the loan funds.[141] As we have seen, the first attempt was made during the first months of the al-Mulqi administration when the proposal emerged to transfer responsibility for the scheme from the JDB to the Agricultural Bank. The proposal was subsequently dropped in part because the bank, whose funds had been frozen as a result of the debt moratorium imposed in 1947, was ill-equipped to handle the loans scheme administratively. In the midst of the tension and violence which surrounded the question of Jordan's accession to the Baghdad Pact, Farhan revived the proposal hoping to capitalize on the renewed influence of nationalist sentiment. This time, he was backed up by a report on agricultural credit by al-Gritli which criticized the multiplicity of rural lending institutions in the country and recommended their amalgamation under one roof.[142] In response to that report, Farhan convened a series of meetings in the Ministry of Economy to which neither Eyre nor Kaibni were invited.[143]

In addition to the more general political challenge, at stake here were fundamental questions about the process of development. Farhan believed that these funds could be put to more effective economic purpose by pooling and rechannelling them into larger-scale and more capital intensive projects such as the development of the oasis in Azraq or irrigation development in the Jordan Valley.[144] The British were concerned, however, that such project-oriented use of the funds would do nothing to enhance the development of viable credit institutions in the country which they considered to be of greater long-term value. From an administrative point of view no less than from an economic one, the Village Loans Scheme had proved a success combining low delivery costs with a high rate of repayment. In the first year of collection, 1956, it was able to collect 74 per cent of its debts. Because it was based on a revolving credit basis, this meant that the scheme had made an important step towards achieving self-sufficiency and thus sustainability, important in a country with limited financial capacity.[145] Indeed, in commenting on the administrative success of the Village Loans Scheme, Crawford remarked that 'I know of no other development scheme in the Middle East which has achieved so much at so little capital cost'.[146]

Of course, by refusing to hand over responsibility for the loans scheme to the Agricultural Bank, it could be argued, as Farhan no doubt did, that the British were contradicting their stated goal of institution-building in Jordan. Their reply, however, was that Jordan was not ready to administer one central credit institution. 'It is the old story of the desirable and the attainable' wrote Russell Edmunds. 'I quite agree that . . . the amalgamation of all agricultural credit facilities in one single institution is a very desirable thing; but an effective instrument to do the job properly . . . cannot be brought about by the single stroke of the pen. I fear in the Jordan scene, there are too many factors militating against an efficient and properly run single institution.'[147] The British also accused Farhan of deliberately distorting al-Gritli's report for his own purposes, arguing that its main focus had not been on the immediate unification of all sources of credit so much as on the need to reform the Agricultural Bank which was described as being in a 'shocking and useless state'.[148] Thus, buoyed by the administrative and economic success of the scheme, Crawford argued that 'if by any chance Farhan and Kheiri get their way . . . I think we should say we will not play'.[149]

The appointment of Sulayman Nabulsi as prime minister and the outbreak of the Suez War seemed to give Farhan the opportunity he was looking for to capture the capital locked up in the JDB's Village Loans Scheme. As part of a purge of pro-British officials in the country, Ibrahim Kaibni, the Director of the Jerusalem office of the JDB, was dismissed from his position in December 1956, and replaced by the Ba'athist, Ahmad Saba. That, however, was as far as the challenge went. The British threat not to turn over the remainder of the loan capital[150] was enough to force the Nabulsi government to agree to continue the scheme as designed on a revolving credit basis.[151] With the reassertion of political control by King Hussein in April 1957, economic nationalists subsequently lost the initiative. Kaibni was reinstated as the director of the Jerusalem office of the JDB, allowing the loans scheme to continue without much loss of continuity. By the summer of 1957, after a successful second round of collections, Eyre was able to boast that it was well on its way to achieving full self-sufficiency.[152] Three years later, long after Farhan was gone from the Ministry of Economy, the Village Loans Scheme was finally transferred from the JDB and amalgamated along with the old Agricultural Bank into the newly created and centralized Agricultural Credit Corporation (ACC). Interestingly, it was Kaibni who became the ACC's first director.

The BMEO obviously achieved its greatest successes in Jordan. This was facilitated by several factors: the resiliency of British political influence in the country up to the late 1950s, the weakened and fragmented domestic political context which gave foreign donors greater leeway in promoting their own development agendas, and the addition of British development capital to complement its technical assistance activities.

However, the BMEO's success was not only the result of greater political power and influence. It was also the result of a strategy and *modus operandi* which seemed better suited to the Jordanian context than those being promoted by other foreign donors, namely the American Point Four programme. Especially after the expansion of their aid programme in 1954, the Americans seemed intent on funnelling large amounts of funds and technicians into the country as a way of creating the conditions for economic 'take-off'. The end result was the overburdening of the small Jordanian political economy, the weakening of nascent development institutions, and the encouragement of patrimonial forms of bureaucratic rule. The BMEO, on the other hand, seemed more sensitive to the importance of building up effective state institutions. Given Jordan's limited resources, this meant adopting a strategy of more modest proportions – 'hastening slowly' as Mooney described. The BMEO failed to implement this strategy with regards to forestry development but they were more successful in the agricultural sector, especially in the fields of rural credit and, more indirectly, irrigation.

However, the achievements of the Jordanians should not be overlooked. While Farhan and his group of technicians failed to implement their own agenda to its fullest in the 1950s, they nonetheless did lay some of the foundations for future successes in the next decade. A whole generation of technicians gained valuable experience under the dynamic leadership of Farhan in the Ministry of Economy and many of them went on to some of the commanding heights of the Jordanian economy in the 1960s. Moreover, the Ministry of Economy itself was built up from scratch into one of the lead ministries of the state. In that sense, the more strict parameters imposed by the British on Farhan may have allowed (forced) him to concentrate his efforts on a few essentials and make better use of the limited financial and human resources at his disposal. Combined with British efforts at building institutions in the development field, the result was a Jordanian political-economy better able to absorb the more significant infusions of capital assistance which began to flow in the next decade.

Conclusion: 'hastening slowly'

One of the most striking features of the work of the Development Division of the BMEO in the Middle East in the 1940s and 1950s is its awareness of the limitations to promoting growth. This attitude found its roots in the various failures and frustrations of the immediate postwar period, especially in Iran and Iraq. These frustrations continued in Jordan as shown by the struggles to scale down the extent of development policy in the fields of forestry and irrigation. However, the addition of a modest aid budget in Jordan combined with the continuation of a waning but still influential British diplomatic presence in the country gave the BMEO a chance to implement its own counter-approach, based on the premise that sustainable economic progress would best evolve from small-scale, incremental changes. As Crawford stated in a letter to the Foreign Office justifying the rather unspectacular approach of his band of technicians in that country: 'For years, development in the Middle East has been bedeviled by the fetish of long-term planning for large development works. The Village Loans Scheme ... [is] proof that development in the Middle East is generally at its best when it is the sum of a number of smaller projects.'[1]

For the BMEO, small-scale development held out several advantages. It reduced the possibility that British assistance would become the target of political opposition and, therefore, allowed for a more unfettered environment within which to work. It also allowed a country like Jordan with limited capacity, financial and otherwise, to assume greater responsibility for its own development, thus promoting, in a gradual way, self-reliance. Moreover, when targeted at the state, as was the approach of the BMEO, it allowed for the development of more effective state institutions built on 'rational-legal' rather than on 'patrimonial' lines (although one could also argue that the British were equally intent on building their own, albeit more limited, patrimonial channels). Finally, small-scale development works were by their very nature experimental and, therefore, could more easily be adjusted to suit the inherently uncertain context in which most development takes place, certainly a feature of the Middle East in the late 1940s and 1950s.

However, it was not only the BMEO's strategy which proved conducive to locally based development. So too did its procedural approach and it is here that the Development Division perhaps made its most important contribution. Situated as it was in the volatile, if not hostile, political climate of the postwar Middle East and devoid of the kind of resources which would have given it more immediate power and influence, the BMEO was forced to develop a less-imposing way of delivering technical and financial assistance conspicuous for its lack of formality, agreements, conditions, and publicity. This was facilitated by the presence of the BMEO within the region itself, a system of aid delivery which the Department of Technical Cooperation and subsequently the Overseas Development Administration (ODA) chose to duplicate, as well as by the experience and long-standing service of its advisors which earned them a reputation for impartial and quality advice. In fact, so successful did this approach become that, in the late 1950s, some in the Foreign Office began to suggest that the BMEO was becoming too closely associated with some of the local governments of the region.[2]

Having elucidated the approach of the BMEO throughout this text, it might be interesting in conclusion to try and locate it more precisely in the context of current debates about development approach. Where, for example, does the BMEO fit in with respect to the wide array of development critics, or 'neo-populists' as Gavin Kitching has called them,[3] that have arisen since the development business began? We have already drawn parallels between the ideas of Peter Bauer and those of the Development Division, particularly in their dismissal of over-ambitious, large-scale planning and their advocacy of a more modest approach which concentrates on the determinants of development, namely the development of dependable local institutions. But, how far does this critique of the BMEO go and what are the assumptions behind it?

One of the more popular critiques of development planning arose out of Fritz Schumacher's book *Small is Beautiful* (1973) and, on the surface, his ideas bear strong resemblance to those of the Development Division. Like the BMEO, Schumacher takes full aim at the attempt by western aid agencies to impose western concepts of development onto the Third World. This, wrote Schumacher, merely pushed the developing world 'into the adoption of production methods and consumption standards which destroy[ed] the possibilities of self-reliance and self-help. The results [were] unintentional neo-colonialism and helplessness for the poor.'[4] Instead, Schumacher called for an approach based on the use of small-scale, intermediate technology which would be more in tune with local techniques and capacities, much along the lines of Michael Ionides who was himself involved in the subsequent formation by Schumacher of the Intermediate Technology Development Group (ITDG) in London.[5]

However, while both approaches are clearly similar, their underlying assumptions are much different. Schumacher's critique, for example, is much more extensive and global in nature. He took aim at western notions of development based upon the use of western technology not only because they fostered economic and social dualism in Third World countries, characterized by unemployment and mass migration, but also because they failed to recognize the importance of a 'self-limiting' principle. Development should use more modest models not only because it would work better that way; it should also do so – indeed, had to do so – because it would place less pressure on the world's finite supply of resources. In short, Schumacher's agenda was ultimately based on an environmental and moral imperative. That of the BMEO, however, was motivated purely by practicality, not morality. There was no real sense from its work that development and growth *per se* had to be limited; only that attaining fast-paced and balanced growth was difficult and best achieved on a more gradual basis, especially in countries endowed with limited resources and unstable political equations. In that sense, the BMEO must be situated in that category of 'modernizers' who believed that change along western lines was ultimately possible. Like Samuel Huntington,[6] however, they were not the optimistic modernizers that so characterized the early development decades and this is what makes their work so interesting from an historical point of view.

The limited extent of the BMEO's critique is even more apparent if compared to the ideas of Robert Chambers, especially those in his most recent series of essays entitled *Challenging the Professions* (1993). Again, there are some noted similarities in the approach of both, particularly in their appeal for reduced scale and greater simplicity. Chambers, for example, is very critical of 'abstractions' which, he argues, 'leads away from reality, from what is feasible and from the cumulative increments of change which can gradually transform performance'[7] and calls instead for more practical and empirical approaches to development, much in the same way that Ionides did when he criticized large-scale irrigation planning in Iraq and Jordan. Chambers also argues strongly for development programmes which build into their models an assumption that local administrative capacity is weak, again, much along the lines of the Development Division. However, here the similarities end. Chambers's approach calls for a more grass-roots philosophy characterized by broad-based, social participation in the development process whereas that of the BMEO remains firmly 'statist'. As such, while the BMEO may have articulated some progressive ideas in the context of the 1950s, they do not add up to the kind of 'development reversals' being advocated today by Chambers.[8]

The Middle East Development Division no longer exists. It was disbanded in 1981 by the Thatcher Government in part due to fiscal constraints and in part due to the changed conditions of development in the Middle East, now awash with oil revenue. Even before its demise, the kind of approach which it championed in the 1950s became increasingly difficult to maintain in the Middle East of the 1960s and 1970s. For example, the administrative and financial capacities of the region in these later decades were much enhanced though, as Howell insisted in his final despatch, this did not result in a reduction of the direct and more informal technical assistance work of his advisors.[9] Equally significant was London's greater willingness to lend development capital to the region which inevitably resulted in the emergence of more formality, stricter criteria of aid administration, and eventually, moves toward the tying of aid to the procurement of British goods and services. All of this meant that the Development Division began to lose its regional reputation for impartiality and became increasingly associated with British policy in the region. Crawford had predicted so much in his own final despatch to the Foreign Office in 1960.[10]

However, when placed back in context of the 1950s, the BMEO, while perhaps not radical for its time, certainly comes out looking enlightened in comparison to its various counterparts. That this was so despite its origins as an instrument of British imperial diplomacy in the region makes this achievement all the more surprising. Its critique of the dominant development strategies of the day raised some crucial questions about the nature of the development process, ones which remain relevant to this day; and its approach to the provision of technical and financial assistance, distinctive for its decentralization and sensitivity to local conditions and capacities, provides a model of aid administration which continues to warrant greater attention by the donor governments of the West. As such, the creation of the BMEO with its Development Division may have been the one diplomatic initiative taken by Bevin in 1945 that fulfilled his goal of establishing a new relationship between Britain and the Middle East based on the ideas of partnership and mutual cooperation.

Notes

INTRODUCTION

1 Both titles will be used interchangeably throughout the text.
2 Myrdal, *An Approach to the Asian Drama*, 188. See also 'International Inequality and Foreign Aid in Retrospect' in *Pioneers in Development*, 151–65.
3 Louis, *The British Empire*, Monroe, *Britain's Moment in the Middle East, 1914–1971*, and 'Mr. Bevin's "Arab Policy"' in Hourani (eds.) *St. Antony's Papers*, and Sacher, *Europe Leaves the Middle East, 1936–1954*, for various accounts of postwar British policy in the Middle East.
4 Louis, *The British Empire*, 1–50 and Bullock, *Ernest Bevin*.
5 See Bauer, *Dissent on Development*, 112. See also *Equality, The Third World and Economic Delusion*, 'Remembrance of Studies Past: Retracing First Steps' in *Pioneers in Development*, 27–41, Lipton's commentary on Lord Bauer's paper in *Pioneers in Development*, 44–50, and Toye, *Dilemmas of Development*.
6 Toye, *Dilemmas of Development*.
7 Ibid., 92.
8 See Ibid., 47–70.
9 Ibid., 67.
10 Baster, 'The Introduction of Western Economic Institutions into the Middle East', January 1960, 17, Pamphlet Collection, MEC St Antony's College.
11 See Crawford, 'A Note on Land Tenure and Rural Conditions in the Middle East', 28 October 1947, FO 371/61574.
12 See Conference minutes, September 1945, FO 371/45253/E7151.
13 Israel, *Institutional Development*, ix.
14 Hellinger, *Aid for Just Development*, 31.
15 Rondinelli, *Development Projects as Policy Experiments: An Adaptive Approach to Development Administration*, and Caiden and Wildavsky, *Planning and Budgeting in Poor Countries*.

1 BRITAIN, PEASANTS, AND PASHAS: DEBATING APPROACHES TO MODERNIZATION IN THE POSTWAR MIDDLE EAST

1 Gallagher, *The Decline, Revival and Fall of the British Empire*.
2 Lord Altrincham memo, 2 September 1945, FO 371/45252/E6640.
3 Conference Minutes, September, 1945, FO 371/45253/E7151.
4 Sacher, *Europe Leaves the Middle East*, 408.

5 The MESC was established in April 1941.
6 By 1944, the amount of shipping tonnage entering the Middle East had been reduced from a pre-war level of 5.5 million tons per year to 1.5 million tons. (See MESC, *Some Facts About the MESC*.)
7 Warriner, *Land and Poverty in the Middle East*, 2.
8 Skillbeck memo, 'Middle East Council of Agriculture' February 1945, 1, MESC Papers, MEC, St Antony's College.
9 See MESC, 'Problems of Statistical Enumeration in the Middle East' in *Middle East Economic and Statistical Bulletin*, no. 12, April 1944.
10 Hunter, 'Economic Problems: The Middle East Supply Centre' in Kirk, *The Middle East in the War, 1939–1946*, 179.
11 Iraq's wartime inflation rate was estimated at 390 per cent, Iran's at 699 per cent and Syria and Lebanon's at 520 per cent.
12 Hunter, 'Economic Problems', 187.
13 Wilmington, *The Middle East Supply Centre*, 142.
14 Ibid., 127.
15 See Elliot, 'Civil Transport Problems in the Middle East in Wartime', paper presented to the Institute of Transport, 1945, MESC Papers, HE201, MEC, St Antony's College.
16 Wilmington, *The Middle East Supply Centre*, 137.
17 Wilmington, 'The Middle East Supply Centre: A Reappraisal' in *Middle East Journal*, 1952, 161.
18 Ibid., 161.
19 Skillbeck memo, 'Middle East Council of Agriculture', February 1945, 4, MESC Papers, MEC, St Antony's College.
20 Allen, *Rural Education and Welfare in the Middle East*, Keen, *Agricultural Development in the Middle East*, and Worthington, *Middle East Science*.
21 Lloyd, *Food and Inflation in the Middle East, 1940–1945*, 157.
22 Skillbeck memo, 'Middle East Council Agriculture', February 1945, 2, MESC Papers, MEC, St Antony's College.
23 See Thompson to Eden, 24 July 1944, FO 922/6 for more details on the Bayliss incident.
24 Skillbeck memo, 'Middle East Council Agriculture', February 1945, MESC Papers, MEC, St Antony's College, 2.
25 See MESC, *Proceedings of the Conference on Middle East Agricultural Development*.
26 Skillbeck to Jackson, 'Final Report on the Middle East Council of Agriculture', 1 April 1945, 6, MESC Papers, MEC, St Antony's College.
27 Skillbeck memo, 'Middle East Council Agriculture', February 1945, 7, MESC Papers, MEC, St Antony's College.
28 Wilmington, *The Middle East Supply Centre* 1971, 161.
29 DeNova, 'The Culbertson Economic Mission and Anglo-American Tensions in the Middle East' in *Journal of American History*, 1977, 922.
30 See FO 371/45267/E2046.
31 Wilmington, 'The Middle East Supply Centre: A Reappraisal', 155.
32 Godfried, *Bridging the Gap Between Rich and Poor*, 124.
33 Landis, 'Middle East Challenge' in *Fortune*, September 1945, See FO 371/45254.

34 Ibid.
35 Wilmington 'The Middle East Supply Centre: A Reappraisal', 69.
36 Godfried, *Bridging the Gap Between Rich and Poor*, 1987, 126.
37 Skillbeck memo, 'Middle East Council Agriculture', February 1945, 9, MESC Papers, MEC, St Antony's College.
38 Murray, 'Some Regional Economic Problems in the Middle East', in *International Affairs*, 1947, 18.
39 See Porath, *In Search of Arab Unity, 1930–1945* for background information on the events leading to the creation of the Arab League in 1945.
40 Skillbeck to Jackson, 'Final Report on the Middle East Council Agriculture', 1 April 1945, 6, MESC Papers, MEC, St Antony's College.
41 Ibid.
42 Skillbeck memo, 'Middle East Council Agriculture', February 1945, 10, MESC Papers, MEC, St Antony's College.
43 Louis, *The British Empire*.
44 Wark, 'Development Diplomacy: Sir John Troutbeck and the British Middle East Office, 1947–50' in John Zametica (ed), *British Officials and British Foreign Policy, 1945–1950*, 230. Also, see Conference Minutes, 5 September 1945, FO 371/45253/E6641.
45 Lord Altrincham memo, 2 September 1945, FO 371/45252/E6640.
46 Conference Minutes, 5 September 1945, FO 371/45253/E6641.
47 See Lord Altrincham memo, 2 September 1945, FO 371/45252/E6640.
48 Conference Minutes, 5 September 1945, FO 371/45253/E6641.
49 Ibid.
50 Conference Minutes, 6 September 1945, FO 371/45253/E6804.
51 Note by HM Embassy, Cairo, 24 September 1945, FO 371/45253/E7130.
52 See Hare to Secretary of State, 30 November 1945, 741.83/11–3045.
53 Louis, *The British Empire* for a more thorough examination of the non-interventionist nature of Bevin's Middle East diplomacy in the postwar world.
54 Bevin's speech in the House of Commons, 23 November 1945; See FO 371/45255/E9161.
55 Hare to Secretary of State, 6 May 1946, 741.90/5–646.
56 Greenhill, 'Progress Report on Recommendations of the September Conference on Middle East Affairs', 15 January 1946, FO 371/52318/E1140.
57 Overton to Armstrong, undated, FO 371/45254/E8058.
58 See Henderson memo, 'Lord Altrincham's Motion', 26 March 1946, FO 371/52318.
59 'Minutes of Meeting held in Sir Orme Sargent's Room on 28 June 1946', FO 371/53388/J2946.
60 Boardman to Lewis-Jones, 'Middle East Secretariat', 2 December 1948, 741.90/12–1348.
61 Ibid.
62 These advisers covered the fields of labour, statistics, agriculture, forestry, health, entomology, and animal husbandry.
63 Elwood to Hudson, 'The British Middle East Office', 3 June 1947, 890.50/6–2447.
64 See Tuck to Henderson, 20 August 1945, RG 84, Cairo, General Records, 1945, Box 140; and 'Comments of His Majesty's Embassy, Cairo, on Items of

the Agenda of the Middle East Economic Conference, April 1945', 29 March 1945, FO 371/45250.
65 Lampson to Eden, 6 April 1945, FO 371/45250/E2514.
66 See Commanders in Chief to Sir A. Overton, 22 March 1946, FO 371/52318.
67 Crawford, 'The Development Division', 29 December 1953, FO 957/192.
68 Memo of Conversation with Dennis Greenhill, 20 March 1947, 741.90/3–2147.
69 Crawford, 'The Development Division', 29 December 1953, FO 957/192.
70 Ibid.
71 Crawford, upon hearing of the magnitude of the request, remarked that 'I still have not recovered from my amazement.' See Crawford to Greenhill, 14 June 1947, FO 371/61607/E5376.
72 MEOC(47)22, 'Note by Foreign Office', 27 August 1947, FO 371/61623.
73 Greenhill's Progress Report on Recommendations of the September Conference on Middle Eastern Affairs, January 15 1946, FO 371/52318. At the bottom of this report, Bevin scrawled 'I am disappointed...Are we casting our net wide enough for experts?'
74 MEOC Working Party, 'Development Possibilities in Iraq', enclosed MES to BMEO, 12 April 1949, FO 371/75084.
75 Bevin minute, 15 July 1947, FO 371/61622/E6362.
76 Windett memo, 19 October 1950. FO 957/110.
77 Overton to Howe, 20 December 1946, FO 371/61509/E183.
78 See MEOC, 21 May 1947, FO 371/61499/E4486.
79 See Uvarov and Waterston, 'MEALU General Report of Anti-Locust Campaign, 1942–1947', 19 September 1947, FO 371/61564/E8755.
80 Ibid.
81 The last vestiges of direct technical participation by the British in desert locust control in the Middle East disappeared with the expulsion of their anti-locust unit from Saudi Arabia in 1956 during the Buraimi incident. (See Lampen memo, 'British Desert Locust Team in Saudi Arabia', 10 April 1956, FO 371/121385/V1281/50.)
82 Overton to Howe, 30 December 1946, FO 371/61509/E183.
83 Crawford, who felt that personal contacts were the only things allowing Britain to 'hang on' to the Middle East, went so far as to suggest the building of more tennis courts at embassies as a way of facilitating contact! (See Crawford to Bevin, 9 June 1947, FO 371/61538/E5248.)
84 Overton to Howe, 30 December 1946, FO 371/61509/E183.
85 Crawford, 'The Development Division', 29 December 1953, FO 957/192.

2 IMPERIAL DREAMS AND DELUSIONS: THE ECONOMICS OF PROMOTING MIDDLE EAST DEVELOPMENT

1 Troutbeck to Wright, 31 December 1947, FO 957/60.
2 See MEOC(47)14, 'Economic Policy in the Middle East', 15 May 1949, CAB 134/500.
3 See Conference minutes, September 1945, FO 371/45253/E7151.
4 Rowe-Dutton minute, 27 March 1947, T236/1185.
5 MEOC(47)3, 16 July 1947.

6 Ministry of Food, 'Possibilities of Obtaining More Foodstuffs from the Middle East', FO 371/61509/E183.
7 Stewart to Crawford, 25 June 1947, FO 371/61511/E5824.
8 Gandy memo, 12 December 1946, FO 371/52329/E10803.
9 Crawford, 'Economic Policy in the Middle East', 10 June 1947, FO 371/61499/E5377. Crawford was also adamant that, if a policy of promoting food production for export was encouraged in the Middle East, then it would be incumbent on Britain to ensure that markets for those products would be guaranteed. He correspondingly recommended that London consider the idea of signing long-term contracts with potential Middle East suppliers. (See Crawford to Greenhill, 26 April 1947, FO 371/61511/E3490.)
10 Polk, Sterling: Its Meaning in World Finance, 58.
11 He had previously headed the Treasury Mission to India in February of the same year.
12 Eady to el Kabir, 'Iraq', 6 March 1947, T236/1189.
13 'Sterling Balance Negotiations Between Iraq and U.K.', Agreed minutes of the second meeting, 20 June 1947, T236/1190.
14 El Kabir, 'Iraq: Sterling Balance Negotiations', undated, T236/1189.
15 Sassoon, Economic Policy in Iraq, 1932–1950.
16 'Sterling Balance Negotiations Between Iraq and UK', Agreed minutes of the fourth meeting, 1 July 1947, T236/1190.
17 Busk to FO, 'Negotiations with Iraq', 23 October 1947, FO 371/61653/E9952.
18 Burrows memo, 27 April 1948, FO 371/68461/E6109.
19 Mack to FO, 13 May 1948, FO 371/68461/E1256.
20 Baghdad to MES, 3 August 1949 FO 371/75158/E9936.
21 See Trevelyan to Burrows, 12 August 1949, FO 371 75157/E10246.
22 See Stewart, 'The Present Position of Irrigation and Agricultural Development In Iraq', 19 March 1949, FO 957/140.
23 Trevelyan to Burrows, 22 July 1949, FO 371/75157 E9320. With regards this issue, Crawford wrote to his agricultural advisor, Sir H.Stewart: 'I hope that to recover the expenditure the Iraqi Government will not have to resort to the selling of State Domain lands, though they may be forced into this. The result will certainly be that the land will go to the rich merchants, etc. and little or nothing will be done for the peasantry. One would hope that the Government would keep control of the State Domain land by long leases with conditions against fractionation of economic sized plots and a good husbandry clause which would enable the Government to break the lease and get control of the land if conditions justified it.' (See Crawford to Stewart, 7 March 1949, FO 957/96.)
24 As one negotiator stated with respect to negotiations over sterling balances in India, the suggestion of a link was made to Indian leaders in order that 'they could assure their public that the releases were being devoted to capital development while making sure that they did not, in fact, get anything more in the next few years...than they [were] getting now...Our object, after all, is not to finance capital development but to secure an acceptable agreement on long-term releases.' (See Tomlinson, 'Indo-British Relations in the Post-Colonial Era: The Sterling Balance Negotiations, 1947–1949' in Porter and Holland (eds), Money, Finance and Empire, 1790–1950.)
25 See Walter Lippman in The Washington Post, 9 February 1946.

26 See Henderson memo, April 4 1946, FO 371/52318.
27 'Memo of Conversation with Dennis Greenhill', 20 March 1947, 741.90/3–2147.
28 See 'Minutes of Informal Meetings Between British and United States Officials Held at the Department of State October 23 to 28 Inclusive Concerning the Raising of Living Standards in the Middle East', DOS to London, 24 November 1947, 890.50/10–347.
29 McGuire to Lewis-Jones, 'Middle East "Balance Sheet"', 25 March 1946, 890.51/3–2546.
30 See Wark, 'Development Diplomacy'
31 See *Al-Ahram*, 1 February 1949; and Conference Minutes, 21 July 1949, FO 371/75052/E9043.
32 See Crawford, 'Rough Forecast of Cost of Principal Projects in the Middle East', undated, FO 371/75085/E5505.
33 ED(OS)(49)21, 'Draft Report to Ministers on Economic Development in the Middle East', 1 September 1949, CAB 134/194.
34 FO memo, 'Middle East Development: Immediate Objectives', FO 371/75087/E7213.
35 See ED(OS)(49)21, 1 September 1949, CAB 134/194.
36 See ME(O)(49) 14, 10 May 1949, CAB 134/501.
37 See Seale, *The Struggle for Syria: A Study of Postwar Arab Politics, 1945–1958*.
38 Furlonge to Clough, 26 January, 1951, FO 371/91864/EY1151.
39 Pappe, *Britain and the Arab-Israeli Conflict, 1948–1951*, 133.
40 Furlonge to Clough, 26 January 1951, FO 371/91864/EY1151.
41 Evans memo, 25 April 1951, FO 371/91864/EY1151/3.
42 Shephard to Younger, 18 September 1950, FO 371/82342/EP1119/21.
43 See Walmsley, 'Economic Conditions in Arab Palestine Including Arab Jerusalem', February 1952, FO 371/104473; and Baster, 'The Economy of Jordan' in *Middle East Journal*, 1955.
44 Louis, *The British Empire*, 345–79.
45 FO to Amman, 17 November 1948, FO 371/68826.
46 Kirkbride to FO, 17 September 1948, FO 371/68825/E12135.
47 The loan was for the Iraqi Railway Commission, partly to finance old debts, many of which were owed to the British firm Holloway Brothers Limited.
48 The loan, in fact, was followed by a letter to all British embassies and legations in the region instructing them to keep the arrangement quiet. (See FO to Cairo, Jedda, Amman, Damascus, Benghazi, Beirut, Tripoli and Tehran, 5 December 1949, FO 371/75159/E14330).
49 See Howell to Dudley, 16 February 1962, ODA.
50 Maitland, Stewart, and Murray were part of the IBRD mission to Lebanon, Crawford joined their mission to Ethiopia and a preliminary one to Syria and Threlkeld was part of their original mission to Iraq.
51 Crawford memo, 28 April 1949, FO 371/75097/E3346.
52 Rapp commented in his memoirs 'that of all the US and UN technicians that began to flow into the region in the 1950s, more than one found that in our library there was all the material required for the reports they had been employed to make and decided that it was unnecessary to travel further'. (See Sir T. Rapp Papers, 372, MEC, St Antony's College).
53 See FO to Hall Patch (IBRD), 22 April 1953; Stevens (Bank of England) to

Stevenson (Treasury), 5 May 1953; Fogarty memo, 'Proposed IBRD Loan to Jordan', 30 May 1953; and Hall Patch to Sir H. Brittain, 12 August 1953, FO 371/104912/ETI117.

54 Crawford memo, 28 April 1949, FO 371/75079/E3346.
55 Ebtehaj, who on the whole was sympathetic to the IBRD's approach, was critical of this excessive conservatism with regard to oil-rich Iran, stating that 'it is now clear that the I.B. was simply a device for helping the European powers and not the impoverished peoples of the Middle East who really needed it'. (Pyman memo, 15 September 1950, FO 371/68731/E12379.)
56 Mason, *The World Bank Since Bretton Woods*, 383.
57 Meeting between BMEO and IBRD, Cairo, 25 April 1949, FO 371/75086/E5994.
58 Ibid.
59 Troutbeck to Wright, 20 May 1949, FO 371/75086/E6666.
60 Wright memo, 'Visit of Mr. Eugene Black', 16 February 1953, FO 371/105091/UEE81/14.
61 Crawford to Richmond, 18 December 1952, FO 371/98272/E1112.
62 Ibid.
63 See Waight, 'Report on Persian Gulf Tour of Treasury Representative', May to June, 1949, T236/4152; and ME(O)(49)35, 'Economic and Social Development in the Middle East: Persian Gulf States', 19 December 1949, CAB 134/501.
64 Hay to Furlonge, 13 November 1951, FO 371/91300/EA1117.
65 See Makins, 'Report on a Visit to the States of the Persian Gulf Under British Protection with some Observations on Iraq and Saudi Arabia and with Conclusions and Recommendations', 20 March 1952, FO 371/98343/EA1051/53. For a copy of Makins' report as well as a useful summary of British policy in the Gulf in the 1950s, see Burrows, *Footnotes in the Sand: The Gulf in Transition, 1953–1958*.
66 Flett to Coulson, 28 November 1952, FO 371/98400/EA1112.
67 Makins, 'Report on a Visit to the States of the Persian Gulf', 20 March 1952, FO 371/98343/EA1051/53.
68 See Serpell to Ross, 14 October 1952, FO 371/98343 EA1112 and Rose to Laver, 27 October 1952, FO 371/98399/EA1112.
69 Scott memo, 4 October 1952, FO 371/98399/EA1112/64.
70 Waterlow memo, 14 July 1953, FO 371/104341/EA1111/64.
71 See Pelley to Sir R. Hay, 10 March 1953, FO 371/104341/EA1111.
72 Murray, 'Notes on a Regional Development Bank in the Middle East', 17 June 1953, FO 371/104200/E1112/2.
73 Troutbeck to FO, 23 November 1953, FO 371/104341/EA1111.
74 Burrows suggested several schemes: education in Sharjah, irrigation in Dhaib and port improvements in Dubai and Sharjah. This was the beginning of British involvement in the development of the Trucial States, involvement which became reasonably intensive in the mid to late 1960s. (See Burrows to Lord Marquess, 29 September 1953, FO 371/104341/EA1111/68.)
75 FO to Baghdad, 9 March 1953, FO 371/104684/EQ1102/5; and Gardiner to Falla, 7 June 1954, FO 371/111014/VQ1116/2.
76 Conference of United Kingdom Representatives in the Middle East, 19 June

1952, FO 371/99032/VEE176 and '1952 Review of Economic and Social Conditions in the Middle East', FO 371/104198.

77 See Waterlow, 'Minutes of Development Division Conference', 21 December 1950, FO 371/91197/E1053.

78 Crawford to Wall, 14 July 1950, FO 371/81950/E11345/14.

79 Warriner, *Land Reform and Development in the Middle East*, 71–112.

80 Troutbeck to Wright, 3 January 1950, FO 957/109.

3. THE BRITISH MIDDLE EAST OFFICE AND THE ABANDONMENT OF IMPERIAL APPROACHES TO MODERNIZATION

1   Troutbeck to Wright, 31 December 1947, FO 957/60.

2   See Gallagher, *Egypt's Public Health Wars, 1942–1949*.

3   Greenhill memo, 18 August 1947, FO 957/4.

4   Crawford to Greenhill, 31 May 1947, FO 957/4.

5   Wright to Troutbeck, 2 March 1948, FO 957/15.

6   See 'Relationship between the BMEO and the Executive Organisations of the United Nations', 24 March 1947, FO 957/4.

7   Dundas memo, 'BMEO in relation to UNO in the Middle East', undated, 1948, FO 371/68387/E4385; and Wright to Troutbeck, undated, 1948, FO 371/68387.

8   Crawford to Greenhill, 31 May 1947, FO 957/4.

9   Ibid.

10 Crawford to Overton, 11 April 1947, FO 957/4.

11 Houstoun-Boswall to Bevin, 19 June 1948, FO 371/68388/E8596.

12 Creswell to Bevin, 25 June 1948, FO 371/68388/E9023.

13 Mack to Bevin, 30 June 1948, FO 371/68388/E9432.

14 Ibid.

15 Godfried, *Bridging the Gap Between Rich and Poor*, 152–3.

16 See Thornburg and Spry, *Turkey: An Economic Appraisal*.

17 Murray to Bevin, 25 January 1949, FO 371/75083/E1345.

18 See FO memo, 'Middle East Development', 21 February 1949, FO 371/75083/E2443.

19 FO memo, 20 January 1949, FO 371/75083/E2446; and BMEO to MES, 8 February 1950, FO 371/81952/E1152.

20 See 'Meeting Held in Crawford's Room at BMEO on 16 April 1949', FO 371/75085/E5504.

21 Trevelyan memo, undated, FO 624/151.

22 Interview with R.S. Porter, 23 November 1988.

23 Asher, and Associates, *The United Nations and Economic and Social Cooperation*, 435–93.

24 See 'Economic and Social Development in the Middle East', 28 April 1950, FO 371/81919/E10210/1.

25 Threlkeld, 'Technical Assistance in Middle East Countries', 21 November 1950, FO 371/91211/E1104/3.

26 Threlkeld, 'Coordination of Point Four Experts and BMEO', 23 January 1950, FO 957/109.

27 Crawford to Evans, 18 February 1950, FO 371/81942/E1103.

28 Bozman memo, 21 January 1950, FO 957/109.

29 BMEO to MES, 9 January 1950, FO 957/110.

30 Ibid.

31 Ibid.

32 See Nash to Trueman, 30 March 1950 FO 371 81924/E1051; and 'Recruitment of Experts for Employment by Middle East Governments', undated, FO 957/110.

33 Crawford to Waterlow, undated, FO 957/110.

34 See Chapman, 'Memorandum on Forest Technical Assistance in Middle East Countries', 15 May 1950; and Wall to Evans, 24 July 1950, FO 957/106.

35 See Sargent, 'Cultural Relations With Eastern Countries: A New Line of Approach', FO 957/110.

36 Among the positions subsidized were the British seats on the Iraqi Development Board held successively by Sir Eddington Miller and Michael Ionides, Walpole's position as Director-General of the Department of Lands and Surveys in Jordan, Davidson's position as Forestry Adviser to the Syrian Government and Dr Scott's position in the Medical School in Damascus.

37 See Waterlow to Windett, 11 August 1951, FO 957/147.

38 Waterlow to Windett, 22 August 1951, FO 371/91210/E1058.

39 See 'Record of Meeting in Mr Wright's Room on 28 January 1949', 29 January 1949, FO 371/75083/E1771; and Memo of Conversation, 'Economic and Social Development in the Middle East', 4 March 1949, 500.00/3–449.

40 Greenhill to Evans, 14 April, 1950, FO 371/81942/E1103/10.

41 NEA Files, Lot 55–D36.

42 The seconded advisers were Stewart in agriculture and Murray in economics and statistics. See Crawford to Evans, 18 February, 1950, FO 371/81942/E1103/6.

43 Rapp to Morrison, 29 March 1951, FO 371/91210/E1103/3.

44 See Windett, 'Regional Meeting on Coordination of Technical Assistance held in Alexandria, 29 June, and Present Position of British Middle East Office Development Division in Middle East Technical Assistance', 17 July 1951, FO 957/143.

45 See 'Summary of Discussions During the Office Conference held at British Middle East Office, Cairo, 21 to 22 December 1951', FO 957/151.

46 Ibid. At this point, the Development Division is separated from the BMEO which itself is transferred to Cyprus. However, we shall continue to make use of both terms in the text.

47 Ibid.

48 Threlkeld, 'Technical Assistance in Middle East Countries', 21 November 1950, FO 371/91211/E1104/3.

49 'Summary of Discussions During the Office Conference held at British Middle East Office, Cairo, 21 to 22 December 1951', FO 957/151.

50 See Waterlow, 'Minutes of Development Division Conference', 21 December 1950, FO 371/91197/E1053.

51 Rapp to Bevin, 15 January 1951, FO 371/91197/E1053/2.

52 Evans to Crawford, 2 January 1952, FO 371/91218/E11345.

53 'Development Division Report for 1953', March 1953 FO 371/110777/E1052/10.
54 Crawford to Sterndale Bennett, 4 November 1954, FO 371/110006/EP1107/1.
55 Crawford to Selwyn Lloyd, 'Final Despatch', 14 June 1960, ODA.
56 One of the more interesting requests from the fund was for a Lebanese football trainer to serve as an apprentice with a professional football club in Britain. In light of a competing offer from the Soviets, the request was justified on the grounds that 'football is becoming increasingly popular here and is an excellent thing because it means that street crowds let off steam and are less likely to get excited about politics'. The request was ultimately refused. See FO 371/115477/V1052.
57 Crawford to Selwyn Lloyd, 'Final Despatch', 14 June 1960, ODA.
58 Crawford, 'The Development Division', 29 December 1953, FO 957/192.
59 Crawford to Simpson, 12 November 1953, FO 371/104193/E1051.
60 Troutbeck to Wright, 3 January 1950, FO 957/109.
61 Bozman memo, 21 January 1950, FO 957/109.
62 Gardiner to Bowker, 7 July 1953, FO 371/104258/E10345. See also Geren, 'Why A Point IV Agreement Has Not Been Concluded With Syria', 28 May 1951, 883.00TA/5–2851.
63 Pinkerton memo, 'Point IV Agreement with Lebanon', Beirut to DoS, 28 February 1951, 883A.00–TA/2–2851.
64 Crawford to Evans, 6 February 1950, FO 371/81942/E1103/5.
65 Crawford, 'Report on the Regional FAO Pre-Conference Meeting at Bludan, 1951', 17 September 1951, FO 371/91198/E1053.
66 Windett to Ledyard (Geneva), 18 August 1951, FO 371/91212/E1104/28.
67 Maitland to Evans, 20 March 1951, FO 371/91217/E11345/9.
68 Windett to Evans, 26 November 1951, FO 371/91218/E11345.
69 Maitland to Evans, 9 June 1951, FO 371/91217/E11345/9; and Waterlow memo, 'US Mutual Security Programme: Economic Aid to M.E. Governments', 31 July 1951, FO 371/91213/E1104/32.
70 Crawford described Locke, formally a Vice-President with Chase Manhattan Bank, as 'one of the brightest guys to hit this part of the world'. (Crawford to Evans, 23 January 1952, FO 371/98276 E11345/5).
71 'Development Division Report for 1952', FO 957/178. See Kingston, '"Ambassador for the Arabs": The Locke Mission and the Unmaking of American Development Diplomacy in the Near East, 1951–1953' in David Lesch (ed.), *The Middle East and the United States: A Historical and Political Reassessment*.
72 Much of what follows is taken from Windett, 'Regional Meeting on Coordination of Technical Assistance held in Alexandria, 29 June, and the Present Position of British Middle East Office Development Division in Middle East Technical Assistance', 17 July 1951, FO 957/143.
73 See Crawford memo, October 1951, FO 957/149 with regards to Iraqi suspicion of Development Division involvement with the Iraqi Development Board. See also 'Visit of British Forester', Director-General of Police and Security (Qamishli) to Ministry of Interior (Damascus), 19 May 1951, Markaz al-Watha'iq al-Tarikhiya, Damascus (in arabic).
74 MEDD to MES, 5 March 1953, FO 371/104193/E1051/5.

75 Crawford was formerly Governor in the Northern Provinces of the Sudan, Sir Herbert Stewart had been the Chief Agricultural Adviser to the Indian Viceroy, Maitland had been Chief Conservator of Forests in the Central Provinces and Eyre had been Director of Agriculture in Palestine under the Mandate.
76 Crawford to Selwyn Lloyd, 'Final Despatch', 14 June 1960, ODA.
77 Crawford, 'The Development Division', 29 December 1953, FO 957/192.
78 Davidson to author, 22 November 1989.
79 Crawford, 'The Development Division', 29 December 1953, FO 957/192.
80 Interview with Dr. Paul Howell, 21 February 1989.
81 Crawford, 'The Development Division', 29 December 1953, FO 957/192.
82 Rapp to Bowker, 17 January 1951, FO 371/91197/E1053.
83 Davidson to author, 22 November 1989.
84 Maitland, 'Forestry and Soil Conservation in Egypt', 8 June 1949, FO 957/89.
85 Davidson to author, 22 November 1989.
86 Waterlow, 'Minutes of Development Division Conference', 21 December 1950, FO 371/91197/E1053; and Rapp to Morrison, 3 April 1951, CO 67/371/4; and 'Economic Development in Cyprus in Relation to the Middle East', CAB 134/501.
87 Porter to author, 12 December 1989.
88 Ibid.
89 In Syria, he paved the way for the appointment of the FAO expert, Henry; in Iraq, he first convinced the Iraqis to appoint another FAO expert, Haig and, later, the Palestinian, Brair; in Iran, Wordsworth brought in specialists from Cyprus; and in Jordan, another Palestinian working in the Sudan was convinced to return, Husseini.
90 Interview with Ayoub Betarseh, 24 March 1990, Amman.
91 See Windett, 'Regional Meeting on Coordination of Technical Assistance in Alexandria, 29 June, and Present Position of British Middle East Office Development Division in Middle East Technical Assistance', 17 July 1951, FO 957/143.
92 Ibid.

4. THE BRITISH MIDDLE EAST OFFICE AND THE POLITICS OF MODERNIZATION IN IRAN, 1945–1951

1 Keddie, 'Is there a Middle East?' in *International Journal of Middle East Studies*.
2 Banani, *The Modernization of Iran, 1926–1941*, 147.
3 See Floor, *Industrialization in Iran, 1900–1941* and Lambton, *Landlord and Peasant in Persia*.
4 See Azimi, *Iran: Democracy in Crisis, 1941–1953* and Abrahamian, *Iran Between Two Revolutions*.
5 See Bullock, *Ernest Bevin*.
6 Abrahamian, *Iran Between Two Revolutions*, 246.
7 See Fawcitt, *Iran and the Cold War: The Azerbaijan Crisis of 1946*.
8 Maitland, 'Confidential Notes', June 1948, FO 371/68752/E10336.
9 Ibid.
10 Ibid.

11 Baxter to Le Rougetel, 20 May 1946, FO 371/52763/E3678.
12 See Greenhill memo, 9 May 1946, FO 371/52763/E3678.
13 Le Rougetel to FO, 28 March 1947, FO 371/62001/E4007.
14 See FO 371/62001/E2939 for translated text of speech.
15 Crawford to Greenhill, 10 May 1947, FO 371/62001/E4007.
16 See Abrahamian, *Iran Between Two Revolutions*, 225–35 and Azimi, *Iran*, 152–78 for discussions of Qavam's premiership.
17 Pyman to Copeman, 16 December 1946, FO 371/52696/E11741.
18 See Millspaugh, *The American Task in Persia* and Millspaugh, *Americans in Persia*.
19 Le Rougetel to Howe, 5 February 1947; and Le Rougetel to Crawford, 7 January 1947, FO 371/62001/E11392.
20 Swann to Baxter, 17 February 1947, FO 371/62001/E11449.
21 Ibid.
22 See Minutes of the Meeting held in the Treasury Chambers, 19 August 1946, FO 371/52734/E8427 for discussions of financial questions concerning the Lars Valley Dam scheme.
23 Baxter to Swann, 22 March 1947, FO 371/62001/E11392.
24 FO to Tehran, 14 April 1947, FO 371/62001/E2939.
25 See Bostock and Jones, *Planning and Power in Iran*.
26 Also associated with the BMEO at this time was a labour advisor, Audsley, whose main preoccupation was to work with British-owned oil companies in the Middle East to improve their labour relations in their host countries. At the time of Qavam's speech, Audsley had already been active in Iran working directly with the AIOC as well as assisting the Iranian Government in the drafting of a comprehensive new labour law.
27 See Stewart, 'Karun-Zayandeh Rud Irrigation Project', 21 June 1947, FO 371/62002/E6005.
28 Ibid.
29 Ibid.
30 Stewart, 'Notes on Persia' 17 June 1947, FO 371/62002/E5683.
31 See Maitland, 'Preliminary Report on Forestry Development in Iran with Special Reference to the Seven Year Plan for Forestry and to the Northern Forests (Caspian Sea Belt)', June 1948 FO 957/55.
32 Maitland, 'Confidential Notes', June 1948, FO 957/55.
33 See Champion and Osmaston, *The Forests of India*.
34 Pridie, 'Report on Tour of Persia', 31 July 1947, FO 371/62060/E7313.
35 Le Rougetel to Bevin, 3 September 1947, FO 371/62060/E8371.
36 Pridie, 'Report on Tour of Persia', 31 July 1947, FO 371/62060/E7313.
37 FO to Le Rougetel, 21 October 1946, FO 371/52786/E9523.
38 Le Rougetel to Bevin, 31 December 1946, FO 371/52786/E12480.
39 Waterlow memo, 2 January 1947, FO 371/52786/E12480.
40 See Wright to Hoyer-Millar, 14 December 1948, FO 957/63.
41 Washington to Chancery, 11 February 1949, FO 371/75482/E2147.
42 Clinton-Thomas memo, 16 February 1949, FO 371/75842/E2127.
43 Ibid.
44 Wright to Hoyer-Millar, 14 December 1948, FO 957/63.
45 See Maitland Diary, 'Tour of Azerbaijan', 6 May 1949, FO 371/75484/E4662

and Maitland and Burns (OCI) memo to Bookwalter, 'Tour of Zabul in Sistan', 5 April 1949, FO 371/75484/E5174.

46 Tehran to FO, 28 May 1949, FO 371/75485/E6929; and Crawford to MES, 21 April 1949, FO 371/75484/E5174.

47 Troutbeck to Dundas, 27 September 1948, FO 371/68754/E12732 and Troutbeck to Burrows, 13 December 1948, FO 371/68754/E16033.

48 Trevelyan to Dundas, 14 October 1948, FO 371/68754/E13880.

49 Le Rougetel to Troutbeck, 23 October 1948, FO 371/68754/E14095. See Troutbeck to Burrows, 13 December 1948, FO 371/68754/E16033.

50 Maitland to Troutbeck, 31 January 1950, FO 957/107.

51 Maitland, 'Report for Period 7 to 29 March' (during work with OCI), FO 371/75485/E7815.

52 Bostock and Jones Planning and Power in Iran, 89.

53 Clinton-Thomas memo, 19 February 1949, FO 371/75483/E2499.

54 See FO 371/75483/E3909 for a translation.

55 Maitland, 'Confidential Notes About Tour' (between 18 April and 3 June 1948), June 1948, 23, FO 957/55.

56 Le Rougetel to Bevin, 24 March 1948, FO 957/63.

57 Le Rougetel to Burrows, 19 April 1948, FO 957/63.

58 See Thornburg to Naficy, 19 May 1948, RG 84, Tehran, 1948, Box 120; and Baldwin, Planning and Development in Iran, 29.

59 Creswell to Bevin, 26 May 1948, FO 957/63.

60 Azimi, Iran, 191.

61 Creswell to Bevin, 26 May 1948, FO 957/63.

62 Crawford to Troutbeck, 18 May 1948, FO 957/63.

63 Creswell to Bevin, 'Selected Projects in Connection with the Seven Year Plan', 14 June 1948, FO 957/63.

64 Azimi, Iran, 197.

65 Le Rougetel to Burrows, 19 April 1948, FO 957/63.

66 Furlonge memo, 10 January 1951, FO 371/91482/EP1102.

67 Baldwin, Planning and Development in Iran, 32.

68 Bostock and Jones, Planning and Power in Iran, 99.

69 Ross to Bevin, 31 May 1949, FO 371/75485/E6932.

70 Maitland to Lawford, Tehran, March 1950, FO 957/107.

71 Lawford to Bevin, 10 March 1950, FO 957/114.

72 Jackhill memo, 29 June 1949, FO 371/75485/E7845.

73 Shephard to Younger, 9 September 1950, FO 957/114.

74 Ibid.

75 Lawford to Burrows, 12 September 1949, FO 371/75486/E11286.

76 Lawford to Bevin, 10 March 1950, FO 957/114.

77 Ibid.

78 Ibid.

79 Baldwin, Planning and Development in Iran, 33.

80 See Ghods, 'The Rise and Fall of General Razmara' in Middle Eastern Studies, 29, 1993.

81 Furlonge memo, 10 January 1951, FO 371/91481/EP1102.

82 Carr memo, 'Impending Reorganization of Statistical Services in Iran', 1 February 1951, RG 84, Tehran, 1951.

83 Wright memo, 'Persia: Notes for the Treasury', 3 March, 1951, FO 371/91485/EP1112.

84 Shepherd to Bevin, 19 February 1951, FO 371/91482/EP1103.

85 Maitland, 'Report on OCI: 28 February to 13 March 1949', FO 371/75484/E4662.

86 Maitland, 'Report for Period 7th to 29th May 1949', FO 371/75485/E7815.

87 Ibid.

88 Ibid.

89 Murray to Crawford, 29 December, 1949, FO 957/114.

90 Crawford, 'Observations on Tour of Persia', FO 371/82333/EP1102.

91 Maitland, 'Notes on Visit to Persia, 28 February to 5 April 1949', 4, FO 371/75484/E6102.

92 Thornburg, 'Apostles of American Democracy', 15 May 1948, RG 84, Tehran, 1948, Box 120. See also Thornburg, *People and Policy in the Middle East* and Lutz, 'Problems and Prospects' in *Middle East Journal*, 1950.

93 Ibid.

94 Maitland, 'Report for Period 7 to 29 May 1949', FO 371/75484/E7815.

95 Maitland, 'Tour of Azerbaijan from Diary 26th of April to 6th of May 1949', FO 371/75484/E4662.

96 Maitland and Burns, memo to Bookwalter, OCI, 'Tour of Zabul in Sistan', 5 April 1049, 4, FO 371/75484/E5174.

97 Ibid.

98 See Maitland, 'Tour of Azerbaijan from Diary 26th of April to 6th of May 1949', FO 371/75484/E4662.

99 Maitland, 'Confidential Notes About Tour, 18th April to 5 June 1948', 23, FO 957/55.

100 Maitland, 'Preliminary Report...', June 1948 9, FO 957/55.

101 Ibid, 16.

102 Maitland, 'Confidential Notes...', June 1948 FO 957/55.

103 Maitland, 'Preliminary Report...', June 1948 6, FO 957/55.

104 Ibid, 7.

105 Maitland report for OCI quoted in Troutbeck to Attlee, 15 December 1949, FO 371/75493/E15410.

106 In a meeting in London in July, 1948 with British timber firms who were interested in the possibility of exploiting Persian timber, Maitland cautioned them that such commercial activity would be premature in the absence of a properly organized forestry service. See Maitland, 'Notes on Work Done in London, July 3 to 30 1948', FO 957/51.

107 Maitland, and Stewart, 'Report on Forestry for OCI', May 1949, FO 371/75493/E15410.

108 See Kernan, 'A Policy of Conservation for the Caspian Forests of Iran' in *Middle East Journal*, 1953, 229.

109 Maitland, 'Preliminary Report...', June 1948, 16, FO 957/55.

110 Maitland, 'Confidential Notes...', June 1948, 8, FO 957/55.

111 Maitland, 'Preliminary Report...', June 1948, 32, FO 957/55.

112 Ibid.

113 Maitland, 'Confidential Notes...', June 1948, 8, FO 957/55.

114 Maitland to Crawford, 30 January 1950, FO 957/107.

115 Maitland to Troutbeck, 31 January 1950, FO 957/107.
116 Maitland to Shepherd, 'Second Progress Report', 27 March 1950, FO 957/107.
117 Maitland to Lawford, 1 March 1950, FO 957/107.
118 Tehran to MES, 25 May 1951, FO 371/91512/EP1281.

5. THE BRITISH MIDDLE EAST OFFICE AND THE POLITICS OF MODERNIZATION IN IRAQ, 1945 TO 1958

1 Jwaideh, 'Midhat Pasha and the Land System of Lower Iraq' in *St Antony's Papers*, 106–35 and Owen, *The Middle East in the World Economy, 1800–1914*, 180–88 and 273–86.
2 Zubaida, 'Community, Class and Minorities in Iraqi Politics' in Louis (ed.), *The Iraqi Revolution of 1958*, 197–210.
3 See Marr, *The Modern History of Iraq*, 50–4.
4 See Hourani, 'Ottoman Reform and the Politics of Notables' in *The Emergence of the Modern Middle East*, 33–66 and Yapp, *The Near East Since the First World War*.
5 See Birdwood, *Nuri al-Said*.
6 These included the right to appoint the prime minister, the power of veto over legislation emanating from the parliament, the right to prorogue parliament and to call elections and autonomy in foreign policy and treaty making.
7 Batatu, *The Old Social Classes and the Revolutionary Movements of Iraq*, 55.
8 The Slugletts, in their comments on Batatu's work, suggest that the socio-economic gaps were not just between the wealthy merchants, industrialists and landowning families and 'the poor' but between the wealthy and 'most of the rest of the population'. See Farouk-Sluglett and Sluglett, 'The Social Classes and the Origins of the Revolution' in Louis (ed.), *The Iraqi Revolution of 1958*, 118–41.
9 The working class in Iraq at this time were described as being 'still in the making' and the emerging national bourgeoisie as being plagued by 'wide disparities in political thinking and social consciousness'. See Farouk-Sluglett and Sluglett, *Iraq Since 1958: From Revolution to Dictatorship*, 36–7.
10 Batatu, *The Old Social Classes and the Revolutionary Movements of Iraq*, 470.
11 For a debate in the context of pre-revolutionary Iraq, see Owen, 'Class and Class Politics in Iraq before 1958: The 'Colonial and Post-Colonial State' and Batatu's comments on Owen's article in 'The Old Social Classes Revisited' in Louis (ed.), *The Iraqi Revolution of 1958*.
12 See Sassoon, *Economic Policy in Iraq, 1932–1950*.
13 Batatu, *The Old Social Classes and the Revolutionary Movements of Iraq*, 472.
14 Ibid., 622.
15 Baker memo, 18 July 1946, FO 371/52563/E6756.
16 Bevin to Stonehewer Bird, 19 July 1946 and Bevin to Stonehewer Bird, 18 September 1946, FO 371/52402.
17 Chancery to FO, 16 July 1946, FO 371/52315/E7045.
18 Louis, *The British Empire*, 310.
19 Stonehewer Bird to Eden, 3 May 1945, FO 371/45324/E3116.

20 Lord Altrincham memo, undated and Stonehewer Bird to Eden, 3 May
     1945, FO 371/45324/E3116.
21 Greenhill to Baxter, 6 May 1946, FO 371/45324/E4204.
22 Ibid.
23 Minutes of Informal Meetings Between British and United States Officials
     Held at the Department of State, October 23 to 28, Inclusive Concerning the
     Raising of Living Standards in the Middle East, enclosed in State
     Department to London, 24 November 1947, 890.50/10–347.
24 MES, 'Irrigation Proposals for Iraq', 3 January 1947, FO 371/61621/E606.
25 FO memo, 'Irrigation Development in Iraq', 20 March 1947, FO
     371/61509/E1183.
26 See 'Notes for the Secretary of State's Talk with the Iraqi Foreign Minister
     about the Development of Irrigation in Iraq', 1 February 1947, FO
     371/61621/E606. It states that 'in Egypt, 17 million people live off 6 million
     acres; Iraq's population today is only 5 million.'
27 Crawford memo, 21 November 1946, FO 957/3.
28 Stewart memo, 28 November 1946, FO 957/3.
29 Pridie memo, undated, FO 957/3.
30 Overton to Stonehewer Bird, 20 December 1946, FO 371/61621/E79. Due to
     his expertise on Iraqi agriculture, Skillbeck was also contacted by the MES
     and his views supported those of the BMEO. He cited the Hawija scheme as a
     'living example of the horrors of failure to plan not only the irrigation but the
     needs of the community', in particular the organization of land tenure. He also
     added a new twist when he highlighted Iraq's foremost need to be administra-
     tors and not technicians; 'if the administration cannot cope with the new
     obligations it will be better not to embark on them for another hundred years.'
     See Skillbeck to Waterlow, 23 January 1947, FO 371/61621/E936.
31 The first development plan was passed in 1927, it was replaced by a five year
     capital works programme in 1931, a new one in 1934, a three year *and* five
     year plan in 1935, a five year plan in 1937, another in 1938, and two more in
     1939, the 'April' one being replaced by the 'August' one. For more details,
     See Sassoon, *Economic Policy in Iraq, 1932–50*, 57–61.
32 See Willcocks, *The Irrigation of Mesopotamia*.
33 Stonehewer Bird to FO, 10 July 1946, FO 371/52463/E6759.
34 FO to Stonehewer Bird, 14 March 1947, FO 371/61621/E11936.
35 Stonehewer Bird to Bevin, 25 April 1947, FO 371/61621/E3836. See also
     'Record of a meeting held at the British Embassy in Baghdad on 22 April
     1947, to discuss the economic development of Iraq', FO 371/61621/E3774.
36 Batatu, *The Old Social Classes and the Revolutionary Movements of Iraq*, 546.
37 Jabr took stringent action against the political opposition by banning the two
     left-wing parties and arresting and putting on trial Fahd, the head of the Iraqi
     Communist Party.
38 Troutbeck to Wright, 31 December 1947, FO 957/60.
39 Troutbeck to Bevin, 22 April 1948, FO 371/68387.
40 Murray, 'Interim Report by Statistical Adviser on Work in Iraq', 11 March
     1947, FO 957/8 and Murray to Crawford, undated, FO 957/8.
41 Murray, 'Notes on Progress of Work During Stay in Iraq, January and
     February 1948', 16 February 1948, FO 957/45.

42 Crawford to Whitehall, 1 May 1959, FO 371/141107/EQ2201.

43 Haigh to Gamble, undated, FO 957/96.

44 Maitland, 'Note on Mr F.F.Haigh's letter to Mr F.H.Gamble', 10 January 1949, FO 957/96.

45 See Maitland, 'Excerpt from Diary', 21 April 1949, FO 371/75150/E5046 and Stewart to Waterlow, 20 May 1949, FO 371/75150/E6436 and Crawford, 'Visit to Iraq', 19 May 1948, FO 371/68409/E6898.

46 See Axelgard, 'US Support for the British Position in Pre-Revolutionary Iraq' and Thatcher, 'Reflections on US Foreign Policy Towards Iraq in the 1950s' in Louis (ed.), *The Iraqi Revolution of 1958*.

47 Maitland, 'Diary Notes: Visit to Iraq and Iran', 29 September to 26 October 1948, FO 371/68383/E15073.

48 Walker memo, 17 February 1949, FO 371/75177/E1553.

49 Crawford memo, 5 April 1949, FO 624/151 and Mack to Wright, 11 April 1949, FO 371/75150/E5511.

50 Trevelyan to Evans, 17 August 1950, FO 371/82420/E1102.

51 See Mack memo, 5 April 1950, FO 371/82419/EQ1102 and Troutbeck to FO, 25 November 1952, FO 371/98735/EQ1016.

52 Ionides to Monroe, 7 January 1958, Pamphlet Collection, MEC, St Antony's College.

53 Ibid. Ionides is referring here to the writings of Doreen Warriner on land reform and development in the Middle East. See Warriner, *Land and Poverty in the Middle East* and *Land Reform and Development in the Middle East*.

54 Wiens, 'Land Development and Distribution Program', 14 April 1955, RG 286, TCA-Iraq, Office of the Director, Subject Files, 1951–58, Box 24.

55 Ionides to Monroe, 7 January 1958, Pamphlet Collection, MEC, St Antony's College.

56 Ibid.

57 Ionides, *Divide and Lose*, 1960, 200.

58 See Crawford memo, October 1951, FO 957/149, Troutbeck to Eden, 31 October 1951, FO 957/149 and MES to Baghdad, 27 November 1951, FO 957/149.

59 Chapman, 'Forests and Forestry in Iraq', 21 March 1950, FO 957/176.

60 Mooney, 'Summary of Notes on Tour of Iraq', 6 June 1951, FO 957/139.

61 Ibid.

62 Mooney to Crawford, 'Note on Meeting of Dr H.F.Mooney with H.E. Arshad Pasha', 3 November 1951.

63 FAO, Mediterranean Development Project, Interim Report, Country Study: Iraq, October 1957, Pamphlet Collection, MEC, St Antony's College.

64 Memorandum of Conversion: Arshad al-Umari and Lewis H. Rohrbaugh, 28 February, 1953, RG 286, TCA-Iraq, Office of the Director, Subject Files, 1951–58, Box 23.

65 Ionides, *Divide and Lose*, 201.

66 Porter, 'An Economist Looks at the Arab Middle East', March 1958, Pamphlet Collection, MEC, St Antony's College.

67 'Economic Review: Iraq, 1951', 887.00/undated.

68 Troutbeck to Eden, 16 October 1953, FO 371/104666/EQ1016.

69 Ireland to DoS, 'Press Criticisms of Development Board', 887.00/9–2851.

70 Salter, *The Development of Iraq: a Plan of Action*, 114.
71 Discussions between Salter and Shuckburgh, enclosed in Shuckburgh to Troutbeck, 18 October 1954, FO 371/111006/VQ1102.
72 See 'Summary of *The Development of Iraq: A Plan of Action* by Lord Salter', 16 August 1955, FO 371/115765/VQ1103.
73 Hooper to Rose, 19 October, 1955, FO 371/115748/VQ1015.
74 Ionides, *Divide and Lose*, 198.
75 Wright, to Selwyn Lloyd, 'Annual Review', 8 February 1957, FO 371/128038/VQ1011.
76 Ionides, *Divide and Lose*, 198.
77 Troutbeck to Eden, 'Final Despatch', 9 December 1954, FO 371/110991/VQ1015. Troutbeck went on to state that Nuri believes 'in paternal government, the strong hand distributing gifts of welfare which can be paid for not by taxing the rich but rather by extracting further revenues from the oil companies'.
78 Wiens, 'Land Development and Distribution Program', 14 April 1955, RG 286, TCA-Iraq, Office of the Director, Subject Files, 1951–58, Box 24.
79 Hancock, J.D. to Sayid Hassan Mohammod Ali, 10 January 1953, RG 286, TCA-Iraq, Office of the Director, Subject Files, 1951–58, Box 24.
80 See Internal memo, FO 624/149.
81 Gumm, C.L. to Hancock, J.D., 'Land Reform', 2 December 1952, RG 286, TCA-Iraq, Office of the Director, Subject Files 1951–58, Box 24.
82 Ionides to Monroe, 7 January 1958, Pamphlet Collection, MEC, St Antony's College.
83 Troutbeck to Falla, 27 January 1954, FO 371/110988/VQ1015.
84 Ibid.
85 Bromley to Richmond, 11 August 1953, FO 371/104685/EQ1103.
86 See Windawi, 'Anglo-Iraqi Relations, 1945–58', 194–9.
87 Shuckburgh memo, 4 October 1954, FO 371/111006/VQ1102.
88 Wright to Rose, 'Background Information: Progressive Internal Legislation in Iraq', 18 June 1955, FO 371/121642/VQ1015.
89 'Development in Iraq', *The Economist*, 1957.
90 Ionides to Monroe, 1 October 1957, Pamphlet Collection, MEC, St Antony's College.
91 Ibid.
92 Ibid.
93 Ibid. Wilson was the American representative on the Iraqi Development Board and Vernon was a senior member of Point Four's staff in Iraq.
94 Louis, 'The British and the Origins of the Iraqi Revolution' in Louis (ed.), *The Iraqi Revolution of 1958*, 55.
95 See Robinson, 'A Reconnaissance Survey, Agricultural and Economic, of the Miri Sirf Dujaila Resettlement Project in the Kut Liwa', May 1953, RG 286, TCA-Iraq, Office of the Director, Subject Files, 1951–58, Box 23. See also Crawford, 'The Dujaila Scheme', 10 April 1951 and Cheesman, 'Iraq: Cooperation in the Dujaila Scheme', April 1951, FO 371/91662/EQ1285.
96 Ionides, 'Help From the West', 174.
97 Ionides to Monroe, 7 January 1958, Pamphlet Collection, MEC, St Antony's College.

98 Ionides, 'Help From the West', 173.
99 Ionides to Monroe, 1 October 1957, Pamphlet Collection, MEC, St Antony's College.
100 Crocker to Washington, 'Approach of Point IV in Iraq', 887.00–TA/1–3152 and Locke to Secretary of State, 15 February 1952, 887.00–TA/2–1552.
101 Rohrbaugh memo, 'MSLD Conference', 5 August 1952, RG 286, TCA-Iraq, Office of the Director, Subject Files, 1951–58, Box 24.
102 See Hancock memo, 'Conversation with Darwish Haidari', 11 December 1952, RG 286, TCA-Iraq, Office of the Director, Subject Files, 1951–58, Box 23.
103 Ibid.
104 Berry, 'Acceleration of the Miri Sirf Lands in Iraq', 29 August 1952, 887.00–TA/8–2952.
105 Ibid.
106 See Ireland to DoS, 887.00–TA/3–1952 and Rohrbaugh 'Highlights of the Week', 21–27 December 1952, 887.00–TA/12–2752.
107 Hancock memo, 'Revision of Miri Sirf Land Development Legislation', 2 June 1953, RG 286, TCA-Iraq, Office of the Director, Subject Files, 1951–59, Box 23.
108 Hancock to Rohrbaugh, 'Recast MSLD Program', 4 March 1953, RG 286, TCA-Iraq, Office of the Director, Subject Files, 1951–58, Box 23.
109 Belgrave memo, 'Point IV', 24 July 1953, FO 371/104694.
110 Ibid.
111 See Hancock memo, 'Discussion with Badi Raphael Butti, Acting Director, Department of Cooperatives', 25 March 1952 RG 286, TCA-Iraq, Office of the Director, Subject Files, 1951–58, Box 4.
112 See Robinson to Hancock, 'Organisation of Cooperative Credit Societies on the Hawija Project', 18 March 1953 RG 286, TCA-Iraq, Office of the Director, Subject Files, 1951–58, Box 23.
113 Haig to Wordsworth, 3 January 1955, FO 957/214.
114 Wordsworth to Crawford, 6 October 1954, FO 371 111010/VQ11010.
115 Belgrave memo, 15 January 1954, FO 371/111010/VQ11106.
116 Hammar to Wiens, 'Agricultural Credit Survey', 22 March 1954, RG 286, TCA-Iraq, Office of the Director, Subject Files, 1951–58, Box 4.
117 Crawford to Faber, 11 January 1954, FO 371/111010/VQ11106.
118 Salter, *The Development of Iraq*, 58.
119 Wordsworth to Crawford, 6 October 1954, 6 October 1954, FO 371/111010/VQ11010.
120 Crawford memo, 'Miri Sirf Schemes (Iraq)', 31 May 1955, FO 957/214.
121 Faber to Simpson, 29 March 1955, FO 957/214.
122 Wordsworth to al-Pachachi, 'Iraq: Cooperatives, 1955', 28 October 1955, FO 957/214.
123 TCA-Iraq memo, 'Credit Project', 13 July 1956, RG 286, TCA-Iraq, Office of the Director, Subject Files, 1951–58, Box 4.
124 Wordsworth to al-Pachachi, 'Iraq: Cooperatives, 1955', 28 October 1955, FO 957/214.
125 Wordsworth to al-Jamali, IDB, 28 October 1955, FO 957/214.
126 Ibid.

127 Crawford to Faber, 11 January 1954, FO 371/111010/VQ1106.
128 See Hancock to Abdul Jabbar Chalabi, 30 March 1953, RG 286, TCA-Iraq, Office of the Director, Subject Files, 1951–58, Box 23. After thanking al-Chalabi for a report on the Sudan Gezira Scheme, Hancock expressed his hope that 'serious thought' was not being given to its adoption. He felt it did not promote the development of self-reliant, economically independent farm operators. In fact, 'as I understand it,.this scheme actually nets a considerable profit to the government. I believe that any net profit from schemes such as this should accrue to the people.'
129 Salter, *The Development of Iraq*, 59.
130 Crawford memo, 'Miri Sirf Schemes (Iraq)', 31 May 1955, FO 957/214.
131 Wordsworth to al-Jalali, 28 October 1955, FO 957/214.
132 Crawford memo, 'Miri Sirf Schemes (Iraq)', 31 May 1955, FO 957/214.
133 Simpson to Kellas, 13 October 1955, FO 371/115785/VQ1461.
134 Kellas to Simpson, 1 November 1955, FO 957/214.
135 Ibid.
136 Simpson to Kellas, 17 November 1955, FO 957/214.
137 Crawford to Ross, 3 May 1957, FO 371/127765/V1103/6.
138 Wordsworth, 'Visit to the Miri Sirf Schemes at Hawija, Shahrazoor and Latifiyah', 2 May 1956, Pamphlet Collection, MEC, St Antony's College.
139 Ibid., 8.
140 Ibid., 12.
141 Howell to Lord Home, 'Report on Activities During Last 12 Months', 20 June 1961, ODA.

6. THE BRITISH MIDDLE EAST OFFICE AND THE POLITICS OF MODERNIZATION IN JORDAN, 1951 TO 1958

1 Wilson, *King Abdullah, Britain, and the Making of Jordan*, 3.
2 Aruri, *Jordan: A Study in Political Development, 1921–1965*, 89.
3 Satloff, *From Abdullah to Hussein*, vii.
4 Vartan Amadouni, "Infrastructural Development Under the Transjordanian Mandate" in Rogan and Tell (eds.), *Village, Steppe, and State*.
5 Ibid. Amadouni has described British military expenditure in Transjordan as being a type of 'military Keynesianism'.
6 Monroe, "Mr Bevin's 'Arab Policy'" in Hourani (ed.), *St Antony's Papers*, 1961, 9.
7 Windett, 'Report on Tour of Statistical Adviser, 26 May to 16 June 1951', FO 371/91257/E2207; and Know, 'Official Statistics of the Hashemite Kingdom of Jordan', 20 May 1952, RG 286, Jordan, Executive Office, Subject Files, 1952–56, Box 1.
8 Interview with Saleh Abu Zaid, 25 April 1990, Amman. Abu Zaid was an employee in the Statistical Department at the time of Farhan's transfer. See also Windett, 'Priorities in Advisory Work: Statistics', 20 July 1951, FO 957/152.
9 Amman to Drake, 17 November 1955, FO 371/115668/VJ1151.
10 Walpole to Evans, 29 August 1950, FO 371/82722/ET1102; and Drew to DoS, 'Administration of British L 1,000,000 loan to Jordan', 885.411/7–1051.

11 Interview with Hamid al-Farhan, 10 July 1988, Amman.
12 BMEO, 'Investment Possibilities in Jordan', 21 September 1951; and Crawford, 'Financial Aid to Jordan', 17 July 1951, FO 371/91806.
13 See 'Notes of a Meeting with the Jordanian Financial Delegation', 28 November 1951, FO 371/91806.
14 Rapp to Bowker, 26 January 1953, FO 371/104917/ETI151.
15 Ross memo, 22 April 1952, FO 371/98875/ETI151.
16 Furlonge to Richmond, 27 November 1952; and Waterlow memo, 5 December 1952, FO 371/98876/ETI151.
17 Amman to DoS, 885.00–TA/10–1152.
18 See Welling to Mallory, 'Brief History of the Development Board', 13 January 1954, RG 286, US Operations Mission, Jordan, Executive Office, Classified Subject Files, 1951–56, Box 1; and The Joseph Green Papers, 26 June 1953.
19 Ibid.
20 See Satloff, *From Abdullah to Hussein*.
21 Furlonge to Ross, 30 June 1953, FO 371/104902/ETI107.
22 Furlonge to Richmond, 5 May 1953; and Russell Edmonds to Richmond, 26 May 1953, FO 371/104902.
23 Satloff, *From Abdullah to Hussein*, 76.
24 Furlonge to Ross, 30 June 1953, FO 371/104902/ETI107.
25 Furlonge to Ross, 16 June 1953, FO 371/104902/ETI107.
26 Porter to author, 1 August 1990.
27 Furlonge to Richmond, 25 January 1953, FO 371/104491/ETI151/19.
28 Furlonge to Eden, 15 January 1953, FO 371/104917/ETI151.
29 Welling to Green, 'Development Board', 8 October 1952, RG 286, US Operations Mission, Executive Office, Classified Subject Files, 1951–56, Box 1.
30 Amman to FO, 4 February 1954, FO 371/110900/VJ1109.
31 Interview with Farhi Obeid, 26 March 1990, Amman who was one of the initial recruits into the economic planning unit.
32 Interview with Moraiwid at-Tell, 26 April 1990, Amman.
33 Furlonge to Richmond, 5 May 1953, FO 371/104902/ETI107.
34 Ibid.
35 See The Joseph Coy Green Papers, 'June 22 1953' and 'June 26 1953'.
36 Welling memo, 'Possible Withdrawal of UNTAA from Jordan', 22 January 1954, RG 286, US Operations Mission, Jordan, Confidential Files, Box 12.
37 Satloff, *From Abdullah to Hussein*, 87.
38 Interview with Farhi Obeid, 25 March 1990, Amman.
39 See Lindberg, 'Report on Economic Development Problems in Jordan', 14 July 1954; and al-Gritli, 'General Economic Survey of Jordan', 29 October 1956.
40 Crawford to Simpson, 19 July 1954, FO 371/110892/VJ1104.
41 Dudgeon to Simpson, 18 November 1954, FO 371/110893/VJ1104.
42 al-Gritli, 'General Economic Survey of Jordan', 29 October 1956; and Amman to DoS. 'Some Observations of IBRD Mission on Jordan Development Problems', 1 September 1956, RG84, Jordan, Confidential Files, Box 12.

43 Crawford memo, 7 December 1954, FO 371/110900/VJ1109; and Simpson to Russell Edmunds, 12 August 1953, FO 371/104902/ET1107.

44 Russell Edmonds to Simpson, 5 March 1956, FO 371/121511/VJ1102.

45 See Oren, 'A Winter of Discontent: Britain's Crisis in Jordan, December 1955 to March 1956' in *International Journal of Middle East Studies*, 22, 1990.

46 See Duncan to DoS, 885.00/1–356.

47 Amman to DoS, 'Some Observations by IBRD Survey Mission on Jordan Development Problems', 1 September 1956, RG 84, Jordan, Confidential Files, Box 12.

48 Duncan to DoS, 885.00/1–356.

49 Ibid.

50 Interview with Amin al-Hassan, 27 March 1990 and Patai, *The Kingdom of Jordan*, 63.

51 See Lindberg, 'Report on Economic Development Problems in Jordan', 14 July 1954; al-Gritli, 'General Economic Survey of Jordan', 29 October 1956; and Amman to DoS, 'Some Observations by IBRD Survey Mission on Jordan Development Problems', 1 September 1956, RG 284, Jordan, Confidential Files, Box 12.

52 In 1950, the staff consisted of Salti as the Inspector, one assistant inspector, two clerks, six district forest officers, ten enclosure guards, three nursery officers and three forestry officers in training. See Chapman, 'Notes on Forestry in Jordan', 19 May 1950, MEDD Papers, Box 8, MEC, St Antony's College.

53 Chapman, 'Notes on Forestry in Jordan', 19 May 1950, MEDD Papers, Box 8, MEC, St Antony's College.

54 Mooney, 'Notes on a Tour of Jordan', 15 July 1951, MEDD Papers, Box 8, MEC, St Antony's College.

55 Mooney, 'A Short Note on Forestry in Jordan', 18 December 1951, MEDD Papers, Box 8, MEC, St Antony's College.

56 Richmond to Falla, 13 February 1954, FO 371/110896/VJ1106.

57 Edgecombe to Duke, 2 July 1954, FO 371/110896/VJ1106.

58 See 'Annual Report of the Development Board of the Hashemite Kingdom of Jordan', 1954; and Edgecombe to Duke, 2 July 1954, FO 371/110896/VJ1106.

59 Mallory to Parker, 'Technical and Economic Assistance to Jordan: A Preliminary Appraisal', 885.00TA/2–854.

60 See Graham to Simpson, 11 May 1954, FO 371/110891/VJ1104.

61 Salti, 'Annual Report for the Department of Forestry, 1 April 1954 to 31 March 1955', 1 April 1955, 17 (in arabic).

62 See RG 286, Jordan, Office of the Director, Subject Files, 1952–56, Box 3.

63 Minister of Economy to Nelson, 14 June 1955, RG 286, Jordan, Program Division, Subject Files, Box 1.

64 Patai, *The Kingdom of Jordan*, 62.

65 Davidson, 'Notes on a Visit to Jordan: June 1961', 6 July 1961, ODA.

66 Waterer, 'Some Observations on the Forests and Land Use in General in Jordan', July 1949, MEDD Papers, Box 8, MEC, St Antony's College.

67 See FO 371/75308 for an outline of the scheme (in arabic).

68 Crawford 'Memo of Discussion', 4 May 1949, FO 371/75290/E9606; See also

Walpole to Crawford, 'General Observations on the Settlement of Refugees on the Land in Transjordan', 3 April 1949, FO 371/75289/E5036.

69 See Sir Murdock MacDonald and Partners, 'Report on the Proposed Extension of Irrigation in the Jordan Valley', London, July 1951.

70 Ionides to Evans, 17 October 1951, FO 371/91832/ET1421.

71 Ionides to Furlonge, 27 January 1950, FO 371/82722/ET1102.

72 Ionides to Waterlow, 2 October 1952, FO 957/158. In fact, a subsequent report by Porter on Bunger's Jordan-Yarmouk project revealed some of his claims about its employment effects to have been 'exaggerated'.

73 Crawford to Furlonge, 16 October 1952, FO 957/158.

74 Wakefield to Evans, 10 July 1952, FO 957/157.

75 See The Joseph Coy Green Papers, 11 February 1953.

76 See The Joseph Coy Green Papers, 28 January 1953.

77 See The Joseph Coy Green Papers, 4 December 1952.

78 Bergus to Gardiner, 3 August 1953, RG 286, TCA Jordan, Executive Office, Classified Subject Files, 1951–56, Box 2.

79 See The Joseph Coy Green Papers, 31 July 1953.

80 Lynch to Secretary of State, 885.21/9–1553.

81 Murray memo, 11 December 1952, FO 957/158.

82 Ionides to Simpson, 'Memo on the TVA Report on the Jordan Valley', 29 September 1953, FO 371/104949/ET1421/100.

83 Ibid.

84 Furlonge to Bowker, 4 May 1953, FO 371/104948/ET1421.

85 Ionides to Simpson, 6 November 1953, FO 371/104950/ET1421.

86 For a particularly bitter recrimination of the American 'mishandling' of the Jordan Valley scheme, see Walpole to Monroe, February 1954, Elizabeth Monroe Papers, MEC, St Antony's College.

87 Nelson to Mallory, 'Report on the Development Board, November 16 1955', 19 November 1955, RG 84, USAID Jordan, Confidential Files, Box 12.

88 Interview with Sweillem al-Haddad, 28 March 1990, Amman. Haddad played a large part in both the formation of this team and in its subsequent technical work. In the early 1950s, he had been part of Simanski's small irrigation team stationed at both Addasiya and Deir Alla.

89 Simanski, 'Preliminary Brief Notes on the Proposed Yarmouk Pilot Scheme', 12 July 1956, FO 371/121583/VJ1421.

90 Crawford to Dudgeon, 28 July 1956, FO 371/121529/VJ1153.

91 Crawford to Dudgeon, 20 August 1956, FO 371/121583/VJ1421; and Crawford to Dudgeon, 28 July 1956, FO 371/121529/VJ1153.

92 Interview with Najeeb Tleil, 5 April 1990, Amman.

93 Crawford to Dudgeon, 28 July 1956, FO 371/121529/VJ1153.

94 Ibid.

95 Lampen to Russell Edmunds, 18 September 1956, FO 371/121529/VJ1153.

96 Interview with Moraiwid at-Tell, 26 April 1990, Amman, who was placed in charge of this committee. For some reason, the committee lost touch with Ionides after his departure from Baghdad.

97 Interview with Sweilum Haddad, Project Engineer in charge of the East Ghor Canal Scheme, 25 March 1990, Amman.

98 See East Ghor Canal Scheme, Technical Team, 'Monthly Progress Report for the Oct. 1958 Period 1 to 31/10/1958', 15 November 1958.

99 Interview with Sweilum Haddad, 25 March 1990, Amman.
100 Figure based on a report by the Department of Lands and Surveys. See Gritli, 'Agricultural Credit in Jordan', undated, FO 371/121577.
101 Ibid.
102 Ibid.; and Cheesman, 'Founding of the Jordan Cooperative Central Union Ltd. and Future Cooperative Possibilities in Jordan', FAO, 1959, 7, MEDD Papers, Box 6, MEC, St Antony's College.
103 Cheesman, 'Cooperative Possibilities in the Hashemite Kingdom of Jordan', February 1952, 3, MEDD Papers, Box 6, MEC, St Antony's College.
104 The moratorium was to last for four years but was extended in 1951 for another four years.
105 The Arab Mortgage Bank gave up agricultural lending altogether and by 1954, its agricultural loans accounted for less than 10 per cent of its outstanding business. Most of its work was transferred to mortgage lending in urban areas. (See Gritli, 'Agricultural Credit in Jordan', undated, FO 371/121 577, 1).
106 See Bennsky, 'Report on Jordan's Economy and Credit Structure', 20 May 1953, 13–14, RG 286, USAID-Jordan, Office of Director, Subject Files, 1952–56, Box 1.
107 Cheesman, 'Cooperative Possibilities in the Hashemite Kingdom of Jordan', February 1952, 4, MEDD Box 6, MEC, St Antony's College.
108 Ibid.
109 See Bennsky to Welling, 'Cooperative Sub-Committee of the Jordan Development Board', 1 April 1953, RG 286, USAID-Jordan, Office of Director, Subject Files, 1952–56, Box 5.
110 Cheesman to Nuseibeh, Minister of Reconstruction and Development, 2 April 1953, FO 371/104901/ETI106/3.
111 Interview with Amin al-Husseini, 1 April 1990, Amman.
112 Ibid. Later, some Jordanians were sent on FAO and Point IV money to Loughborough College in the United Kingdom.
113 Crawford to Evans, 12 June 1952, FO 371/98874/ETI109.
114 Lindberg to Crawford, 18 October 1953, FO 371 104920/ETI153/15A.
115 Amman to FO, 2 October 1953, FO 371/104920/ETI153/16.
116 Cheesman memo, 'Note by Cooperative Adviser', undated, FO 371/104920/ETI153/15.
117 Rapp to Churchill, 29 April 1953, FO 371/104901/ETI106.
118 Cheesman, 'Report on Cooperatives in Jordan', October 1953, FO 371/104901/ETI106/6.
119 Wordsworth, 'The Cooperative Movement in Jordan', 11 January 1955, FO 957/209.
120 Brair to Cheesman, 11 November 1953, FO 371/104901/ETI106.
121 IBRD, *The Economic Development of Jordan*, 144.
122 See Wordsworth, 'The Cooperative Movement in Jordan', 11 January 1955, FO 957/209.
123 Wordsworth, '1955 Loan Funds for Cooperatives', 8 October 1954, FO 371/110893. For this purpose, Wordsworth drew up a Five Year Plan. See Wordsworth, 'Note on Higher Training of Staff', 11 January 1955, FO 957/209.

124 Cheesman, 'Suggestions for a Cooperative Supervising and Audit Union for the Hashemite Kingdom of Jordan', 4 March 1954, MEDD Papers, Box 6, MEC, St Antony's College.

125 Ibid.

126 Ibid.

127 Johnston to FO, 22 January 1959, FO 371/142166/VJ1281. Johnston made the interesting comment that 'the movement is a striking example of the progressive social legislation which is possible even in a country which has been distracted by political turmoil as Jordan has in the last eight years and which is now in the grip of a "frankly" authoritarian regime'.

128 Cheesman, 'Founding of the Jordan Cooperative Central Union Ltd. and Future Cooperative Possibilities in Jordan', FAO, 1959, MEDD Papers, Box 6, MEC, St Antony's College.

129 Ibid.

130 Eyre, 'The Frontier Villages of Arab Palestine', 8 May 1952, MEDD Papers, Box 2, MEC, St Antony's College.

131 The Jerusalem Office of the Development Board was in the former office of the Custodian of the Holy Places, Its telephone number was 7!

132 Eyre, 'Progress Report on Frontier Villages of Jordan Development Scheme', January 1953, MEDD Papers, Box 2, MEC, St Antony's College.

133 Interview with Farah Abu Jabber, 8 April 1990, Amman.

134 Ibid.

135 Rapp to Crawford, September 30 1952, FO 957/164.

136 Eyre, 'Second Progress Report on the Village Loans Scheme', 1954, MEDD Papers, Box 2, MEC, St Antony's College.

137 Eyre, 'Third Progress Report on the Village Loans Scheme', 1956, MEDD Papers, Box 2, St Antony's College.

138 IBRD, *The Economic Development of Jordan*, 86 and 148.

139 See Porter, 'Economic Trends in Jordan, 1954–1959', Beirut, July 1961, ODA.

140 Porter, 'Foreign Aid and Economic Development in Jordan', Beirut, 24 July 1961, ODA.

141 Crawford to Simpson, 9 February 1956, FO 371/121577/VJ1283.

142 al-Gritli, 'Agricultural Credit in Jordan', undated, FO 371/12157.

143 FO memo, 14 February, FO 371/121577/VJ1283.

144 Crawford to Simpson, 9 February 1956, FO 371/121577/VJ1283.

145 Eyre, 'Third Progress Report on the Village Loans Scheme', 1956, MEDD Papers, Box 2, MEC, St Antony's College.

146 Crawford memo, undated, FO 371/121514/VJ1107.

147 Russell Edmonds to Simpson, 18 February 1956, FO 371/121577/VJ1283.

148 Crawford to Simpson, 9 February 1956, FO 371/121577/VJ1283.

149 Ibid.

150 Eyre to Mason, 18 December 1956, FO 371/112514/VJ1107.

151 Bullard to Lampen, 29 January 1957, FO 371/127913/VJ1102.

152 Eyre, 'Report on Village Loans Scheme for the Jordan Development Board', 20 July 1957, MEDD Papers, Box 2, MEC, St Antony's College.

CONCLUSION

1 Crawford to Selwyn Lloyd, 3 July 1956, FO 371/121514/VJ1107.
2 Lampen memo, 21 May 1957, FO 371/127765/V1103.
3 See Kitching, *Development and Underdevelopment in Historical Perspective*.
4 Schumacher, *Small is Beautiful*, 167.
5 Interview with Bob Porter, 23 November 1988.
6 See Huntington, *Political Order in Changing Societies*.
7 Chambers, *Challenging the Professions*, 16.
8 Ibid. See also Chambers, *Rural Development*.
9 See Howell to Prentice, 'Final Despatch', 9 July 1969, ODA.
10 Crawford to Selwyn Lloyd, 'Final Despatch', 14 June 1960, ODA.

Bibliography

PRIMARY SOURCES

BRITISH GOVERNMENT DOCUMENTS

Public Records Office, London

CAB 134
CO 64 (Cyprus)
FO 371 (General, Iran, Iraq and Jordan, 1945–59)
FO 624 (Consular Files, Baghdad)
FO 922 (MESC, 1941–45)
FO 957 (BMEO, 1945–55)
FO 800 (Bevin Papers)
 T 236

Overseas Development Administration, London

MEDD Papers (1961–81)

UNITED STATES GOVERNMENT DOCUMENTS

National Records Center, Suitland, Maryland

US State Department (Consular files for Egypt, Iran, Iraq and Jordan)
Point IV (Iran, Iraq and Jordan)

National Archives, Washington D.C.

US State Department

PRIVATE PAPERS

Green Papers, Princeton University Library
Elizabeth Monroe Papers, MEC, St Antony's College
MEDD Papers, MEC, St Antony's College
MESC Papers, MEC, St Antony's College
Sir Thomas Rapp Papers, MEC, St Antony's College

INTERVIEWS AND CORRESPONDENCE

Farhah abu Jabbar, Salah abu Zaid, Omar Abdullah, Zaid Aynab, Ayoub Batarseh, Donald Davidson, Hamad Farhan, Sweilum Haddad, Amin al–Hassan, Paul Howell, Barry Hudson, Amin al-Husseini, Adel Khalidi, Kamil Kowar, Sa'ad an–Nimri, Hasim Nuseibeh, Farhi Obeid, Hannah Odeh, Bob Porter, Kamal Sha'ir, Moraiwid at-Tell, Njeib at-Tleil.

(II) SECONDARY WORKS

Abrahamian, E., *Iran Between Two Revolutions* (Princeton, 1982)

Allen, H.B., *Rural Education and Welfare in the Middle East* (London, 1946)

Amin, G., *The Modernization of Poverty* (Leiden, 1972)

Aruri, N., *Jordan: A Study in Political Development, 1921–1965* (The Hague, 1972)

Asher, R. and Associates, *The United Nations and Economic and Social Cooperation* (Washington DC, 1957)

Axelgard, F., 'US Support for the British Position in Pre-Revolutionary Iraq' in W.R. Louis (ed.), *The Iraqi Revolution of 1958* (London, 1991)

Azimi, F., *Iran: Democracy in Crisis, 1941–1953* (London, 1989)

Baldwin, J., *Planning and Development in Iran* (New York, 1967)

Banani, A, *The Modernization of Iran, 1926–41* (Stanford, 1961)

Baster, J. 'The Economy of Jordan' in *Middle Eastern Affairs*, 1955

Bauer, P.T., *Dissent on Development* (London, 1971)

Equality, The Third World and Economic Delusion (London, 1981)

'Remembrance of Studies Past: Retracing First Steps' in G. Miers and D. Seers (eds.), *Pioneers in Development* (Oxford, 1984)

Batatu, H., *The Old Social Classes and the Revolutionary Movements of Iraq: a Study of Iraq's Old Landed and Commercial Classes and of its Communists, Ba'thists, and Free Officers* (Princeton, 1978)

Birdwood, Lord, *Nuri al–Said: A Study in Arab Leadership* (London, 1959)

Bostock, F. and G. Jones, *Planning and Power in Iran: Ebtehaj and Economic Development under the Shah* (London, 1989)

Bullock, A., *Ernest Bevin: Foreign Secretary, 1945–1951* (London, 1983)

Burns, N., 'The Dujaylah Settlement' in *Middle East Journal*, 1951

Burrows, B., *Footnotes in the Sand: the Gulf in Transition, 1953–1958* (London, 1990)

Caiden, N. and A. Wildavsky, *Planning and Budgeting in Poor Countries* (Toronto, 1974)

Chambers, R., *Rural Development: Putting the Last First* (London, 1982)

Challenging the Professions: Frontiers for Rural Development (London, 1993)

Champion, A.G. and F. Osmaston, *The Forests of India* (London, 1962)

Dann, U., *King Hussein and the Challenge of Arab Radicalism: Jordan, 1955–1967* (Oxford, 1989)

Darwin, J., *Britain and Decolonisation: The Retreat from Empire in the Postwar World* (London, 1988)

DeNova, J.A., 'The Culbertson Economic Mission and Anglo-American Tensions in the Middle East, 1944–1945' in *Journal of American History*, 1977

Farouk-Sluglett, M. and P. Sluglett, *Iraq Since 1958: From Revolution to Dictatorship* (New York, 1989)

Fawcitt, L. *Iran and the Cold War: The Azerbaijan Crisis of 1946* (Cambridge, 1992)

Floor, W., *Industrialization in Iran, 1900–1941* (Durham, 1984)

Gabbay, M., *Communism and Agrarian Reform in Iraq* (London, 1978)

Gallagher, J.A., *The Decline, Revival and Fall of the British Empire* (Cambridge, 1982)

Gallagher, N.E., 'Egypt's Public Health Wars, 1942–1952' (PhD, University of California, Santa Barbara, 1989)

Gallman, W.J., *Iraq under General Nuri* (Baltimore, 1964)

Gerber, H., *The Social Origins of the Modern Middle East* (London, 1987)

Ghods, M., 'The Rise and Fall of General Razmara' in *Middle Eastern Studies*, 1993

Glick, P., *The Administration of Technical Assistance: Growth in the Americas* (Chicago, 1957)

Godfried, N., *Bridging the Gap Between Rich and Poor: American Economic Development Policy in the Arab East, 1942–49* (New York, 1987)

Headrick, D.R., *The Tentacles of Progress: Technological Transfer in the Age of Imperialism, 1850–1940* (Oxford, 1988)

Hellinger, M. et al., *Aid for Just Development* (Washington DC, 1992)

Holland, R.F., *European Decolonization: an Introductory Survey* (London, 1985)

Hourani, A., 'Ottoman Reform and the Politics of Notables' in *The Emergence of the Modern Middle East* (London, 1981)

Hunter, G., 'Economic Problems: The Middle East Supply Centre' in G. Kirk, *The Middle East in the War, 1939–1946* (Oxford, 1952)

Huntington, S., *Political Order in Changing Societies* (New Haven, 1968)

International Bank for Reconstruction and Development, *The Economic Development of Iraq* (Baltimore, 1952)

The Economic Development of Jordan (Baltimore, 1957)

Ionides, M.G., 'Objects and Implications of Economic Development' in *Administrative Organisation for Economic Development* (London, 1957)

'Help from the West' in *Engineering*, 1958

Divide and Lose: the Arab Revolt, 1955–58 (London, 1960)

Israel, A., *Institutional Development: Incentives to Performance* (Baltimore, 1987)

Jwaideh, A., 'Midhat Pasha and the Land System of Lower Iraq' in *St Antony's Papers*, 16:3, 1963

Keddie, N., 'Is there a Middle East' in *International Journal of Middle East Studies*, 1973

The Roots of Revolution (New Haven, 1981)

Keen, B.A., *Agricultural Development in the Middle East* (London, 1946)

Kernan, H.S., 'A Policy of Conservation for the Caspian Forests of Iran' in *Middle East Journal*, 1953

Kingston, P., '"Ambassador for the Arabs": The Locke Mission and the Unmaking of American Development Diplomacy in the Near East, 1951–53' in David Lesch (ed.), *The Middle East and the United States: A Historical and Political Reassessment* (Boulder, 1996)

Kirk, G., *The Middle East in the War, 1939–46* (Oxford, 1952)

The Middle East, 1945–1950 (Oxford, 1952)

Kitching, G., *Development and Underdevelopment in Historical Perspective* (London, 1982)

Krassowski, A., 'Development Divisions: British Aid Administration in the Middle East and the Caribbean' (Overseas Development Institute, 1973)

Lambton, A.K.S., *Landlord and Peasant in Persia* (London, 1952)

Lloyd, E.M.H., *Food and Inflation in the Middle East, 1940–45* (Stanford, 1956)

Louis, W.R., *The British Empire in the Middle East, 1945–1951: Arab Nationalism, The United States and Postwar Imperialism* (Oxford, 1984)

'The British and the Origins of the Iraqi Revolution' in Louis (ed.), *The Iraqi Revolution of 1958* (Texas, 1991)

Lutz, J.D., 'Problems and Proposals' in *Middle East Journal*, 1950

Marr, P., *The Modern History of Iraq* (London, 1985)

Mason, E., *The World Bank Since Bretton Woods* (Baltimore, 1973)

MESC, *Some Facts About the Middle East Supply Centre* (Cairo, 1944)

'Problems of Statistical Enumeration in the Middle East' in *Middle East Economic and Statistical Bulletin*, no. 12, April 1944

Proceedings of the Conference on Middle East Agricultural Development (Cairo, 1944)

The Work of the Middle East Supply Centre During the European War (Cairo, 1945)

Millspaugh, A. C., *The American Task in Persia* (London, 1925)

Americans in Persia (Washington DC, 1946)

Monroe, E., 'Mr. Bevin's "Arab Policy"' in Hourani (ed.), *St Antony's Papers* (London, 1961)

Britain's Moment in the Middle East, 1914–1971 (London, 1981)

Morgan, D.J., *The Official History of Colonial Development: Reassessment of British Aid Policy, 1951–65* (London, 1980)

Murray, J., *A Report on Statistical Organisation in the Government of the Kingdom of Iraq* (Baghdad, 1947)

Murray, K., 'Feeding the Middle East in Wartime' in *Journal of Royal Central Asian Society*, 1945

'Some Regional Economic Problems of the Middle East' in *International Affairs*, 1947

Myrdal, G., *An Approach to the Asian Drama* (New York, 1968)

'International Inequality and Foreign Aid in Retrospect' in G. Meiers and D. Seers, *Pioneers in Development* (Oxford, 1984)

Oren, M.B., 'A Winter of Discontent: Britain's Crisis in Jordan, December 1955 to March, 1956' in *International Journal of Middle East Studies*, 22, 1990

Owen, R., *The Middle East in the World Economy, 1800–1914* (London, 1981)

Pappe, I., *Britain and the Arab-Israeli Conflict, 1948–1951* (London, 1988)

Patai, R., *The Kingdom of Jordan* (Princeton, 1958)

Penrose, E. and E.F. Penrose, *Iraq: International Relations and National Development* (London, 1978)

Polk, J., *Sterling: Its Meaning in World Finance* (London, 1956)

Porath, Y., *In Search of Arab Unity, 1930–1945* (London, 1986)

Porter, R.S., 'Statistical Services in the Middle East' in *Middle East Economic Papers* (Beirut, 1955)

Qubain, F.I., *The Reconstruction of Iraq, 1950–57* (London, 1957)

Rogan, E. and T. Tell, (eds.), *Village, Steppe, and State: the Social Origins of Jordan* (London, 1994)

Rondinelli, D., *Development Projects as Policy Experiments: an Adaptive Approach to Development Administration* (London, 1993)

Sacher, H., *Europe Leaves the Middle East, 1936–1954* (New York, 1972)

Salter, Lord, *The Development of Iraq: a Plan of Action* (Baghdad, 1955)

Sassoon, J., *Economic Policy in Iraq, 1932–1950* (London, 1987)

Satloff, R., *From Abdullah to Hussein: Jordan in Transition* (Oxford, 1994)

Schumacher, F., *Small is Beautiful: Economics as if People Mattered* (London, 1993)

Seale, P., *The Struggle For Syria: a Study of Postwar Arab Politics, 1945–1958* (New Haven, 1986)

Thacker, N., 'Reflections on US Foreign Policy Towards Iraq in the 1950s' in W. R. Louis (ed.), *The Iraqi Revolution of 1958* (London, 1991)

Thornburg, M.W. and G. Spry, *Turkey: an Economic Appraisal* (Washington DC, 1947)

People and Policy in the Middle East (New York, 1964)

Tomlinson, B.R., 'Indo-British Relations in the Post-Colonial Era: The Sterling Balance Negotiations, 1947–49' in A. Porter, and R. Holland, *Money, Finance and Empire, 1790–1950*, (London, 1985)

Tothill, J.D., *Agriculture in the Sudan* (London, 1953)

Toye, J., *Dilemmas of Development* (London, 1989).

Trevelyan, H., *The Middle East in Revolution* (London, 1970).

Wark, W., 'Development Diplomacy: Sir John Troutbeck and the British Middle East Office, 1947–50' in John Zametica, (ed.), *British Officials and British Foreign Policy* (Leicester, 1988)

Warriner, D., *Land and Poverty in the Middle East* (London, 1948)

Land Reform and Development in the Middle East (London, 1957)

Willcocks, W., *The Irrigation of Mesopotamia* (London, 1911)

Wilmington, M., 'The Middle East Supply Centre: A Reappraisal' in *Middle East Journal*, 1952

The Middle East Supply Centre (London, 1971)

Wilson, M., *King Abdullah, Britain, and the Making of Jordan* (Cambridge, 1987)

Windawi, M.I.K., 'Anglo-Iraqi Relations, 1945–1958' (PhD, Reading University, 1989)

Worthington, E.R., *Middle East Science* (London, 1946)

Yapp, M., *The Near East Since the First World War* (London, 1991)

Zubaida, S., 'Community, Class and Minorities in Iraqi Politics' in W.R. Louis (ed.), *The Iraqi Revolution of 1958* (London, 1991)

Index

Abd al-Ilah (Regent of Iraq): 96, 98–100
Abdullah (King of Jordan): 39, 123
Abu'l Huda, Tawfiq: 128
Abu Jabber, Farah: 150
Agriculture: 14, 31–2, 47, 74–5, 79, 85, 88–9, 94, 100, 104, 115–17, 145–52
al-Ahali group (Iraq): 96, 101
Altrincham, Lord: 10, 19–22, 27, 99
American University of Beirut (AUB): 64
Anglo-Iranian Oil Company (AIOC): 37, 69, 70, 74, 80, 83, 85–6, 92
Anglo-Iraqi Treaty: 20, 95, 97
Anglo-Jordanian Treaty: 134
Arab Development Bank (ADB): 31, 42–4
Arab League: 17–18, 42; economic committee of, 43–4
Arab Legion: 130, 133
Arab Revolt: 94
Ataturk, Kemal: 67, 103, 109

Baghdad Pact: 57, 133, 151
Balfour Beatty and Co.: 30, 35, 108
Bauer, Peter: 5, 155
Bayliss, Colonel: 15
Bevin, Ernest: 3, 10–11, 18, 20–3, 25, 28, 30, 32–5, 44, 46, 50, 70–1, 98–102, 125, 157; Bevin Plan, 36–9
Blandford, John: 141
Britain: 2–5, 10–28, 29–31, 31–2, 36, 40, 44–5, 69–78, 97–104, 125–35, 157
BMEO (British Middle East Office): approaches to modernization, 4, 9, 46–66, 154–7; creation of, 20–1; and IBRD, 41–2; in Iran, 38, 67–93 passim; in Iraq, 39, 94–122; in Jordan, 39, 123–153
British Council: 53
Bunger, Miles: 129, 140–1

Chambers, Robert: 156
Chapman, G.W.: 53, 56, 136

Clapp Mission (Middle East Economic Survey Mission): 51, 54–55, 59, 141
Colombo Plan: 44
Cheesman, W.J.W: 65, 146–9
Cooperatives: 65, 113, 116–20, 146–9
Crawford, Bill: 24–5, 32, 36, 40–1, 44, 48, 51–60, 62–3, 72–5, 82, 100–3, 117–20, 122, 128–9, 143–7, 151–4, 157
Culbertson Mission: 16–17;
Cyprus: 12–13, 18, 53, 64–5, 135, 147

Davidson, Donald: 64, 138
Development Division of the British Middle East Office. *See* BMEO
Dundas: 22, 48

Eady, Sir W.: 33
Ebtehaj, Abol Hassan: 74, 83, 81n.55
Eden, Anthony: 23
Edgecombe, Arthur: 129, 131–2, 137
Edmunds, Russell: 133, 151
Egypt: 10–13, 17, 20–4, 29, 33, 47–8, 52–7, 64–5, 76
Entomology (Locusts): 14, 26–7, 57
Evans, Trefor: 22, 37, 143
Expanded Technical Assistance Program (UN). *See* United Nations
Eyre, Jack: 62, 149–51

Faisal (King of Iraq): 94–5
FAO (Food and Agricultural Organization). *See* United Nations
Farhan, Hamid: 126–7, 130–5, 143, 150–3
Fellahin. *See* Peasants
France: 13, 76
Fowler, Dr: 75–6
Forestry: 63–4, 75–6, 88–93 106–7, 135–8
Ford Foundation: 42, 64, 148
Furlonge, Geoffrey: 37, 130–2, 143

Gezira Scheme: 119–20, 119n.128
Glubb Pasha: 130

Green, Joseph: 129, 141–2
Greenhill, Dennis: 22, 36
Gibb, Sir Alexander and Partners: 30, 50, 73, 75–6, 101
al-Gritli: 133, 151
Groundnuts Scheme (Tanganyika): 54

Habbaniya Lake Project: 103, 104
Haig: 117–18, 120
Haigh, F.F.: 99–102
Hancock, J.D.: 115–16 ·
al-Hassan, Amin: 134
Hay, Sir Rupert: 42
Hijaz Railway: 135
Houstoun-Boswall, W.E.: 48
Howell, Paul: 63, 157
Huntington, Samuel: 156
Hussein (King of Jordan): 124, 127, 129, 148, 152
al-Husseins, Amin: 147

IBRD (International Bank for Reconstruction and Development): 31, 40, 43, 48, 51, 55, 72–73, 77, 81, 83, 103, 133–4, 147, 150
Iliff, William: 19, 40, 77
India: 75, 88, 90, 99
Intermediate Technology Development Group (ITDG): 156
International Statistical Education Centre (ISEC): 65
Ionides, Michael: 104–5, 109–14, 120, 122, 124, 140–4, 155–6
Iran: 38, 67–93, 96, 100, 103, 154; Capital Development Commission, 71–2; Plan Organization 38, 64, 74, 80–5, 91, 107; Majlis, 68–71, 73, 77, 179–82, 84–5; Seven Year Plan, 29, 38, 72, 74, 78–92, 107; Sterling Balances, 38
Iraq: 8, 14–15, 20, 29–30, 39, 92–122, 154, 156; Iraq Development Board, 40, 51, 64, 101–12; Irrigation Development Commission, 25, 29, 33, 35, 99, 102; Sterling Balances, 33–5, 39
Iraqi Communist Party (ICP): 98
Iraqi Petroleum Co.(IPC): 97
Irrigation: 25, 29, 33, 35, 71, 71, 76, 99, 102–5, 107–108, 120, 135–44
Istiqlal Party (Iraq): 98

Jabr, Salih: 101, 102
Jackson, Robert: 14
Johnston Plan: 144
Jordan: 8, 37, 39, 123–153, 154, 156; Agricultural Credit Institutions, 130, 145–53; Development Board 125–35,

143–51, 153; Irrigation Division, Department of Lands and Surveys, 135–45; Sterling Balances, 38–9

Kaibni, Ibrahim: 149, 152–3
Kashani, Ayatollah: 68
al-Khatib, Anwar: 126, 132
al-Kheiri, Khalusi: 126, 128, 138, 152
Kirkbride, Alec: 39, 125
Kirkuk Massacre: 98
Kitching, Gavin: 155
Kuwait: 42–4, 57

Lampson, Sir Miles: 23–4
Land Reform: 79, 89, 96–101, 110–21, 145–147, 152–3. See also Miri Sirf Land Development Programme (MSLD)
Landis, James: 16–17, 49
Lars Valley Dam Scheme: 73–6
Lebanon: 13, 41, 47, 51, 64, 139
Le Rougetel, Sir John: 71–2, 76–8, 81–2
Lindberg, John: 131
Locke, Edwin: 61, 141
Lutz, J.D.: 77

MacDonald, Sir Murdock and Partners: 140
Mack, Sir Henry: 34,.
Maitland, Victor: 64, 70, 75–8, 83, 86–92, 102–3, 106, 113
Makins, Sir Roger: 42–3
Mallory, Lester: 137
Marshall Plan: 18
Mansur, Ali: 84–5
Middle East Council of Agriculture (MECA): 15, 17–18, 26, 47
Middle East Development Board: 18, 21
Middle East Economic and Statistical Bulletin: 13, 26 ·
Middle East Official Committee (MEOC): 20, 22, 25–6, 32
Middle East Secretariat (MES): 20–4, 27, 35, 37, 48, 53, 77, 99
Middle East Supply Centre (MESC): 9–24, 26, 32, 35, 47, 49, 54, 71–2, 86, 98, 119; medical division,13; scientific advisory mission, 14
Miller, Eddington: 111
Millspaugh, Arthur: 72
Miri Sirf Land Development Programme (MSLD): 97, 105, 108, 110, 113–14, 118–21, 139
Mohammad Reza Shah Pahlavi: 68–71, 79–86, 91, 103
Monroe, Elizabeth: 112, 125
Mooney, Herbert: 62, 64, 106–7, 122, 136–7

Mossadegh, Mohammed: 38, 85–6, 92
·Morrison-Knudson Mission: 72, 73, 74
al-Mulqi, Fawsi: 129–31, 150
Murray, John: 43, 64–5, 75, 85, 87, 102,
     142
Murray, Keith: 17

Nabulsi Sulayman: 134, 144, 151
Naficy, Hassan Mosharef: 74, 85
Nasser, Gamal Abdul: 95
Nationalism : 19, 29, 43, 95, 126–7, 130,
     132
National Front (Iran): 80, 84–5

Old Gang (Notables): 11, 95
Oil: 10, 38, 41, 42, 44, 49, 67, 69, 96, 103–4,
     110
Overseas Consultants Incorporated (OCI):
     50–1, 56, 72, 77–8, 81–4, 87, 113
Overseas Development Administration
     (ODA) (formerly the Department of
     Technical Cooperation): 46, 155
Ottoman Empire: 67. 94
Overseas Technical Service: 53
Overton, Sir Arnold: 22, 26–7, 32, 71, 100

al-Pachachi, Hamdi: 99–100, 103
Palestinian Refugees: 37, 39, 51, 56, 100,
     123–4, 136, 139, 141, 149
Peasants: 11, 28, 36, 39, 46, 68, 71, 96, 100,
     105, 114
Point Four Programme (Technical
     Cooperation Administration): 2, 6, 8,
     52–3, 58–61, 90, 108, 113–17, 126,
     128–9, 132, 134–5, 137–8, 141
Polk, Judd: 33
Porter, R.S.: 62, 64–5, 131, 150
Portsmouth Treaty: 29, 34
Pridie, Dr: 76–7, 100

Qavam, Ahmad: 71–5, 79, 81

Rapp, Sir Thomas: 44, 55, 63, 150
Rashid 'Ali, Husain: 14, 95, 97
Razmarra, General Ali: 38, 85–6
Reza Shah Pahlavi: 67–8, 87, 93
Rowe-Dutton, E.: 31, 40

al-Said, Nuri: 95–6, 109–13
Salter, Lord: 108, 111–12, 118
Salti, Yacoub: 135–8
Sargent, Sir John: 53
Schumacher, Fritz: 155–6
Shepherd, Sir Francis: 38, 83–4, 86
Skillbeck, Dunstan: 14–15, 17–18
Soviet Union: 2, 11, 29, 35, 67–72, 79

Spears Economic Mission: 13
Statistics: 6, 12, 14, 57, 63–5, 76, 102
Sterling Balances: 19, 21, 31–5, 38–9, 125
Stewart, Sir Herbert: 32, 50, 75, 100, 103
Stonehewer Bird, Sir Hugh: 20, 99, 101
Sudan: 12, 32, 75, 147
Suez Crisis: 4, 120, 152
al-Suwaydi, Tawfiq: 99, 100
Syria: 13, 32–3, 37, 41, 44, 47, 56, 59, 60, 64,
     89, 123, 139

Tennesse Valley Authority (TVA): 142
Thatcher, Margaret: 157
Thornberg, Max: 49–50, 81, 85, 87
Threlkeld: 52, 56–8
Troutbeck, Sir John: 29, 41, 43, 45, 47–8,
     102, 111
Toye, John: 5
Trucial States: 44, 44n.74
Truman, Harry S.: 2, 51
Tudeh Party (Iran): 68–72, 79, 98
Turkey: 2, 36, 40, 49, 67

al-Umari, Urshad: 100, 106–7, 111
United Nations (UN): 1–2, 47–8, 53, 57,
     121; Food and Agricultural
     Organization (FAO), 47, 56, 60, 62,
     117, 120, 148; Expanded Technical
     Assistance Program (ETAP), 51, 53,
     57, 148; United Nations Relief and
     Works Administration (UNRWA), 37,
     51, 55–6, 124, 128, 132–3, 135, 141–2,
     147; United Nations Technical
     Assistance Administration (UNTAA),
     31; Technical Assistance Boards, 55
United States: 11, 16–17, 35–6, 49, 53–61,
     72, 77, 81, 86–8, 91, 103, 114–16, 124,
     129, 131, 134–8, 140–4, 152
United States Special Economic Mission to
     Middle East. See Culbertson Mission

Village Loans Scheme (Jordan): 130,
     149–53

Walpole, George: 140
Warriner, Doreen: 12, 112
Waterlow, Charlotte: 22, 53, 77
Waterston, Dr: 26–7
Wathbah: 95–6, 98, 101, 108
Welling, Tracy: 129, 131
Wiens, Henry: 110
Windett, S.: 25, 60–1, 64, 66
Wordsworth, M.C.: 65, 116–20, 120, 147
World Bank: See IBRD

Zaim, Hosni: 37